MY
AFTERWIFE'S
QUEST

Christine Turnbull

Cover designed by Rufus Turnbull

This book is a work of creative non-fiction. Names, characters, places, and incidents are products of the author's recollection and are used with the acknowledgement and or consent of the named individuals, otherwise they have been described obscurely on purpose.

Printed in the United States of America

First Printing: May 2019
Name of Company

ISBN-978-1-64570-114-9

This is dedicated to my husband with whom I spent the last twenty-five years of my life with. I am so pleased that you recalled so many of our stories. Additionally, although my mother and siblings still struggle with my loss, I truly hope this book can be a bridge and provide a level of comfort to help mend the fractured relationship with My Guys. And to my wonderful son - you continue to bring me joy as I watch you grow.

After it is all said and done ... the most important thing is what you choose to believe.
Whether unknown encounters are coincidences or phenomena to be accepted or are meant to deceive.
So ask yourself, "Have you experienced something in your life that was remarkable but still to this day you chose not to believe?"
Yet accepting everything else blindly without vetting the information you receive.

RUFUS TURNBULL

Christine Turnbull

f

CONTENTS

Christine Turnbull

PROLOGUE

As the airplane maintained its slow descent over the Atlantic coast into the South Florida air space, my husband was awakened by the slight change in cabin pressure that often goes unnoticed where at times it causes discomfort in the ears of infant passengers resulting in their uncontrollable cries. Groggily and instinctively he tapped the screen on his cellphone to wake it up so it would show the time and realized that a little more than two hours had transpired since he left Puerto Rico at 6am. At that moment I thought, throughout all the years and the hundreds of times we have traveled together, this was the earliest he had ever boarded an airline flight to anywhere. And unlike all of the others, this trip was a secret.

He then adjusted the Bluetooth earbuds to listen to the playlist he had fallen asleep to for the short remainder of the flight. Anticipating getting another half hour's nap as a result of feeling deprived from the nervous excitement he was feeling - not to mention having to get up so early to be at the airport at 4:00am to clear TSA - he closed his eyes and resumed the appearance of sleep.

You see, sleep had become ephemeral to him - like currency to be spent - and he has been unintentionally denying himself. From the moment I fell ill, of late his sleeping habits had become incessantly unhealthy.

"Anyone who travels through the JetBlue concourse at the Luis Munoz Marin Airport in San Juan Puerto Rico will find it difficult to catch a nap unless they are dressed like eskimos."

He loved repeating this same joke - especially if you made the mistake and laughed. And if you found that statement to be funny, he had a follow-up punchline where he further suggested that,

"No communicable diseases could survive in that terminal due to how cold the temperature is kept." Concluding with, "If anything, diseases are kept dormant."

Having arrived so early at the airport, frost had already developed on the exterior glass wall panels which was an unnoticed invitation to the passengers on the early morning flights. Consequently, he dressed for comfort donning a heavy hooded sweatshirt, black jeans, and Jordans.

On this fateful morning on the 4th of September 2015 - approximately seven and a half months after I passed away - my husband was enroute to see another woman. And to make a case of full disclosure, he had actually made a similar pilgrimage a couple of months before. That first rendezvous was a clandestine weekend to the Bahamas where the only other person that actually knew of the escapade was his best friend. He called him up on the morning he departed and conveyed that his cell phone won't have any service in Nassau and if he didn't hear from him after a few days, he now knows where to start looking.

You see, in my omnipotence - from the metaphysical and spiritual sidelines - I watched as my husband became a recluse while remaining at home alone. Only the weekdays of briefly taking our son to and from school broke the daily monotony in his life where he otherwise suffered emotionally in silence. He would sit in stillness for hours on end, turning off the daily automated audio streams of the syndicated Tom Joyner Morning Show and NPR over the internet that was normally part of his Wake Up program regimen. He constantly sought the balance of laughter and news as he maneuvered his day. The local over air radio format was never appealing. He thought that the local talk radio hosts allowed too many of the same narcissists too much air time where they repeated their same points to nauseam. And the other adult music format feared similarly in the mornings where they purposely played music so old that the station didn't have to pay royalties to the artists because they were mostly dead. So with those mediums now turned off, his life had become disconnected.

Later I observed when he re-established his social media presence and slowly developed friendships online. On Facebook he befriended a Chinese woman who listened - correction - read what he had recently experienced via the Messenger text service. At this point he no longer wanted to share his emotions with anyone that he knew because the conversations quickly became awkward after their commiseration. She was like a sounding board where he could anonymously tell his story and how he was feeling. And to that end, she was a proverbial godsend. The energy that emanated from his honest testimonials brought forth the balance he subconsciously sought from her responses. Being on the other side of the world she provided that sympathetic ear seemingly evoking the kind of wisdom that one possesses when they can visualize the future even though she was only a day ahead of him. It got him through those initial early painful months of emotional despair. After that purpose was served, they remained Facebook friends and later he reluctantly joined an online dating site.

It all started out innocently enough – not really knowing how to navigate the various options available online. He also found the experience to be quite daunting. The dating dynamic was a huge social adjustment he immediately discovered. Women were very assertive in their virtual presence conversely to how they would commonly behave traditionally when they were meeting someone in person like at a singles bar or dance club. The main difference was they felt empowered and less exposed due to the safe confines at home behind their handheld devices and computers.

He never showed interest in younger women even though it was a preference of many – both men and women. Some members even suggested that he would be more appealing if he lowered his age in his profile stating that his posted picture warranted that kind of dishonesty.

The line in Sir Walter Scott's poem, "Oh, what a tangled web we weave when first we practice to deceive" immediately came to mind. No wonder they were so loose with the truth – nobody could call them out on their misconceptions. As a result of that insight, his sense of perception was heightened and in the end opted to be honest even if it would garner less attention. And at the same time, he incorporated the simple axiom that guided him in business when he dealt with his noncommittal clients: he didn't know what he wanted at this point in his life, but he knew what he didn't want. He didn't want to date anyone significantly younger than he was by evidence of how he kept changing the age of compatibility in his search settings, settling for an age disparity of minus 10 and plus 5.

What I thought was particularly peculiar was the fact that he didn't even consider dating anyone locally - the same manner he intentionally chose not to listen to the local radio stations. My intuition was enough to discern that in addition to not being emotionally stable for a new meaningful relationship at that moment, coupled with my ability to garner the points of view of everyone that piqued his interest, I was going to be instrumental in his decision making process. Without him knowing, I was going to influence who was not right for him - and also our son.

Consequently, I quickly ascertained that the Nassau relationship would be doomed if pursued and upon his arrival, I knew he would quickly determine similarly for himself. She wasn't totally honest with her personal situation where many of her photographs weren't current for starters. When he arrived everything quickly materialized before his eyes as her circumstances became clear: He had to rent a car because she claimed that hers was being repaired on the day of arrival. And even though he wanted to check into a hotel, she suggested her home when they chatted - then at the last minute she borrowed a friend's vacant vacation home where landscape maintenance seemed to have lapsed a few months causing him to wonder whether she was too embarrassed about her own circumstances - or worse - whether she still lived at her parent's home. Then by happenstance, they ran into her twenty-six-year-old son. He was taller than my 6ft. 4-inch husband which was a little intimidating at the moment. And from his social media posts, he glorified his recreational abuse of drugs - even on his job. My husband was totally out of the element he was accustomed to although she was totally smitten with him. And after he was introduced to her girlfriend who candidly told him she hoped he won't be like the others on the second evening over dinner, for all intents and purposes, the weekend had already ended.

The second time my husband met with another woman was two months ago. Now this occurrence was absolutely unplanned. He had flown up to Miami two days ahead of a planned summer vacation where he was treating my entire family on a Western Caribbean Cruise. His intention was to visit his mother and sisters in Biscayne Park two days ahead of picking up my mother, sister, niece and our son who were arriving and all disembarking on Saturday.

Having been online on the dating site a few months now, he discovered a new twist in his search options. For the very first time when he opened the Dating App on the mainland, the pool of available women exponentially increased. He immediately realized that it was due to the fact that his tablet and cellphone GPS locations now were in the contiguous United States. Before that time, he was only able to communicate via the dating App Direct Messaging with people exclusively in the Caribbean. So during the down time at his mother's house, he briefly chatted with someone new who lived in the Coral Gables area of Miami. After a prolonged conversation they decided to meet on Friday in the early evening at the Cheesecake Factory for dinner at the mall literally across the street from her high rise apartment. This time like before, he told his nosy sister what he was about to do jokingly saying, "... just in case I don't return, you know where to start looking."

Ms. Coral Gables was extremely late and she wasn't at fault. I would love to suggest that I had nothing to do with all of the arbitrary wrong turns she'd taken to maneuver through 5 o'clock traffic on Friday in south Florida in her attempt to be timely, so I plead the fifth. In the short window of time, I was able to perform the necessary due diligence seeing this meeting was last minute and I selfishly wanted nothing to ensue knowing that his vacation departure was in less than twenty-four hours. I was able to learn about her circumstances where she was unemployed living in a high rise luxury apartment. My intuition again concluded that she was totally wrong for him and he would again soon realize it for himself. After all, I should know who is right for him - we spent the last 25 years of our lives together.

While he waited for her, he passed the time hanging out in the mall and bought a few shirts for the cruise. When she finally got to her apartment it was around 9pm - two hours past their date time - and she told him that she was too tired to have dinner. So he offered to buy her take out from the restaurant and bring it by her apartment. She agreed.

Upon his arrival to the parking garage, she had to allow his entry via the remote access system. He began to feel a little hopeful when he recognized some of the backgrounds of the pictures she posted on the dating site like around the lower level swimming pool as he walked by. That was again short lived when everything went south after he was greeted at the door. She met him wearing the same torn jeans and top from the profile pictures on the dating site. Subsequently her pants appeared more torn than in the posts now showing hints of underwear and derrière which led him to speculate how long ago those pictures were taken. She proudly expressed that they were her favorite jeans and at that moment I knew what he was thinking; they must be her only jeans. Additionally, the only visible furniture in her stark spacious apartment was on the patio from where they eventually ate.

Considering everything that he had been through, he hadn't even been with this woman for an hour when she had the audacity to ask if she could join him on the cruise disembarking the following day. He simply expressed how tired he was without explaining the impossibility of her request and at an opportune time later, excused himself graciously.

But today was going to be different; and as fairy tales suggests, today was going to be charmed - after all - today was going to be the third time. Again, in the 'spirit' of full disclosure, this time his morning date was all of my doing. Today's meeting was the culmination of several months of research and surveillance where a confluence of events that I had meticulously orchestrated and persons I had unknowingly influenced and manipulated were now coming to fruition. I had navigated the cosmos meta-physically and spiritually to align the stars, planets, and moons to bring two lost souls together ... no time too soon. And now, I have the opportunity to rewrite a happier ending to my life's story with him.

With the announcement by the captain to prepare for landing as a cue, I took the opportunity to say goodbye to the love of my physical life and my infinite dreams, my husband and forever universal friend. The conditions were right to attempt what has been described as Electronic Voice Phenomenon where bereaved individuals affirm to hearing the voices of their recently departed loved ones in electronic devices. If the receiver is in a clear and lucid state of mind, they tend to question what they have heard as irrational and totally disregard what they had experienced. But he had just awakened, and still in a semi state of sleep which is perfect for this form of communication. He was about to start over with someone whom over the past several months I had meticulously surveilled to the point where she was also ready to start over and hopefully love him as much as I had.

So as *Corinne Bailey Rae* sang *The Sea* in his ears in her breathy inimitable way, my soul cried joyfully knowing that from this moment forward he was going to be alright - our son was going to be alright. For the past quarter century, he made me very happy. And ultimately, I knew he would make her happy too. https://www.youtube.com/watch?v=BmuzfjaYo4Y

The Sea

I never knew you were standing on this shore.
It says everything .... explains everything.
And then from then on it couldn't be just like before.
It says everything .... changes everything.
So don't just stand there wishing life would fade away.
Don't you go around with anyone that makes you feel ashamed.

The chorus refrains ...

Goodbye paradise.
I hope that someday you could try....

But instead I sang softly in his ears the following ....

"Go Ahead and Cry,
It's Time to Say Goodbye,
Go Ahead and Cry,
It's Time to Say Goodbye,"

Instantly I knew ... he heard me. I knew because – first and foremost – I never was able to sing or carry a tune. On the other hand, I'd like to think that the metaphor 'angelic voices' or 'singing like an angel' was reminiscent of the voice he heard. In my previous existence, I was told numerous times my speaking voice was somewhat angelic, but I knew I couldn't sing and I didn't even try.

He instantly recognized my pitchy voice and softly began to uncontrollably cry. He was seated in an exit row window seat and turned his face away from the persons to the right of him so they would not be able to see how distraught he had instantly become. His sobs were inaudible and prolonged as tears trailed down his face rolling like a stream. Moments after the plane landed he calmed himself behind his sunglasses like mourners do and came to the realization that what he had just experienced was a sign that everything was going to be alright and now began to dry the tears on his face with the back of his hands. As he deplaned, he inaudibly mouthed the words "I love you." knowing that I would see.

In spite of everything he had been through, he desperately needed to move on with his life and raise our son Kevin to be the best man he could be by way of his example. It was the absolute least I could do for my once in my lifetime love and kindred spirit of my everlasting dreams, Rufus Turnbull.

FOREWORD

I hope I'm not getting too ahead of myself in all my excitement. You see, this is a story of hopes and dreams from a unique perspective. It is a story of reflection and recollection of a life lived and the perseverance to carry on. It is a narrative of happenstance that under normal conditions and circumstances would have never occur nor later materialized. It is a story that lends us to think whether situations are actually chanced or whether unknown forces intervene. And it reinforces the fact that love in general terms is everlasting and how it truly conquers all. It also suggests that anyone who seeks clarification to any of life's unanswered questions should simply look within themselves and the truth may be revealed.

This story is also unique because of the point of view it is being told. The following accounts are all accurate with the exception of events clarified later in the *Author's Notes*. Otherwise everything described henceforth were derived from a compilation of first hand conversations and visual accounts by the individuals involved, along with actual journals, video-logs and text message transcription. And if you haven't already ascertained, I no longer exist physically because on that fateful day in January 2015, my life expired and my Afterlife began. Not immediately I must also add because I was coming to terms with the unfolding new realities and possibilities of life after death.

You see, Afterlife is now the reality of my existence. It is also the perspective in which I can share this story. For those that believe that in death life simply ends and everlasting life begins only for the righteous, I am not in the position nor will I attempt to advise anyone what to think, what to believe, or what is right or wrong for them. What I can subscribe is true conviction is solidified at that very moment in one's life when their truth is realized, whatever that truth may be. In other words, clarity is brought forth not from the life lessons being taught but when those lessons are truly learned.

During my physical life I believed many things and perpetuated beliefs that were familiar to my family and friends because they were constantly repeated and seldom questioned – at home, in paroquial schools, and at the different houses of worship I attended. In hindsight it all made sense because I was being spiritually fulfilled. But if hindsight is 20/20, then Afterlife is UHD (Ultra High Definition) because everything now from my perspective is perfectly clear.

Rufus on the other hand always questioned social norms and was very careful how, when, and where he expressed his opinions about topics that were taboo. We respectfully agreed to disagree although from time to time the subject was revisited whenever the news cycle brought attention to the issues of contention like the sexual abuse or infidelity cases with clergy. I was conditioned to defend the *Word* and not the Man, while Rufus chose to question their credibility where they were in judgement of anyone that believes differently.

A perfect example of what I am referring happened when I witnessed the meeting between Rufus and the pastor of the church I attended where before my passing I was also the church's secretary. The meeting was primarily to make the arrangements for my funeral service on St. Thomas. Four days prior there had been a Spanish service at the crematory chapel in Puerto Rico for my friends and family living over there. At this meeting the pastor got to know Rufus personally for the first time and was surprised when he learned what he did for a living because it was totally unconventional to what had been locally established. The pastor also was able to discern that he was not as religious as I was and realize the meeting was not the place to proselytize. What he did convey to Rufus in confidence was 'he did not have any answers and honestly could not tell him where I was.'

A few months later I overheard Rufus telling his best friend Milton that the statement from my pastor was the most honest and truthful thing he had ever heard in a church. They were having another one of their heated discussion at the midnight buffet on the Tom Joyner Fantastic

Voyage Cruise. They were so loud at one point that they became the attention to onlookers in their immediate vicinity who incredulously peered at Rufus with disdain. The beauty of their friendship was they were unwavering in their positions and in the end they always agreed to disagree.

When I was alive Rufus expressed the fact that he did not claim to know anything about the different religions and actually found a little humor that per capita, St. Thomas - in the United States Virgin Islands - has more than its fair share of houses of worship. One time he pointed out all of the churches he recognized while we drove that were in very close proximity – where the newer were in various phases of construction. I even noted churches that were commercial buildings where he hadn't, but I didn't want to help perpetuate his antagonistic comments. He later explained that the population of the island could not sustain all of the churches.

At the same time for a moment, he attended a non-denominational church seeking his truths primarily, but specifically because the service was less than 90 minutes until he stopped going when it no longer served his purpose.

Invariably, the pastor knew at that particular moment with Rufus as his audience of one in that meeting in his office, he basically uttered what my husband needed to hear. And with what was discussed, he was able to provide a small level of comfort. As life continues, on the subsequent Sundays and spiritual holidays to follow, the pastor continued to preached the gospel to his congregation as prophesied in the Bible.

But from my unique point of view and perspective, Afterlife is actually not what I had expected. To this point it has been much more. It wasn't what I expected because of what I was promised during all those years of paroquial schooling and the lessons taught at the various houses of worship I have attended during my short lifetime. What I have learned that over the millennia those lessons and messages have been misconstrued primarily for the preyed profit from those who most likely cannot afford the price of promised salvation. And it seemed that the houses of worship that were less profitable seem to be doing the most good. Without proselytizing any further, I found that The Word is simply a guiding path to circumstances in your life you may or may not fully understand nor appreciate - no matter what religion you transcribe to. But in the end, The

Word is totally realized in Afterlife. What I once sought that was inexplicable and unfathomable is now found. One way I can describe what have now become my reality is in the following example.

Imagine your world as it exists right now metaphorically as the hugest warehouse that you can imagine. The contents of this warehouse contains everything you have seen, heard and learned, including everyone you have ever known. So the more in life you have experienced is how your warehouse is populated. Stay with me now.

When you are alive, the warehouse is dark and void of all natural light. It's synonymous to what you experience when you are sleeping. Close your eyes for a moment to experience the perpetual darkness I am describing.

When you are awake, the warehouse still remains dark but you are able to navigate and negotiate around it with a metaphorical flashlight. So when you speak with your friends, family, mutual and non-mutual acquaintances, you are allowed briefly into their warehouses with your flashlight - and vice versa - they are into yours for as long as you are invited until you are not. If you recall something from your past, your mind shines the flashlight in that general direction and allows you to recall. And if you seem to forget something you have experienced, it is possibly hidden until it is found, or someone that you have invited into your warehouse reminds you where they saw it last with their flashlight. And to make the case for people that experience dementia, the intensity of their flashlight is affected. If I didn't lose you by now, hold on for the kicker.

The moment you take that last breath of life, the flashlight is forever turned off, but your entire warehouse is now illuminated brilliantly. Additionally, all the other warehouses that you were associated with are also lit and accessible for your instantaneous exploration. Everything you have experienced is instantly seen and is accessible at the speed of light - or 186,000 miles per second. To put this into perspective, it takes a little more than a tenth of a second for light to travel around the earth. And every time you see the light of the sun, it took that light 8½ minutes to reach your eyes being 93 million miles away.

Light, by definition is simply electromagnetic radiation that has waves properties. Its electromagnetic spectrum is a form of energy that is divided into several bands of wavelengths that are seen and unseen where the visible spectrum represents a narrow group of wavelengths you see when you are alive via the proverbial flashlight. And in the Afterlife, I am now able to see the entire light spectrum where all can be heard and all can be seen. In essence, I have become omnipotent. And to conflate a biblical reference, at the speed of light, I am always there and on time. That is the premise in which this story derives. My sense of awareness now is not only visual, but it's all encapsulating. At the end of the book, and example of my omnipotence is clearly documented.

To many, I may not have fulfilled my life's purpose although cut 48 years short. But the way I have come to its terms is it was all of the time I had there relatively. The significance of my life can only be found with those whose lives I have personally touched. The impact that I made in the lives of those that shared their deepest condolences with my family were sincerely appreciated and will eventually wane as time passes by. Those truths are synonymous with everyone that has experienced great losses of loved ones. I now only exist metaphysically in the hearts, minds, and fleeting memories of the people whose warehouses I have had the privilege of being invited into. And in that state I am quickly realizing that my life is not over. I still have a huge part to play where I can still be impactful.

I also realize that after I passed, a void was left in the souls of the loved ones whom held me near. Their thoughts are ever-consuming of memories of me in their warehouses: my son, mother, sisters, niece, nephew, aunts, uncles – and for the sake of this book – my husband particularly. Although many of my friends have moved on and are only reminded of me when they see my picture or think about someone in my immediate family, invariably it all wanes as time passes by. And you only die when you are no longer in the thoughts of your loved ones.

Sensing but not actually knowing that my life's end was nearing, I had instinctively taken steps and made decisions to manage crises in my family in Puerto Rico. My grandmother was increasingly becoming an overwhelming burden for my mother to care for after being diagnosed with dementia. After two years my mother showed signs of exhaustion and sleep deprivation. I became very concerned and made the difficult decision along with my siblings to have my grandmother admitted to a nursing home and to help subsidize the cost. Consequently, as a result of dementia, a few months before I passed I realized that my grandmother had already said goodbye to me as the example of the flashlight intensity suggested. Remembering when Rufus and I visited her last at the nursing home, she recognized him but not me. In my presence she called him by name and actually said,

"Rufus, how are you doing......where is your beautiful wife."

That statement tugged at my heart strings, but I persevered and still continued to visit her until the end. I now know that it was the universe's way of rationalizing the situation of my passing with my grandmother. It was no secret I was her favorite grandchild; even my sisters expressed those sentiments to me. And although the family continues to visit her regularly, she was purposely never notified of my circumstances.

Additionally, I asked Rufus to take care of the minor home repairs at my mother's house that had accumulated over time in order that she could get additional rental income now that my grandmother had moved out of the lower level. And to top it off, I went to Sears and ordered the installation of an automatic gate opener so that my mother would no longer have to get out of her car in the rain to enter the carport after forty years.

I did all of this during my cancer treatments when I spent extended weeks at times at the hospital in Puerto Rico. The other arrangements I made were more of a personal nature where I had individual picture albums prepared for my sisters, niece and my son. I had accumulated hundreds of photographs over the quarter century and I felt compelled to catalogue them with momentous pictures with me in them and present them as personal albums. It was my way of leaving physical memories of me with them individually.

But for my husband, I didn't do anything. Not because of any shortcomings, vengeance or being overlooked. I didn't do anything because I felt that he had everything. Now as I observe him grieving continuously for the past months, I see where I was wrong. I see how at home he expects me to walk down the hall at certain times of the day when I routinely did and now I am no longer there. I also observed how my side of our king size bed remains kept where he is content to only continue to sleep on the edge on his side. I quickly learned that if he had everything he wouldn't be in so much emotional pain. For the past months, he has been showing me that I was his everything.

CHAPTER ONE

*"I was willing to take this ride in life without complaints
about the lengths that he took."*

URING THE LAST YEARS OF MY LIFE before my diagnosis, Rufus would from time to time ridicule me for some of the presents I had given him during the holiday seasons. And to be totally fair, I must also admit he has lauded me for the gifts when I genuinely touched his heart or totally surprised him. It was the smallest gestures that seemed to give him the greatest sense of joy and gratitude. And on several occasions he would mentioned repeatedly that our son was the present he was most thankful for.

Now in hindsight - you know - in Afterlife Ultra High Definition, I have also come to the realization where I have gotten some of the presents I have given to him totally wrong. While on the other hand, he has always told me that I gave the best greeting cards for his birthdays and our anniversaries. His comments always raved about whether I spent an inordinate amount of time reading several cards in Kmart to pick the right one or whether I worked part time at Hallmark unbeknownst to him because the cards seem to always strike a chord. Those impressions were so meaningful to the point that he kept the cards in his office until they were replaced by the next year's offerings.

I know that I'm prolonging what I am avoiding to convey, but you can't blame a girl. You see, the last two Christmases, I really messed up - big time. In my heart's spirit - and I am being totally honest now - I was at fault.

My excuse was the traditional cop-out statement most people in prolonged relationships utter summarily saying," he has everything" as far as gifts were concerned. The truth is I had become complacent and frankly, I stopped paying attention.

It is typical that during the infancy of relationships, we are all guilty of being giddy and emotionally delirious; the sun is brighter, the sky is always blue, and we always stop to smell the roses. We pull out all of the stops in making and maintaining good appearances and impressions.

I remember having regular appointments at the hair and nail salons - not to mention being a regular at the shoe stores especially when there were sales. Then as the years go by, we tend to take the important things for granted. The bait that was necessary to catch the 'fish' aren't necessary anymore because we are no longer fishing. The fish are no longer in the ocean because we have provided a proverbial fish tank of sorts in the environments in which we dwell.

This observation is not gender specific. But when it came to my own circumstance, I submit that if I were to make a visual presentation of my relationship in the form of a graph, it would show a steady upward trend that eventually levels out and plateaus. But as the saying goes, 'What goes up, must come down.' Unhealthy relationships trend downwards and some actually crash. On the other hand, many would relish at the concept where relationships that plateaus are a good thing. It suggests routine and stability. But as honesty dictates, in comparison Rufus' graph didn't change - he never plateaued. Yes, definitely, and of course from time to time he'd get on my last nerve, but that was his nature.

Like the time he used to allow every new car he own to run out of gas for the first time just so he will know how many miles he could get on a full tank around the islands. He did not trust the fuel economy rating of the vehicles stating that it was his opinion the manufacturer's provided averages for highway and city driving were inaccurate. His supposition was based on the islands terrain with all of the hills and the maximum speed limit of 35mph. So he filled the tanks and would drive his new cars for the first time until it ran out of gas. Then divide the number of miles driven by the capacity of the fuel tank and give it his own category as 'Island Miles per gallon.' You are going to hear me say this a few times in the book. "I AM NOT KIDDING."

He did it with the Chevy truck I bought him for his birthday in 2003 when it less than 100 yards from the gas station on the waterfront he ran out of fuel by the funeral home. Luckily the that truck included Roadside Assistance. And he did it again when he traded it in for the Ford Explorer. But the time he did it with the Hummer, I had to get involved. I came to his rescue in my cute Infiniti SUV. Kevin warned him he was going to get into trouble when LOW FUEL spelled out before his eyes on the instrument display. He deduced that meant 30 miles of gas was left in the tank when on the following day he broke down on an incline. He called me at my job and took my car returning with a few gallons of fuel and to make a long story short, I did not speak to my husband until the smell of gas was out of my car. After I passed away, he bought a service van and told his best friend Milton to be on call when he runs out of gas.

But other than that, by nature he is a jester and also has been a sustaining sense of stability. And over the quarter century together his graph never leveled out. He always seemed to get me whether it cost hundreds, thousands, or simply his time.

Like on our second date, he told me that we were going to a Kenny G concert. Truth be told, I was excited and totally impressed. At my second memorial service Rufus stood in front of the church and told everyone that I was new to the island and he could tell me anything and I would have believed it. He explained that he actually had a Kenny G Live cassette where he photocopied the paper casing that had a picture of the box office ticket where the concert was recorded live. He proceeded to cut out the ticket, and repeated the process so he would have two. Then he continued to explained how he called a friend at the supermarket to chill a bottle of Asti Spumante Sparkling Wine in the afternoon and picked up a freshly baked island favorite 'butter bread' from Weeks and Weeks Bakery on Back Street before picking me up. When he said 'butter bread', one of his friends actually cheered him on from the back of the church. The tenor of the memorial service immediately changed when he concluded that it was indeed a Kenny G concert, the only difference was the venue was at the Drake's Seat lookout where the seating were the front seats of his car under the open sunroof that allowed the view of the moon and stars with champagne and warm bread. After that, quite frankly, I didn't know what to expect from him because I was willing to take this ride in life without complaints about the lengths that he took.

Or the time when he flew my mother in to surprise me on my birthday at the end of December a little more than a month after we were married when I commented that I was feeling homesick. He made all the detailed arrangements like booking her reservations from Puerto Rico down to having a chauffeur pick her up from the airport, delivered her to the Chart House Restaurant and somehow had her seated at our table by the time we returned from the salad bar. Are you kidding me? He even had the foresight to catch my salad plate as my hands instinctively went to my face in disbelief as I cried and the other diners applauded after I said, "Mother, what are you doing here?" And this was achieved way before cell phones and the internet. Back then, airline reservations were done face to face at travel agencies and at times over the phone. He explained to me later that the hired car was the easiest task only because of his island notoriety of being a minor celebrity as a local musician. Hundred$$$.

Another time he led me to believe he was going away for the weekend to see his mother and I decided to call one of my girlfriends over to hang out with me. Rufus anticipate that decision like a chess movement and preemptively notified her of his true intentions. So on the day of travel, I drove him to the airport with my girlfriend in tow. I was about to kiss him goodbye when he asked,

"Aren't you coming along?"

"I don't have a ticket," I replied immediately. Then on cue he showed me two boarding passes to which I continued incredulously, "But I don't have any clothes!"

"I haven't packed anything either," he demonstrated having no luggage. Before I could ask what we were going to wear – I swear – without the camera production, Rufus quoted the catch phrase to the following advertisement campaign saying while holding his wallet,

"With American Express, you're always packed." He then further explained that after we get our rental car in Miami we were going to make a beeline to the mall for weekend clothes.

"I don't have my makeup!" I complained when I realized that my face was naked to which he continued smiling and casually pointed to my girlfriend who dangled my makeup purse behind me. It finally hit me that he got me again and I punched him hard in the gut after I said,

"And look at how I am dressed!" to which I came to the realization that we should always be ready for any and every eventuality outside our homes.

I immediately went to the restroom after my girlfriend left with our car to apply my makeup. When we boarded I had no idea that we were flying 1st Class and again I felt self-conscious about my attire so I covered myself with the complimentary blanket. Before takeoff Rufus motioned to the passenger across the aisle from him where he asked for additional hot towels where he wiped his hands, face, under arms and exposed legs. Rufus suggested that I should do similarly joking and I punched in again, this time in the arm.

Or the Christmas when he sacrificed part of our huge deck and built me a walk-in closet seeing that I had exhausted the small space of our existing. Another time he bought me a larger new SUV when he saw me struggling to put Kevin - while in his car seat - in the backseat of my 2-door Explorer. He chose the three-row 7-passenger Montero for when my family visited.

We were always on the same frequency back then because we had a rule to curtail our spending - or specifically his proclivity towards buying new electronics. We decided that each other's approval was needed if we were going to spend more than a hundred dollars. So if he wanted to buy me a car, I had to be informed. On the same day he visited the St. Thomas dealership and later call to inform me what he was about to do, I told him that I had just hung up with the dealer on St. Croix and had chosen the exact make and model car where after they delivered it by barge was a better deal. Thousand$$$$.

Or the Christmas when he got the desired effect of me becoming very emotional when he spent the previous evening chronicling our life with framed pictures and hung them in our hall to be revealed when I awoke. Time.

But the best presents I actually received was when I became ill. He told me, "I got you." and to take the year off and get better. I was always concerned about money then, but the way he expressed his determination reassured me.

One time when I was away for my treatments, he purposely shocked the hell out of me when he forwarded pictures of my kitchen totally trashed and destroyed. The cabinets were all indiscriminately smashed to chronicle the before of the renovation he began after he returned from dropping me off at the airport. The after would be revealed upon my return. He built all of the cabinets himself on our patio after work every day having accumulated just about all of the necessary table and power tools over the years. And when he needed a hand to help him carry the large cabinet carcasses, Milton was a phone call away. I even took the opportunity to choose the type of sink I preferred so I purchased it and had it delivered to St. Thomas. And when I returned he also allowed me to pick the counter top.

Although the following example wasn't a gift, it was a celebration where Rufus challenged himself to arrange a date that was worthy of bragging on the local radio station. In the past there was a Valentine's Day competition where the listening audience could call in and toot their own horn about how romantic a date they had planned. Rufus told me their accounts weren't imaginative. So he simply said we were going out for dinner on Valentine's Day. So after work, the evening was young and we both dressed for a romantic time on the town. We were in the car when he said he had forgotten the keys and would be right back. I waited...and waited...and waited, until I became annoyed - then concerned.

Fifteen minutes later I returned to our apartment to find all of the lights off with the exception of a flashlight on the floor illuminating our small glass dining table from beneath. Earlier in the day he bought takeout from the restaurant we were supposed to be dining at, had it stored in the refrigerator and oven, reheated and plated our favorites from the menu, and he simply waited for my return because he actually had the keys.

But the most memorable present by far was the time upon my return from another three weeks of cancer treatment, Rufus recorded my astonishment for perpetuity. I was totally astounded upon my return to find our 20-year-old wooden 26-step stairway, that steeply lead down to the house, replaced with a concrete staircase with three landings. It had deteriorated naturally over the years and was repaired and reinforced from time to time to keep it safe to traverse. I was actually recorded saying, "I can't believe that I am crying over stairs."
https://vimeo.com/334324335

Even my last Christmas gift from Rufus was special even though we were apart. Kevin and I were in Puerto Rico spending the holidays with my family while he had to remain home because he had to work on St.

John. It was simply magical when I was presented with a gift of a Microsoft Surface from under my sister's Christmas tree. "No way!" I exclaimed. I immediately called him and asked him how could he have known. He nonchalantly stated that while we sat up in bed watching television, I made the comment of how cool it was to write with the stylus on a tablet during a commercial on television. That was the seed I had planted in his mind. He then activated Santa's elves – in the form of our 19-year old niece and 14-year old son – to purchase it from the Microsoft store in Plaza Las Americas Mall in Puerto Rico. At the end of the year I returned alone on the 30th of December to celebrate my birthday and the New Year with him. It was the last holiday celebration we would spend together.

Now my offerings were equally surprising and mostly appreciated initially: his first flying lesson – (hundred$$$), his first pickup truck – (thousand$$$$), our son – (love & time). I even loved the expression he had when I presented him with a diecast model of a miniature Corvette at one of my office Christmas parties. At that time, it was his favorite car. I told him that I couldn't afford the real one, but someday I would.

Then I reciprocated for the surprise of flying my mother in for my birthday when I had to incorporate subterfuge to truly surprise him. It was the weekend of his birthday when I told him we were going away.

"Where are we going?" he asked.

I simply replied, "Away."

He became juvenile stating that it was his birthday and he wasn't going to drive to the airport nor carry our luggage bag. I simply played along.

On the way, I detoured to the Emerald Beach Hotel next to the airport. He commented to say he thought we were going away. I told him that the hotel was 'away' and since he was being stubborn, go ahead and wait in the lobby so I could park the car and bring our luggage bag.

While he waited he took the opportunity to ask the front desk whether I had checked into a room. They not only confirmed that a room was booked for the evening, they added that a lot of my friends were waiting in the room for the guest of honor. When I returned with the roller carryon in tow, Rufus looked like a Cheshire Cat that ate a canary bird. There were six couples of friends and family who all celebrated Rufus that evening while he let everyone know that he was the smartest person in the room and we all played along.

The following morning, we left and headed towards the airport where I left Rufus at the departure curb and told him I was going to park the car. He was amenable and cooperative as he retrieved the carryon and waited for me. What happened next was described best when Rufus told me later,

"I thought I was being 'punked' when I saw the car getting smaller and smaller as it left the airport."

Moments later our landlord and owner of the local flying school Cleo tapped him on the shoulder and said,

"Are you ready to go up?"

"Go up where?" Rufus asked.

Cleo pointed to the sky.

An hour and a half later I returned smiling and laughing knowing that I got him good and kissed him for being such a good sport. But my moment of glory was short lived. Cleo was also hired to fly us to Tortola in the British Virgin Islands for the rest of the weekend. He said Rufus did such a great job in his first lesson, he was going to let Rufus fly most of the way to Tortola. I objected,

"OH NO HE'S NOT!"

♦ ♦ ♦

Back then I was really paying attention. Now for the moment of truth. On the other hand, can I take a break for a moment or two to gather my thoughts? You guys are going to be a tough audience huh? Alright then.

Then there were those presents that warranted ridicule; the disastrous stories about me buying him Live Salsa Concerts on DVDs for a recent Christmas when he already had them. How was a girl s'posed to know? Come on ladies...are you going to help a girl out...or y'all gonna leave me hangin'? But in all seriousness, that was an indication where I was not paying attention.

Again the myth that suggest that after someone dies, they see their entire life pass before their eyes is partly true. In addition to being able to transport myself anywhere at a moment's notice in my life's warehouse, I am quickly realizing that I also have total recall of everything that I have ever seen or experienced down to the minute detail. As a result, I am now recognizing where I fell short and see exactly when and why I had plateaued in my choices and decisions.

During our twenty-five years together, we have actually traveled several hundreds of times for business, pleasure, and simply just to get away. I even overheard Rufus telling Kevin after I passed that he had flown at least 100 times in his short 14 years of life - 18 times before he was the age of one going to our pediatrician in Puerto Rico and visiting family on the mainland.

Anyway, whenever we had a layover at the airport in Puerto Rico, I could always find Rufus in the Gifts Shop buying a magazine and the latest Live Salsa DVDs. His favorite was undoubtedly the 2003 Live performance of Bobby Valentin 35th Anniversary, *Vuelve A La Carcel.* (Goes Back to Jail) His orchestra performed in the penitentiary in Puerto Rico where he once resided. Bobby wore the same jumpsuits that the audience of inmates wore. They were treated to a star studded lineup of the Caribbean and Latin America's notable musical guest artists.

https://www.youtube.com/watch?v=8s3bVqswaic

Rufus appreciated Bobby Valentin for his virtuosity on the bass. And during the Father's Day weekend in 2015, my sister and niece took him out to dance when he had a brief moment to speak with him when he was pleasantly surprised that he spoke English very well. Bobby told him that he has been to St. Thomas a few times and Rufus reminded him that he was present the last time in the stadium when there were fewer than fifty people in the audience due to multiple events simultaneously scheduled. They had a laugh and my sister took their picture.

When he wasn't watching Salsa on DVD's, he was watching it on broadcast television. Especially on New Year's Eve, he would watch and record WAPA and WKAQ - the Puerto Rico television stations - because they would broadcast live parties from the hotel ballrooms where the best Salsa Orchestras were bringing in the new year at corporate parties.

One particular New Year's Eve when we were in New Jersey at my aunt Debbie's, before we watched the ball dropped at Time Square at midnight, Rufus had already watched the Puerto Rican celebration on his smartphone via our satellite TV system because of Daylight Saving Time. He also remotely recorded it so he could really enjoy the fidelity of the music when we returned.

Or the Christmas evening we spent in our new home theater watching a music documentary produced by Banco Popular de Puerto Rico that featured the history of the Latin Orchestra, El Gran Combo. It was compelling to him because when we met he was working for BPPR twenty years prior. The program was entirely in Spanish and I sat beside him in our designated recliners translating so he could comprehend exactly what was being said. I remember how much of a kick he got when I explained the part when the band leader went to the local university to recruit new musicians and some of the instructors immediately quit and joined the band. They expressed it was the best decision in their lives.

Inexorably, the best gifts are unplanned. They organically materialize and leave indelible impressions. Which reminds me of a vacation he planned in 1998 and at the last minute without Rufus knowing, I invited my grandmother to travel with us from Puerto Rico to Miami. She wanted to visit a childhood friend she hadn't seen in over forty years and since our travel arrangements conveniently included a layover, I booked similar flights for my granny. The reason we were departing from Puerto Rico was because it was the only way we were able to arrive at the stadium before the 1pm kick off to attend a Miami Dolphins game to begin our vacation. Now don't ask me who was playing because I didn't understand the game and still don't. I just loved the atmosphere and the fact that he always had a great time.

My first football game with him wasn't as enjoyable as I expected especially when a little girl sitting behind us kept stepping on my hair that hung behind my seat. Her parents didn't attempt to reprimand her until Rufus stood up and told them if it happened again he was going to toss them into the empty seats below. I have enjoyed the games ever since.

Now my two most memorable NFL games for me were the time we scheduled our vacation to New Orleans to see his second cousin Renaldo Turnbull play in the Superdome for our anniversary in 1996. Two words: Air Conditioning. We arrived earlier on Halloween night and stayed at Le Meridien for four days so I could enjoy the kind of hotel décor I preferred and we spent the remainder at the Hyatt because Rufus found out it was connected to the stadium. We hung around in our seats while the other 50,000 fans made a mad dash for the exit and at our leisure strolled back to our hotel room. The other game that held significance was in September 2009 in Atlanta in another domed stadium. It was the first time we went to a game as a family of three. And I repeat again - Air Conditioning. I know that I have digressed but I just enjoyed basking in the stadiums' cool.

Anyway, immediately after landing Rufus was perplexed not knowing that we were going to make a quick stop in Hialeah to drop off my granny. From time to time he kept reminding me that we only have two tickets for the game. I purposely became annoyed so he would stop. After we dropped my grandmother off, we were back on the highway, left our luggage in the rental car and arrived at the stadium in time to see the fighter jets fly over after the national anthem.

When the game was over, I told Rufus that we were going to have dinner at my grandmother's friend. He fussed on the way about checking in late at our hotel. During dinner we met our hosts who were similarly aged as my grandmother. Unbeknownst to Rufus, the husband of my grandmother's friend just happened to be the legendary Cuban bassist Israel "Cachao" Lopez. [pronounced Ka-Chow] At that point in time, Rufus didn't even know who he was. After dinner the women retired to the living room leaving the men alone. Their conversation was nonexistent. To maintain the subterfuge, I purposely shouted the following in Spanish to kickstart their dialogue,

"Cachao, él toca el bajo también." translated "Cachao, he plays the bass too." A fuse was lit to their conversation. They just had a great time Rufus told me later about how they talked about music, particularly Salsa. He was impressed that Rufus had so much knowledge about Latin music and all the different musicians and the bands in which they led and played in while Cachao humbly expressed to him that he simply "played a little bass too." He was so unassuming and was primarily interested in the different kinds of music played in a third of his lifetime.

When we returned to our hotel that evening, I purposely tuned to the Latino channels on the television which was again - totally out of the ordinary. We also had a rule about that too. When we traveled the TV remote was always mine unless there was a major sporting event on. Anyway, it didn't take long to see Cachao in a TV commercial. I saw the quizzical look on his face and said nothing. About a half hour later, there was Cachao again playing the Ray Ramirez electric upright bass in a Gloria Estefan music video. https://www.youtube.com/watch?v=WWAWQmhqWGo

After the video ended Rufus asked,

"Who did I just meet?"

His question was magical. I told Rufus about my grandmother's relationship with the Lopez's and what a big deal Cachao was in the Latino community from Miami to Puerto Rico. Born in Cuba and unable to return like most expatriates, he is the co-creator of the Mambo and the master of the Descarga which in layman terms is the two-bar cadence jam session. After that meeting, Cachao always left VIP tickets for Rufus and me whenever he performed in Puerto Rico. Unfortunately, on the two occasions when he did perform we were traveling. But my mother and granny wasn't about to let those first class experiences fall by the wayside. Once they called us from the Lopez's Presidential Suite before his concert where Cachao humbly commented,

"...they keep making a big fuss about me." and continued to complain that the room was way too big.

When Cachao passed away in 2008, Rufus didn't learn about it until months later when he received his subscription to Bass Player Magazine where Cachao was featured on the cover. He felt compelled to call the local talk radio station WVWI AM 1000 he now disdains because of its radical political views and began the conversation with the host at that time Sam Topp asking,

"Have you ever been in the presence of greatness and didn't know it?"

He then told the radio audience about that fateful day I orchestrated back in 1998. After I passed away Rufus spent a lot of time reflecting and wrote about the experience and later posted it on his Facebook page.

The perfect example of how thoughtful Rufus has been as far as paying forward his experiences happened eight years later. It was 2006 and we were up watching television in bed when the trailer to the movie *El Cantante* (The Singer) starring Jennifer Lopez and Marc Anthony played the leading roles. It was a musical docu-drama about one of Puerto Rico's most renowned singers Hector Lavoe (Hector The Voice). The critics commented that the music arrangements were also a character in the movie – not only the musicians. Knowing that demographically the movie won't play locally in St. Thomas - but it would be a blockbuster in Puerto Rico because the two leading stars were Boricuas, (Puerto Ricans living in the US) Rufus said,

"I am going to Puerto Rico to see it when it opens."

I got excited and replied, "Great, I am coming too."
"That's fine, but I don't want to see it with you." Rufus continued.
I was totally affronted until he mentioned,
"I am going to take your grandmother." He further explained
It was so endearing you could imagine what happened next.

◆ ◆ ◆

Even though I totally understood what was being sung in the songs, Salsa music was never on my playlists. I was a very good Salsa dancer and did my thing on the weekends at the various nightclubs in my late teens and early twenties. Shortly after I was married at the age of twenty-three, a month or thereabouts my Matron of Honor who only speaks Spanish called to see how married life was treating me and heard Salsa playing in the background when she said,

"Chica, lo tienes escuchando su musica también?" [Girl, you have him listening to your music too?]

I corrected her explaining briefly the music was Rufus'.

So for a guy that I regarded as having it all relative to his own personal means, I failed to pay attention to him. If I had, not only would I have not repeated what sounded good – "he has it all" – I would have also realized he indeed has all of the Live Salsa DVDs. And if it really mattered whether I really wanted to present him with a DVD that he would enjoy, then I should have taken the time to peruse through his library of video discs that was meticulously cataloged and inventoried. After returning the discs that I purchased to the store for exchanges and found out later he also had those replacements I presented, I simply gave up and gave him a gift certificate.

The following year I added insult to injury when I tried to justify the gift that I left under the Christmas tree was thoughtful when I bought him a huge bag of Mesquite. Can I talk about something else? Okay, it was wrapped and appeared like a pillow in a case. In hindsight, a nice luxurious pillow sounds amazing now that I think of it.

I again recall from my warehouse a weekend when the three of us stayed at the Ritz Carlton on St. Thomas when he commented that the pillows were the best he had ever slept upon. Rufus even inquired about purchasing a set. Anyway, I figured mesquite would be a hit because he loves to barbecue. But he correctly made the analogy that my present was the equivalent to buying someone dishwashing liquid because they just love to do the dishes. He even complained to my mother stating that I bought him a bag of coal. He was correct. I had stopped paying attention. Hindsight now suggests Christmas cards would have sufficed.

CHAPTER TWO

"I couldn't stand to see the deterioration of my family after the
few months had passed without me. I knew that time would heal their
wounds - but at the same time - I didn't want to witness the turmoil."

A S I LOOK AT HIM IN HIS WAREHOUSE for these past months suffering emotionally and depressed, it has been obvious that in addition to missing me, he has been missing adult human interaction. Although our son Kevin was there, he also was enduring the loss of my presence and if it wasn't for the fact that he had to take him to and from school daily, he would have been further down the rabbit hole.

It warmed my spirit when I saw Rufus try his hands at cooking for the very first time. He would spend hours on the computer watching YouTube of video recipes and then he would have a try at them. I remember when he tried Fish-n-Chips and it was a disaster after he added yellow food coloring - which wasn't in any of the recipes - in the batter in what I assumed he was trying to get the color right. I smiled when I saw him smiling as he disposed it in the kitchen trash bin and diligently started over without the food coloring.

Then I remember that he was very proud of the Sriracha Chicken and rice he prepared from the recipe he had gotten from a mainland client staying on St. John. She introduced him to Pinterest explaining that all of her girlfriends in Tennessee rave over her recipes that she has now called her own.

Months later in the year his best friend replaced me on the Tom Joyner Fantastic Voyage Cruise when they had that heated discussion I described and where he sought advice from the various celebrity chefs and was recorded upside down by Milton when he volunteered in the cooking demonstrations. He learned about the temperature flash points of olive oil immediately realizing why he was ruining perfectly cut pieces of salmon at home. He also found that culturally he had been eating portion sizes larger than nutritionally recommended from the recipe servings on food labels. During the cruise stop in Jamaica, he even bought himself a chef's jacket for Two Thousand Jamaican Dollars ($20.00 US) as a personal graduation gift. Later he reveled in the social interaction he created daily after picking up Kevin from school. He would cook dinner every day and post the pictures of his plated entrees to his sisters and my family in a group chat describing everything he cooked to be coming ceremonially from Chrissy's Kitchen.

My sisters actually got jealous and began cooking again. They both ate out more often than not and began presenting their meals just to prove their own limited culinary skills. And at times Rufus would cook for my family when they flew over for the weekend where from time to time he would ask my mother for tips. And since my sister hardly had anything to work with when they were over there, Rufus actually went shopping once in his chef's jacket and everyone treated him differently like he actually knew what he was doing.

I also thought it was so wonderful how his sisters on the mainland – Lena, Linda, Lynnette and Janet would call him at the end of their work week in the evenings to check in on him. But at the same time, I also found something very disturbing. At home My Guys were hardly speaking to each other. Even though Rufus would ask Kevin how he was coping from time to time, Kevin's responses were short and not engaging like we were accustomed.

We used to love watching The Amazing Race and Chopped TV shows together where Kevin would say something like,

"... if you and dad were on the show, you would keep him back mom putting on makeup." or "The both of you guys would be eliminated because you can't swim." knowing that we sent him to a swimming camp.

And we also use the play Chopped at home where they would critique my cooking. One time Kevin was so critical about my presentation he said,

"I can't let you pass to the next round," to which I actually replied,

"You little bugger."

But of late he was quiet and insulated keeping his thoughts to himself. I respectfully refer to his responses as F.O.G. or being foggy when he stated: "I'm Fine," "I'm Okay," "I'm Good." Rufus simply summed it up as Kevin dealing with the situation in his own way. And with the little time during their short ride to and from school where they use to identify the cruise ships in the harbor or discuss the next time both needed to go to the barbershop, the rides were now in silence.

Rufus and Kevin always argued about sports where they found themselves purposely rooting for the different teams. Tim Duncan versus LeBron James was the latest argument but now all was quiet on the homefront. An example of the temperament around the house immediately after my passing and the subsequent months to follow is appropriately described in the following draft to a journal Rufus wrote when he was trying to develop his writing style.

Father and son laid subdued on the sectional sofa as the fourth quarter drive of the Super Bowl XLIX (49) was becoming a foregone conclusion. Ordinarily they would have been enjoying the season's biggest game downstairs in the home theater with full 7.1 surround sound on a 120-inch screen from a brilliant deep color Hi-Def Sony Projector, but the great room 55-inch flat panel display - although a quarter of the size diagonally - sufficed under the circumstances.

Normal circumstances would have a cast of characters whom would have invited themselves over because of the big screen and comfortable reclining seats that they individually claimed annually. But this year was different. In the recent years, hors d'oeuvre had become a welcomed addition to the Super Bowl experience. Exotic finger foods prepared by the hostess had fast become a mainstay. The fellas initially scoffed at the menu amendments several seasons ago: from the pizzas and wings to the skewered meat and poultry shish-kabobs, lemon marinated chicken wings, deviled eggs and the like. 'The nerves of those 'self-invited friends,' the hostess once commented. She added that one of his uncouth friends referred to her presentation as 'horse-divers' instead of hors d'oeuvre. But she knew it was tongue in cheek. His friends soon became instant converts and the eclectic finger foods offerings soon after were the complementary mainstay and permanent addition to the halftime shows.

But this year was different - to say the least. His friends were all present twenty-four hours earlier at the hostess' church of worship and the food that was offered was a catered repast for the memorial ceremony that celebrated the life of a mother of 14 years and a spouse of 25.

Deemed as one of the more exciting Super Bowl in modern history, father and son watched both melancholy and in silence - while at the same time - seeking a sense of normalcy from the recent devastation in both of their lives.

Dad laid out on the chaise end of the sectional while his son rested his head on his father's shoulder stretching his legs out on the couch's perpendicular as the game came to a climax.

The seconds horribly ticked away as déjà vu played the similar cruel joke on the New England Patriots when a perfectly defended pass was miraculously caught by the receiver because the tipped ball landed in his hands while splayed on the five-yard line. The inevitable was visible in the hapless eyes of their offensive team as they all looked defeated on the sidelines while their defense were about to be dominated on the other side of the field. The Seattle Seahawks next play drove them to the one-yard line where everyone viewing were all certain was inevitably going to be consecutive Super Bowl titles. But with seconds left on the clock, and with the most reliable running-back in the league in their arsenal, the script was written for another downtown celebration in Seattle, a Disney World commercial, and a new Corvette for the consensus MVP of the game. Instead, the Seahawks outsmarted themselves when they executed a passing play that was duly intercepted. The instantaneous change of emotions was palpable: exuberance immediately turned to shock and awe. Father and son were both un-enthusiastically routing for the Seahawks. But with no investment in the game - both financially nor emotionally - father told his son that the Seahawks deserved to lose.

"When you call an outrageous play like that on the one-yard line with the best running back in the league in the backfield - who may inevitably sustain head trauma issues later in his career by the way he is reckless with his body.... the coach is an ass."

They both immediately retired to their rooms without the usual fanfare.

Rufus wrote that a few days after the Super Bowl when he spent lots of time in his home office.

During the weeks to follow - and especially on the weekends - Kevin secluded himself in his bedroom. A couple of times when Rufus was lying in bed, Kevin would lay on my side and they would at times watch something on Netflix or Hulu together. And every now and again it pained me when they would lash out at each other.

One time Kevin told Rufus that he needed a tablet for school. Rufus purchased an iPad and later learned from his teacher that it was not true. The teacher explained that she didn't make that request and furthermore their entire curriculum was available online and even accessible on their cellphones.

Another incident was when Rufus overheard one side of a conversation where Kevin told one of his friends on the phone,

"... I don't have a mother ... because she's dead."

Rufus chided reminding him that I would always be with him and how much I loved him as they both seemed to be holding back tears.

And when Kevin's grades slipped, Rufus became livid, revoked all of his privileges and said all the wrong things like Kevin was using my death as an excuse to not do well in his classes.

I couldn't stand to see the deterioration of my family after the few months had passed without me. I knew that time would heal their wounds – but at the same time – I didn't want to witness the turmoil. I now knew that my Afterlife would become a quest – a quest to rescue My Guys. I also anticipated that Rufus will sooner or later be seeking female companionship – and although I trust his instincts, my concerns were also for Kevin's welfare and whether he would be accepting of the person Rufus ended up with.

As I peruse the warehouses of our lives I can honestly say I knew what he would be looking for and what he was deserving of. As one grows older, maturity becomes the mold that is reminiscent of one's life story to be unfolded. One's likes and dislikes are engrained and compatibility without compromise is nonetheless futile.

He told me several times in the past that if the singer Anita Baker was available and just happened to be in St. Thomas, he would have left me a "long - long" time ago in jest emphasizing the word "long" twice while showing three fingers. Coincidentally, 'Caught up in the Rapture of *Love*" was the first song we danced to on our first date.

To say he was an Anita Baker fan was an understatement. He had all Anita Baker's music: initially on cassettes and later the sheet music before we even met when he played in the band. Then later on he got her CD's to replace the cassettes. So I gathered that he had an affinity for great female singers like Chaka Khan, Nancy Wilson, and Diana Krall, to name a few. But in the end, even though she wasn't as vocally accomplished as those I've mentioned, Corinne Bailey Rae currently was his favorite - check.

I also remember finding a binder with magazine clippings of female fitness models in his office around the same time he subscribed me to the fitness magazine Oxygen of which at that time I really had no interest. Additionally, he would complement me when I was in excellent physical shape. Around that time, he used to love to see me getting into my jeans where it was a hilarious struggle with my thighs. One instance he told me to wait and stop what I was doing. Moments later he actually returned with popcorn and a chair from the dining room, sat next to our bed, and instructed me to continue putting on my jeans.

That was before Kevin was born and around the time my employer Theodore Tunick & Company paid for their employees to join fitness clubs around the island to the point where the office even had workout T-shirts designed. Rufus paid for his own membership at the Marriott's Frenchman's Reef Hotel fitness center. We were there every Saturday and Sunday whenever we were not in Puerto Rico. He really enjoyed the steam room to the point where he incorporated one in the design of our master bathroom shower. Hmmm, check.

During our years together, Rufus would from time to time comment when I dabbled in matchmaking. He was always the pessimist predicting the demise in my attempts to set up my friends - male and female. Early in our marriage, I even tried to set up Milton with one of my sisters where Rufus thought it was a very bad idea. But now I realize that every experience in life is a lesson to be learned from and even though I may not have succeeded then, this time I have to get it right for the sake of My Guys. After all, I know his type and I know his likes and dislikes. The typical beautiful and smart is always a great start, and over the decades together there were nuances now in his decision making process. Everything I have seen and heard over the years is something potentially to be discerned and learned from as I now have the capacity to recall every minute memory of my life in UHD detail. My quest was becoming clearer.

◆ ◆ ◆

Over the years Rufus has told me on several occasions that being married to me and the four and a half years he played in the local band Priscilla and Company as the 'Bassmon' were undoubtedly the happiest times in his life. He even told me about some of the dates and relationships he had before we met to which I actually concluded by telling him, "You know I saved you, right?"

One story he offered, he described it was in his early twenties when a girl was willing to give him her new Audi sports car after their 1st date. She was too needy and possessive he surmised. After their second date, he broke it off and she later began harassing him at his job at the bank where he worked during the day questioning his manhood – to explain it diplomatically.

Another girl indicated to him in no uncertain terms that she would kill him if she catches him merely looking at another woman. That was also precipitated after a first date with her. He admitted that he really liked that girl, but there wasn't even a second date. He jokingly stated to me that he saved himself from an autopsy.

But as I peruse his warehouse from his past, what he did not realize at that moment in his life was the fact that The Laws of Attraction was in play and was actually granting his wishes. Consequently, The Laws of Attraction is always in play – you simply have to be aware. People fail to realize that the mind isn't something that just remembers your thoughts. Our minds are literally where all of our hopes and dreams reside. Everything that you desire and require begins with a thought. And if you act upon those aspirations, they eventually will come true.

At that time in his life, Rufus was young, very tall, handsome, and had a seemingly high profile job wearing a suit at the bank during the day and treated like a local celebrity playing music in the clubs at night. He told me about the many times being asked for his autograph from the tourists on weekends when he shopped downtown on Main Street. At the same time, he actually fabricated a license plate frame for his new car that sarcastically screamed for attention stating, "I'm Living the Single Life ... But I'm LOOKING." (The O's in the word LOOKING were Eyeballs. It was inspired by the Cameo's song Single Life) It was a one of a kind frame he designed and made himself. So the energy to attract was all there.

Priscilla – the band leader – told me once that she was his gatekeeper while the band performed. Scores of women showed interest but his persona scared most of them back then. And for those brave enough to approach the stage during the breaks, Priscilla would turn them away if her intuition warranted. So occasionally he would find phone numbers under his windshield wiper blades or specific responses to the license plate frame like, "I am single too...let's both stop looking" where eyeballs were duly incorporated in the words 'too' and 'looking."

So in essence, he was getting exactly what he was unconsciously asking from the universe - attention - and frustratingly in the end he unknowingly came to the realization it wasn't the kind of attention he desired. He wanted love.

◆ ◆ ◆

Then there were those he dated that didn't live locally. One girl he liked a lot lived on the sister island of St. Croix. He met her during a weekend training seminar held by the bank where she worked at one of the St. Croix branches. The subsequent Fridays that followed after work whenever the band wasn't playing, he would travel to St. Croix in order that they could go out and enjoy the local dance clubs. Never lacking for confidence he was an anomaly living on his own terms: single in his mid-twenties, no children, and worked.

At one point there was a talent show being held on St. Croix and Priscilla was competing for the promotional opportunity. It was an American Idol type show way before there was American Idol. Their band recorded her music track and Rufus told Ms. St. Croix that Priscilla was undoubtedly going to win. She notably favored the Crucian contestants but Rufus insisted it would be futile. Then on the night of the show - as he explained to me - they made the colossal mistake by having Priscilla sing first. They figured because of all her hype, she would be forgotten by the end of the evenings performances. She was the only contestant who traveled from St. Thomas for the competition in 1988. He explained that while he sat next to Ms. St. Croix in the audience, he described the way their band arranged the music track for Priscilla. He then predicted when the crowd was going to cheer and when the crowd was going to go wild. She gave him one of those local 'sucking teeth' expression. Rufus ended by saying,

"The weekend is short; I think we should leave to the clubs after Priscilla sings."

Everything transpired as he predicted, but they left midway because the Crucian contestants were as he said, "sad."

Several years after we were married while we were spending a holiday weekend on St. Croix, Rufus actually took me to visit her mother hoping that she might be back visiting for Christmas also knowing she was now living in Washington DC and married. I actually asked to come along in hopes to see who piqued his interest in his past.

Another girl from his childhood was the impetus for us finally making the decision to conceive a child a priority. I remember meeting her at Bluebeards Castle Hotel and I liked her immediately. She was vacationing with her husband, her teenage and infant daughters when I offered to babysit the babies in order that she and her husband could get a break for an evening on the town. Rufus explained that he knew her from elementary school when she was a military brat of sorts that lived around the world in New York, Germany, Oklahoma and was presently a retired military officer living in Hawaii.

For the first five years of marriage, we enjoyed each other - always on a perpetual weekend getaway in the Caribbean and Florida. It wasn't until my taller twin sister - five years my junior - got pregnant and the pressure to do equally was now front and center. And Rufus wasn't any help emotionally; he simply kept saying he was enjoying the process of trying to conceive.

But I seriously got the maternal bug when I took care of Mrs. Hawaii's infant daughter that evening. And when she returned, I even told her that I wasn't giving her back her child. It really could have gotten ugly if I wasn't of sane mind.

The following is something Rufus wrote in 1999 in 1st Person but for the purpose of this book, he recently re-wrote it from my point of view to chronicle the momentous time leading up to when we conceived our son Kevin.

The new millennium began our second decade of marriage. Five years prior, I was with my sister in Puerto Rico when she gave birth to my mother's first grandchild and as a result, the pressure was on for Rufus and I to produce an offspring. The culmination was the turn of the new millennium when our son was born in the fall.

For the past decade we experienced several years of trials and with one of my younger sister already a mother, I felt my clock ticking like Joe Pesci demonstrated with the stomping of his foot in the hit movie *My Cousin Vinny* as it became virtually impossible to conceive – and not for the lack of trying. We even considered adopting when we made a special weekend trip to St. Croix to visit the youth orphanage. We also considered in vitro fertilization.

Everything changed as a result of my shorter sister's research while working for the Health Maintenance Organization Humana, when she recommended that we should visit who was notably Puerto Rico's best OB/GYN Dr. Charles Llenza. Rufus said that he looked like Alfred Hitchcock. He always makes visual associations with people.

I remember how the whole situation could have derailed when Rufus became extremely annoyed when we first sat in his waiting room for hours. In actuality it was a work day where we had to take time off from our jobs on St. Thomas and travel to Puerto Rico. We were there a day earlier to put my name on the appointment list that hung outside the office door and were there promptly at 7am and hour before they opened the office.

Over seven hours past when we were finally called. He asked preliminary questions like 'how long we were married', and 'how long we had been trying to conceive.' A week earlier I had the very difficult conversation with Rufus about the possibility of pointed questions that may or may not be asked at the consultation as it may be relevant to our inability to get pregnant. I remember crying when I told him of what I was ashamed and I asked for his forgiveness for something that occurred over twelve years prior. He simply hugged me like he never had before stating there wasn't anything to forgive. The next day at my job he reminded me how much he loved me by sending the biggest bouquet of roses with a card that simply read, "I love you."

Dr. Llenza lightened the conversation jokingly commenting that he was happy to see that I was accompanied by my husband because a lot of men don't visit his office and I cannot get pregnant all by myself. And on two instances while in his office – which had a picture window with a street level view – two mothers held their infants to the window and yelled, "Tu hiciste esto". I translated for Rufus that they were saying 'Dr. Llenza did it'.

He then called his friend around the corner who was a Urologist and made an emergency appointment and sent Rufus on his way. A half hour later we were back at the hotel sharing stories. I preferred not to be graphic but I was diagnosed with Endometriosis and had to endure 6 procedures of scar tissue removal from my uterus. Rufus - on the other hand - had no qualms telling everyone his business of how he didn't have to wait at the urologist. The secretary led him through to see the doctor when without the formalities he was instructed to drop his pants. The doctor squeezed his testicles, told him that he had varicocele in his scrotum and he could operate the following day.... REALLY???.

During the next three months, we were back in Puerto Rico every other week for my treatment and Rufus scheduled his surgery around the NBA playoffs to get the veins in his scrotum dilated. He finds humor in almost everything.

Again he was angry on the day of the operation because like before we were there a day early to take care of the administrative stuff and meet the anesthesiologist, but again the operation was delayed. We were also told that the operation would be scheduled at 9am, but he went into surgery at 6pm, so as a result he was infuriated for most of the afternoon. Not the kind of state of mind that's preferable before surgery.

Whenever somebody prefaces a statement with one of those sayings like, "we can laugh about it now", something totally stupid had transpired. Rufus proceeded to tell me that before he was rolled into the Operating Room, Dr. Llenza came to see him and wish him luck. He was later administered anesthesia in his spine and left alone on a stainless steel gurney in the freezing operating room to take in the surrounding wearing nothing but a thin paper cloth backwards frock on his cold ass while his ashy feet hung off the edge. He watched the lights and machines that were connected to monitor his vitals via the adhesive sensors and probes.

He told me that over a period of time, he saw that his heart rate was decreasing and he was quickly becoming tired and sleepy. Soon after he couldn't feel nor move his legs. Then he started to hold his breath to try to further manipulate the machines and it worked. His heart rate was slowing down more. He continued until the machine flatlined and caused an alarm where nurses immediately burst into the operating room and was preparing to - as he eloquently described - "Light him up!" with the nearby defibrillator. He struggled to talk and immediately realized he couldn't. He saw that one nurse was charging the defibrillator while the nurse closest to him squeezed a clear gel on the paddles. They had already raised up the paper frock to expose his chest when he garnered enough strength and shouted as loud and hard as he could, "nooooo!!!" He explained that it sounded like a whisper but it was loud enough to get the nurses attention who now saw his eyes were wide opened, thus saving him from a shocking experience.

If that wasn't harrowing enough, he told me that he woke up a little more than halfway through the operation because the anesthesia wore off. He told the doctor "I can feel everything you are doing down there...I need more anesthesia." The doctors explained that it was too risky to administer more anesthesia and he had to endure the pain especially when they closed his lower groin leaving him a bikini cut. He later joked that the hospital was designed for small people: small gowns, small gurney, and small anesthesia doses.

The post-op recovery was just as hilarious. The operation was an outpatient procedure and he was to be discharged as soon as he was able to urinate. Problem was, his entire groin area was swollen and he was in severe pain and was still joking around. As he put it, a male nurse in the recovery room was on Pee-Watch and in less than an hour the NBA Finals were going to be on with the San Antonio Spurs and the New York Knicks. He even asked me for a 'sample' of my urine so we could get out of the hospital. I tried not to laugh but couldn't help myself. The nurse didn't speak any English so I told him what we were laughing about. Then he told me to tell the nurse that he thought the surgeon swapped the connection of his bladder and testicles so instead of urine, it would now be sperm. I didn't know whether or not if it was possible, but I was crying with laughter.

After over an hour later of trying, he was able to painfully drop a small amount of urine in the toilet under the watchful eye of Inspector Pee-Pee and we were literally out of the door in a wheelchair. The healing took another 3 months for both of us.

Then my grandmother began stressing him for riding his bicycle on weekends commenting to me that after all we have been through, he's killing her 'abuelitos' sitting on his bicycle seat. To appease her, he bought a split seat saddle for his bicycle and kept exercising.

The following January 30th 2000, I was ovulating and it just happened to be the afternoon of the Super Bowl, or as he calls it, The Real Father's Day. I never remember any of the games being one to only be interested in the halftime show and the commercials. But I loved preparing the hors d'oeuvre and snacks for his friends. One of his uncouth friends purposely kept referring to my food as Horse Divers. Immediately following the game, I remember calling Rufus into the bedroom and told him to "Get rid of your friends, now!"

A few weeks later on a Saturday when my "visitor" was late, we drove to Kmart and purchased every type of Home Pregnancy Test in the store, returned *home and I passed them all. The next order of business was telling my family. It was another one of the happiest days in my life. I remember calling home when my four-year-old niece answered the phone.*

"Nana, it's Titi on the phone."

"Tell her I will call her back," I heard my mother yelled from another room.

"Nana said that she is going to call you back." my niece reported.

"Tell Nana that I need to tell her something important." I explained.

"Titi said she need to tell you something important." my niece relayed.

"Ask her what she wants to tell me?" my mother instructed again.

"Nana wants to know what do you want to tell her." my niece relayed.

"Tell Nana that I am pregnant." I stated.

"Nana, Titi said I am pregnant." my niece reported.

"You are pregnant? You can't be pregnant.... you're a little girl.... Oh My God! Gimme the phone!" my mother exclaimed.

The thirty-eight weeks of pregnancy were wonderful. I remember when Rufus and I saw the ultrasound for the first time and they determined it was going to be a boy, for the rest of that weekend he didn't speak to anyone. Absolutely not one word. My family was very concerned. He told me later that he was just excited to be a father and was in deep thought about what kind of parent he was going to be. He was simply playing out what our future was going to be like in his mind.

When it became physically obvious that I was pregnant, Rufus found pleasure in all things maternal: my stomach and how it grew - he loved how it felt and enjoyed spooning with me. He made fun of the store Dress Barn's name and implored me not to ever buy any clothes from a store whose name suggests their customers were cattle. So I challenged him to make me a maternity dress; he made me three.

I know what you are probably thinking, "he can actually sew?" Well, I lost another bet a few years earlier when we were on St. Croix enjoying another weekend getaway. We were window shopping when I saw a dress I liked in the local designer Wayne James boutique when Rufus said he could make something similar. I thought he had finally written a check that he could never cash. I never knew whether I was being baited or not, but he had a way of reeling me in. A week later we were in the Fabric Store back home on St. Thomas. I thought he was just going through the motions of grandstanding to save face, so I simply followed and played along. After a few minutes he whispered,

"*Do you notice that nobody is asking me whether I need any help?*" Before I was able to answer he continued saying, "*Because I don't need their help.*"

"*They didn't ask me either,*" I retorted.

He perused further and proceeded to purchase two Vogue patterns, read the back of the envelopes, instructed one of the clerks - who for some reason knew him - to cut linen fabrics to various lengths, bought a sewing machine, needles, treads, scissors, bobby-pins, zippers and buttons. At the cash register the owner greeted us and he introduced me. I still thought I was being 'punked' until the owner commenced to reminisce about the times when Rufus used to frequent the store when he couldn't find suitable clothing in the local stores because he was too tall. I was totally blindsided and I think that was the very first time I said aloud,

"*I think I am going to keep him.*"

For the next subsequent weekends when we were at home, I proudly wore the products of my husband's labor to my job and my co-workers were all incredulous when I told them the story.

So in the fall of 2000 we were all back at the Pavia Hospital in Hato Rey Puerto Rico along with my mother, sisters, niece and two girlfriends from St. Thomas when our son Kevin was born. We spent the following week at the Embassy Suite so it would be convenient for my childhood friends to visit and for Rufus to enjoy the room service. I remember how much my breasts grew and was mortified when my supportive silly husband asked quizzically, "*Can we keep these?*", pointing at my milk filled mammaries.

My mother now had two grandchildren and I felt an enormous amount of relief. Now I actually knew how my other sister was feeling. Five years later when she became pregnant, she was so stressed out that the last trimester of her pregnancy was prescribed to total bed rest. I was back at the hospital when she gave my mother her third grandchild. In the end, it took us ten years for our mother to have a total of three grandchildren.

CHAPTER THREE

"The reason that I initially referred to her as noteworthy
was the fact that I got the opportunity to actually see her."

THEN THERE WAS THE GIRL who preceded me. She was the most noteworthy; you will understand why as I further explain. The part of this story that really stimulated my interest was what happened after they had broken up. Not because it was a correlation towards getting us to meet each other, but the uncanny circumstances that later became the result of our meeting.

Rufus explained how he was supposed to spend a month with her for his vacation in Miami in the spring of 1989. She was a part time student attending college in Broward County while he was on St. Thomas. They had been dating several months where he would travel to the states and she would return to see her grandmother every now and again.

The first sign that things were amidst was when she didn't meet him at the airport as she normally did. Then after renting a car and later arriving at the apartment that he had actually signed the lease for but where she and her two college roommates were paying its rent, he told me how much of a stalker he felt like waiting several hours into the evening for her arrival. He later recalled a quote from the movie *A Perfect Murder* which absolutely summed up their relationship when Michael Douglas told his suspecting cheating wife Gwyneth Paltrow, *"That's not happiness to see me."* Standing outside of the apartment she essentially told Rufus that she needed more space. I remember how incredulous his facial features became when he reenacted what he told her saying,

"...how much more space do you want between Florida and St. Thomas."

He left saying that he would have taken it better if she had told him her intentions a day prior while he was still at home. He would have made other plans. And as he walked away, he instructed her to destroy the credit card he had given to her for her personal use.

He continued to explain that he spent that evening at the Days Inn off I-95 next to the Hollywood Water Tower. The hotel was fully booked and the night manager was an African with an accent equally as unusual as Rufus. They became kindred brothers for the evening after he explained his circumstance and was given the last available room even though it was reserved. He could have driven and stayed at his mother's in West Palm Beach, but he wasn't up for the drive where he even contemplated he was going to return home the following day.

Then on the evening news on the hotel television he learned that the band UB40 was auditioning for a bass player because theirs was being detained for a vehicular incident while on tour in Miami. He expressed confidence in the fact that he knew all their songs, was up on his chops, and could bring a little flavor to the group. He planned in the morning to drive to Thoroughbred Music on NE135th on West Dixie, buy a new bass and a small amplifier for the audition and kill it. It was all planned out. He spent the night touring in his mind. Good riddance from her he thought.

Those circumstances that transpired then I am now able to review forensically like a cold case where I recognize that an actual opportunity was presented by the Laws of Attraction. You see, she could have broken up with him over the phone, but that would have meant that he would not have been in Miami and learn about the audition. So for his sake, The Laws of Attraction dissuaded her from breaking up with him over the phone. And when he asked why she didn't, there was no plausible response. He could have been the interim bassist for UB40 because he absolutely knew it. He felt it as he saw the news report. So there was an opportunity to change the trajectory in his life.

Instead of following through with his plan to audition, he spent the next two days at his mother's and instead of buying a bass and amplifier, he bought an equally expensive computerized self-moving chess set from The Sharper Image store at the Bayside Mall in downtown Miami. He then returned to St. Thomas where he played computer chess every day for the remainder of his vacation. As I think about those circumstances, if Rufus had acted upon that opportunity, it was very likely we would have never met. But then again that's not exactly how fate works.

Then as he continued to explain it, a couple of months later on the afternoon before Hurricane Hugo ravaged the Virgin Islands in September 1989, Ms. Credit Card called him. He had just returned from the bank on a Saturday afternoon before weekend banking was a thing where he had to secured the facility for the imminent storm and was very tired. Not only did she not destroy his credit card as she promised she would, she was now calling months after and asking his permission to use it to purchase a used car in Miami because the cost was way over her spending limit. He explained to me that he was in a sleepy stupor when he actually gave his consent.

His saving grace was the fact that the call was on speaker phone and audible to his sister Linda who overheard the entire conversation. As his sister put it when she told me later, "I woke his ass up" and incredulously asked him, - trust me when I say the following is an actual commonly used term in the islands,

"Are you crazy in your ass???"

He immediately became lucid and called American Express and cancelled his primary credit card to include any other cards associated. Then Rufus and Linda soberly waited for the anticipated follow-up call of disgrace. But wait, there's more. The reason that I initially referred to her as noteworthy was the fact that I got the opportunity to actually see her.

Fast forward a decade and a half later, Kevin, Rufus and I were returning home from another weekend visiting my family and were waiting for Rufus' flight instructor to pick us up in the 4-seat Cessna at the small commuter Fernando Ribas Airport in Old San Juan Puerto Rico.

Although the International airport was a ten-minute drive away from my mother's home, Rufus explained that after lining up in the commercial air space, waiting to be escorted by airport personnel into customs – which at one instant took thirty minutes and God forbid if it was raining and hoping that you are not further delayed by an international flight, the commuter airport in Old San Juan was the prudent decision due to no delays even though it was more than a half hour away.

After 9/11 2001, all air travel was immediately cancelled and aircrafts were grounded until the FAA and the NTSB implemented new flight safety procedures. I had already organized a party for Kevin's birthday in Puerto Rico. Rufus aggravated me about how much of a bad idea it was – not to mention all the 'fun'– Kevin's similarly age 'friends' were going to have celebrating his first birthday.

Of course the party was for me, but I wasn't going to admit it at that time. To add injury to his insults, everything was all prepaid and there wasn't any way to get our money back or for us to get to Puerto Rico. At the behest of our friend, former landlord, and owner of the local flying school Ace Flight Center's Cleo Hodge, he suggested that Rufus could augment his lessons by flying cross country from St. Thomas to Puerto Rico and rack up the flying hours. That's how I was able to salvage the party. And as a result, we have been commuting that way almost twice monthly for almost a decade because it was convenient and more economical than flying commercial.

Every time Rufus learn about a windfall he would notify his best friend, but Milton wasn't having any part of flying. On this particular weekend both our families were going to be in Puerto Rico. Our family of three flew on a Cessna 172 with our instructor while Milton and his family of four took the ferry instead of the commuter airline.

Sometimes I wonder why they are still friends. Rufus was relentlessly razzing him about his slow boat to China belaboring how much longer a boat ride is than flying reminding him that he wasn't going to ever get that time in his life back. And to pour more salt into the wound, Milton added that after the ferry left St. Thomas, it stopped in St. John to pick up more passengers before going to Puerto Rico. So for anyone familiar with the Virgin Islands, St. Thomas is between St. John and Puerto Rico. So instead of originating the ferry ride in St. John, they traveled from St. Thomas, to St. John, passed St. Thomas enroute to Puerto Rico. So what's normally a twenty-minute flight by commuter airline is a three-to-four-hour ordeal by ferry.

On another weekend we spent in Puerto Rico, Milton and his family was going on a cruise embarking from Old San Juan. Rufus volunteered to pick them up from the airport on a Saturday and drive them to the port facility. He took pictures of how much luggage Milton's family was taking with them for a week's cruise. We normally take a full sized carry-on each on our cruises and Milton said that was impossible because he needs at least three pieces of luggage himself. Rufus retorted to tell him he is basically asking the airlines to lose his luggage and it actually happened on their return flight. To make an unfortunate situation more hilarious, he had his favorite pair of shoes in different luggage thus orphaning his shoes when one of his bags wound up missing. That kind of information I would have gladly kept to myself, but those guys are best friends and that is simply what they do.

So on that fateful weekend our family of three were at the small terminal that generally serviced several small commuter airlines and private aircrafts. Most of the times we were the only persons in the terminal at Fernando Ribas Airport and the Customs agents became very familiar with us when we normally arrive the previous Friday after work and school.

On this particular Sunday the terminal was bustling with transportation activity. Rufus could be seen standing at the floor to ceiling glass wall peering out towards the runway to get the first glimpse of our plane as it flew abeam the terminal. Then he would return and inform us that he saw the plane and sit next to me for the anticipated five to ten minutes it would take for the instructor to land the plane, clear customs, take a bathroom break and meet us in the terminal. He also joked about how much longer it was going to take Milton and his family to get back home having to watch St. Thomas pass by on the way to first dropping off the St. John passengers. He even suggested that it was quite possible we would be able to see their ferry at two thousand feet while we flew back.

A short moment later, I heard a female voice calling Rufus' name. Amidst all the of the would be passengers we noticed a hand waving in our direction. Rufus response towards the gesture was totally unexpected of someone receiving a salutation. His disposition was eerily stoic unlike anything I had seen of him to that point in our lives. He peered briefly in the direction of the incoming voice and simply nodded his head. Then in his best ventriloquist voice, he softly mouthed words without moving his lips,

"That's the girl I dated before I met you."

Now there was a face to Miss Credit Card.

"She is pretty" I simply replied.

Rufus nodded in her direction and did something that was totally juvenile, but I totally understood. He asked me for his aviation headset that I always kept in my bag whenever we flew and he put them on around his neck.

Shortly after the instructor met and led us out to the plane. Rufus stowed our one carry-on in the tail of the plane, helped Kevin and me into the back seats before he climbed in front himself with the instructor. Moments later we were taxiing... all in view of the floor to ceiling glass window of the terminal.

And to add fodder for Rufus' enjoyment, after we got home, Milton called to tell him the ferry stopped in St. John first which meant that it took him at least 3 hours to get home. That's exactly like another time he told Rufus that when he went to Hawaii, the flights were as follow: St. Thomas to Miami, Miami to Los Angeles, Los Angeles back to Dallas, then Dallas to Hawaii. Again I ask, why do Milton keep telling him these things?

♦ ♦ ♦

Other clues I am now able to discern about his type was during two comical incidents when he was unknowingly the subject of a friendly disagreement that we just happened upon. As precarious as that may sound, again the following stories actually happened.

It was Carnival time on St. Thomas in the late nineties where Rufus and I were in the festival village in the evening strolling around in hopes that he may see visiting class members to reminisce. We were minding our business slowly strolling holding hands when we grew near to two older men having a dispute about Rufus' facial features.

"He look like ah Turnbull..." one guy argued, and the other countered,

"Naw, he isa Fahie." (Don't ask me why, phonetically it is pronounced with one syllable as Foy, not with two syllables as it appears as Fa-hie)

It was also visibly obvious that they were both inebriated as they went back and forth as we grew nearer. Rufus approach them a stated,

"You guys are both correct," and continued to explain that his father's last name is Turnbull and his mother's maiden is Fahie. Then Rufus attempted to rattle the men when he asked, "What the hell does a Turnbull look like anyway?"

Without missing a beat, one of them quipped, "Ugly, like you!"

The four of us laughed as the other guy ended,

"Yeah, but 'dem' Turnbull boyz like pretty women though," looking at me.

Another time it was 2006, and the three of us were disembarking the Pacific Princess in Tortola BVI. We were about to exit the pier when two British Customs agents were arguing and one blurted out as we passed,

"... look ah Turnbull right deh!"

Rufus turned around and approached them and asked his 'catchy comeback question, "What the hell does a Turnbull look like?"

"Ugly, like you!" The men repeated simultaneously.

That is the kind of interaction that the Caribbean is notorious for. Fun loving and carefree.

CHAPTER FOUR

*"This new sense of awareness now enables me to compare what
he told me and what I actually experienced when I was there."*

I NOW KNEW EXACTLY what I needed to do in my Afterlife. And even though I did not know exactly how, I was quickly learning how to navigate and test subtle ways of making contact without being too alarming.

There's a sense of finality after a loved one dies if you intend to believe what is totally obvious. But for those who have always questioned the social norms and not take everything at face value, an alternate reality can be a welcomed sense of comfort and reprieve. Rufus has always been a wild card of sorts.

From very young he has always been a free thinker. In teaching Kevin about history I would from time to time overhear him explaining and suggesting to imagine a time without electricity and evenings without light. I remember when the three of us watched the movie *National Treasure* starring Nicolas Cage and later made a beeline to visit the National Archives Museum in Washington DC to see the Declaration of Independence for ourselves. Rufus commented that if that treasonous document was drafted more than two hundred years ago on animal skin and it is now stored under low lighting conditions and you can barely see what is written, consider centuries older documents stored under less controlled conditions before they were properly preserved.

With that foresight, I knew that he was opened to any eventuality philosophically. As a result, I had to tread lightly although I desperately wanted him to know that I was 'in a better place' which was now in his consciousness. The following actually happened.

Rufus was taking Kevin to school for the first time as a single parent the day after the Super Bowl he described in the journal. The afternoon before he was saying his goodbyes to his sisters at the airport when Janet told him,

"Don't be wary if funny things begin to happen to you." He asked her to explain, but she just left it at that. It was as if she saw premonitions into the future and was just providing a mere warning not to be alarmed, but to be wary.

So the next day during the short drive to school, Rufus broke their silence and told Kevin that my mother needed to hear his voice. So he speed-dialed her number from the Bluetooth console of the Hummer and my mother actually answered in the following manner,

"Hi Honey."

Rufus heard it immediately - while Kevin didn't.

"Hi Nana." Kevin replied.

Rufus said the following after saying hello and calling my mother by name,

"You sound exactly like Christine."

"Really?" my mother replied.

"Yeah, you just called me Honey" Rufus explained.

"No I didn't" My mother incredulously replied.

"Yes you did Nana," Kevin confirmed.

The three of them were quiet for a delayed moment reflecting on what they experienced and continued to converse until Kevin got to school. They said their goodbyes and Rufus promised to call every day at the same time where they collectively agreed to take each following day at a time.

I actually greeted both of My Guys and I am glad I got through. The fact that Rufus immediately recognized my voice two days after my last memorial service confirmed I was successful very early in my attempt to communicate. You see, Kevin only heard my words, but Rufus also heard the pitch and tenor in my voice. I was undoubtedly the only person that called both of them Honey for as long as they have been the apples of my eyes. And even though I had other terms of endearment for Rufus where my most creative was "My Six Foot Four, Dipped in Dark Chocolate Man", I knew that I really would have spooked them if my mother answered uttering that moniker. Anyway, it was a test and I was learning how to manipulate the contents in our warehouses.

It was also a consolation of sorts. After all, they weren't there when I passed; they were enroute to Puerto Rico. At the exact moment when the doctor recorded the time I expired, Rufus had simultaneously taken a photograph of Kevin's new haircut as he stood on top of the portable stairs as they boarded the plane. The picture was for me since he was not allowed in the Intensive Care Unit.

My sisters contacted him earlier in the morning immediately after he dropped Kevin off to school, but he was not informed how dire my situation was. The ruse my sisters used suggested to him was that I would be requiring a blood transfusion since we both were Type O Positive, with mine at the moment drastically diluted by prescribed blood thinners. I recall how three years' prior my grandmother underwent a similar procedure during her hospitalization and how she made a remarkable full recovery with the exception of signs of early onset Alzheimer.

He had no idea. The last time he actually heard my voice was the evening before when I called from the hospital to check up on My Guys to see how they were doing. We spoke to each other on the daily, and this time I was really looking forward to this conversation. I knew it would be different from the mundane health status reports. I wanted to know whether he enjoyed the Babyface concert I told him to attend in my place. If he enjoyed it, he would have a colorful way of making me feel like I was there. If he didn't, he would express reasons how that time could not be refunded along with my money. Our conversations always began with me saying,

"Hi Honey, how are you doing?"

He would reply accordingly with the usual pleasantries. But after I fell ill, he always interrupted my greeting to say,

"Don't worry about me, how are you feeling?" Then he commenced to tell me about the concert.

As a musician, he has always been very critical about the local music scene as far as their professionalism and performances were concerned. The conversation always began with the preface 'Back in the day...' He hated going to the clubs where the musicians looked like they just got off the day jobs and really loathe the long breaks they took.

He played the electric bass locally during his formative years before we met. And after we were married, I was able to see him perform sparingly because at that point in his life he wasn't playing regularly. But the few times when he did play, I'd invite my grandmother over for visits so she could also see him perform because she loved music and loved watching him play.

Knowing how opinionated he was, I didn't expect him to pull any punches and he didn't. He surmised by first stating the Babyface concert could have been a lot better. He continued to explained that although there was a live band, backup singers were nonexistent. They utilized digital sequencers which also suggests the possibility that the members of the band were also suspect playing along with synched tracking. He lamented saying can you imagine hearing female voices and there weren't even any women on the stage? Then he told me how he spoiled the concert for my girlfriend and her husband. They were recently married four months earlier and I was her matron of honor fresh out of Intensive Care in Puerto Rico. My mother and Rufus were very upset with me for discharging myself from the hospital to live up to that commitment. But I now have no regrets.

The way he put it was they asked him whether he was enjoying the concert and Rufus initially warned them by actually saying he didn't want to spoil the concert for them seeing that they were obviously enjoying the show. They persisted.

On the mainland there's a 'saying' of sorts where retorts come after someone says "Famous last words..." Over the years I have learned that the local equivalent is "Who Tell Dem Say Dat?" or in other words, "Who told them to insist?" So Rufus gave them his impression of the show...they later probably wished they hadn't ask.

"*Whatever you want.*" He began recreating the performance with the chorus and also responded,

"*Whatever you want Baby...*" singing both backup and lead to demonstrate over the phone.

"*It's alright with me.*" Singing the backup and echoing the lead.

"*Cause you got that Whip Appeal ... so work it on me.*"

The he said he asked my girlfriend and her husband,

"Do you guys hear any back-up singers?" to which they both answered affirmatively while grooving to the music and snapping their fingers to the beat. Then he followed up by asking,

"Do you see any back-up singers?"

Upon their disappointment, he continued to suggest that they could have hired models or video vixens to lip sync behind cold microphones.

Then Rufus reminded me of the time a year or two after we were married when me and my sister-in-law Linda did exactly what he was suggesting at a talent show on the same stage at the University of the Virgin Islands Reichhold Center for the Performing Arts. The major difference was we had all the confidence, attitude and swagger like two members of the female singing group En Vogue during the rehearsals in our apartment. But we were both stricken with stage fright on the night of the talent show where our mouths and bodies barely moved. The only thing that moved to the beat was my heart.

I had totally forgotten about that experience. That memory made me laugh so much it definitely distracted me from telling him the truth about how I was feeling that evening. And for that short moment I simply forgot. But again, that is what he does. He makes you feel better with his sincerity. He did it at my funeral.

He also did it when we got the call that his sister Lena was in intensive care in 2012. We were scheduled to travel the following day to Orlando for vacation but decided to forego our commute on the Florida Turnpike and drove from Miami International Airport directly to the hospital in Aventura.

When we saw his sister, Rufus counted thirteen tubes connected to various machines monitoring her vital systems. She was non responsive only able to blink her eyes when asked questions. He was so distraught he said that he wanted to go to the Aventura Mall a short distance away to reflect. I sternly insisted under my breath,

"We Are Not Going Anywhere!" Then I repeated less insistently, "You are not going anywhere."

The next thing that happened I was alive to witness. While we were in the waiting room, Rufus began to draw something on a piece of paper. Then he returned to see his sister and a minute or two later the nurses and doctors were in the room. At that point, Rufus had to leave and we all asked him what happened. He was smiling when he showed me what he drew. He explained that the evening before his sister Janet took a picture of Lena in ICU with all the tubes and IV's and sent it to him via email. It was her way of showing how dire the circumstances had become. In place of one of the

IV bags, he scribbled an upside down bottle of a Ponche Kuba liqueur and drew the hose drip diverted from her arm into her mouth. He simply showed her the picture and the rest was magic. She began to laugh and couldn't stop. Her heart monitor went into alarm that alerted the medical team. Then soon after one of the doctors relayed the message that was exactly what Lena needed...a good laugh and hope.

◆ ◆ ◆

In the hours to follow a relative amount of awareness was slowly presenting itself as if in preparation for what was quickly becoming inevitable. I'd like to say that I was prepared, but I wasn't. I'd like to admit that I wasn't scared, but I was. In the waning moments I fought to stay alive even in restraints when they tried to stabilize and revive me. I felt everything and I felt nothing, I felt pain and I felt relief. But when it was over, I felt at peace.

I do not fully understand what occurred next nor do I possess the knowledge of quantum theory to explain the matter and energy based concepts that I seemingly have become and can now manipulate to navigate in my Afterlife. That knowledge was never in my proverbial warehouse. What I do know is some people are adversely diagnosed as mental cases when they are unwillingly subjected to other worldly phenomena. As a result, I have to be careful and use my new sense of awareness very carefully and sparingly and traverse this new reality of my existence lightly in the future.

At that moment, I became conflicted whether or not to follow through or undo what I had already instigated and set into motion the evening before.

Immediately after dropping Kevin off to school, Rufus met with the Freshman's Principal to apprise her personally about Kevin's week and a half absence. She already knew. After giving Rufus a hug and her condolences and deepest sympathies, he knew she would be an advocate for him because her late brother was Rufus' childhood friend from kindergarten who was also a Vice Principal in the Atlanta school system. She told him she would keep a very close eye on Kevin and the couch in her office was available for him should circumstances become too overwhelming. As a matter of fact, she did call Rufus on two occasions when Kevin needed to be consoled and alone.

After he returned home from taking Kevin to school after hearing my voice on my mother's phone, he checked his email and saw that he had received the following from my Aunt Debbie in New Jersey. It was another attempt to let him know I was going to be fine. Later Debbie told him that she had no idea where she gotten the poem; she explained that she found it randomly in an arbitrary search and felt compelled to forward it to him after reading it. Before that point she had never sent him any emails.

When tomorrow starts without me, and I'm not there to see

If the sun should rise and find your eyes, all filled with tears for me

I wish so much you wouldn't cry, the way you did today

While thinking of the many things, we didn't get to say.

I know how much you love me, as much as I love you,

And each time that you think of me, I know you'll miss me too

When tomorrow starts without me, please try to understand

That God came and called my name, and took me by the hand

And said my place was ready, in Heaven far above

And that I'd have to leave behind, all those I dearly love

But when I walked through heaven's gates, I felt so much at home

When God looked down and smiled at me, from His great golden throne

He said, "This is eternity, and all I've promised you

Today for life on earth is past, but here it starts anew.

I promise no tomorrow, for today will always last,

And since each day's the same way, there's no longing for the past.

So when tomorrow starts without me, don't think we're far apart,

For every time you think of me, I'm right here in your heart.

Author unknown

During the subsequent months I have been paying very close attention. Over the years I've loved him, he has given me insights and clues about his thought process. But in his present emotional state he could run the error by forgetting those qualities that attracted us to each other. I needed to first make sure that he was ready for a new relationship. And at the same time, I was going to make sure who ever came into his life was going to be right for him. I simply was not going to allow him to have another bag of mesquite.

Now first and foremost, it is imperative that this person must reside abroad because he simply craves the need every now and again to get off the island. Don't get me wrong, St. Thomas is his place of birth and his home. He is also a proud ambassador of the Virgin Islands always mentally comparing it to the other islands as far as it unique qualities are concerned.

His sister Janet stayed away for 25-years where the last time she came to the Caribbean was for our wedding and again for my funeral. When he drove her around she nagging-ly inquired what happened to a landmark, a building or commented on the new developments to which Rufus told her, "Do you think you're in Cuba?"

The island's self-governance is questioned from time to time with its unicameral legislative system where elections are popularity contests where no one wants to make the tough decisions. At the same time, he is of the opinion that if the islands were to exploit its natural resources in the past and reverse adverse US policies - specifically as it relates to rum and oil revenue, the islands would be in a better position to handle its own affairs.

He takes great solace knowing that he lives in one of the most naturally beautiful places in the world. Even though I was raised in Puerto Rico, initially I thought our shoreline were beautiful until I came to St. Thomas and St. John and saw the white sand beaches of which all of the islands are aplenty – not to mention our home overlooks the beautiful Magens Bay beach.

Every now and again he would tell me a little Virgin Islands history from his point of view. Like the major landmark in the capitol Charlotte Amalie is the 1671 Fort Christian or now locally referred to as The Fort. The

Danish fortress was built 100 years before the United States was a country. It is now a museum. But Rufus told me it got its notoriety when it was the police station and the jail. When he was young he said everyone that got into any kind of trouble wound up at The Fort.

I know my sister-in-law Lena would kill me for telling the following story but double jeopardy suggests I haven't anything to lose.

Rufus began the story saying he was four years old when I stopped him for clarification. He confirmed his age stating he has only lived at two addresses as a child having moved to the second house at the age of 5.

Anyway, he said it was a Sunday where as a big family, his oldest brother would make two trips to and from church. The younger siblings always fought for the window seats and since he was the youngest and physically smallest, most of the time he would lose that pre-church battle. This particular Sunday he was happy to have lost.

The short three-minute ride from the airport housing development nicknamed Green Acres to the mid town Methodist Church by the bungalow where slaves used to be traded and sold, the following hilarious story occurred.

Rufus explained at a traffic light stop, their recently divorced father pulled the closest child from the backseat and kidnapped his sister Lena at the age of five. His older brother made a U turn back home to report to their mother. Rufus was laughing when he reenacted how he sounded at the age of four saying,

"Mommy, Daddy stealed Lena."

Since there wasn't any telephone at home, he explained that his brother drove his mother to The Fort to file a police report. He stayed in his brother's car while his mother was inside and moments later he saw his father's car with Lena in the front seat. He went to her rescue until he learned that there was a handcuff around her ankle and the base of the front seat. Rufus said he laughed so much and suggested to her,

"That's what you get for pulling me away from the window seats."

She told him afterwards, "I'm going to beat you up when I get back home."

♦ ♦ ♦

On March 31, 1917, the United State of America bought the Danish Virgin Islands: St. Thomas, St. Croix, and St. John from Denmark for Twenty-Five Million Dollars to act as a military outpost as a result of the war effort. The status of the residence was tenuous and one hundred years later it remains an unincorporated territory of the United States.

As the post-economy changed from the slave trade, to agricultural, to tourism, the first hotels on the islands were represented by their in-land placement. They were primarily boarding facilities with hillside views within close proximity to the harbor which was the transportation hub of the time. One of the first hotels still remain today as a historical preserved real estate treasure still goes by its original name of Hotel 1829 perched on a hill overlooking The Fort and other iconic historic properties like the Grand Hotel, the Emancipation Garden and the Legislature Building. Now in recent time, prime ocean front properties are sought by hoteliers.

Rumor has it that the now defunct Virgin Islands Hotel where Rufus played during the 1980's for a minimum of four evenings nightly was built as a result of a dare. Elliott Fishman and his family were visiting the islands in the mid-20th century when they complained about the service at another local hotel. The management told him that if they didn't like the service, feel free to open their own. So in addition to purchasing a big swath of property overlooking the harbor in the Upper Contant area where their homes were built, they also constructed the largest hotel to that point.

The Fishmans were also the landlord at the industrial park where Rufus worked at his cousin's electrical contracting firm when he subsequently heard the tale of the hotel. He had the opportunity to work at the Fishmans home where in their older ages the story about building the hotel always seemed to be evolving.

But after all that history, at the same time the island also stifles him. I was very fortunate that traveling had become a lifestyle with us; by default, it afforded me countless visits with my family. In the year before we got married when I lived in Puerto Rico, we saw each other every other weekend where we were either in one of the many night clubs or casinos. Whenever we traveled in the winter it would take him a couple of days to acclimate to the temperature change. So cold weather locale was out. On the other hand, he had nothing but great things to say about his friend on St. Croix where he invited me to see her and instead we spent a few minutes in the living room with her mother. The problem is the only other person that he knows on St. Croix is their class valedictorian who is a male doctor.

Now that I had gotten to be socially acquainted with my coworkers on St. Croix from the weekly trips required of me by my job, there may have been one or two with the qualities I was looking for initially. But the more that I consider the possibilities, my list of qualities got longer than one should actually ask of anyone: An independent thinker who equally questions social norms, pretty, charismatic, intelligent, ambitious, can sing, willing to challenge his notions and finally, love my son too...or at least be his advocate. But most importantly, she had to be health conscious because Rufus physical condition was slowly deteriorating and he wasn't paying attention.

So in my inimitable way I was able to compel my former coworker Vicky to come over to the house and get Rufus to purchase life insurance policies because I was becoming very concerned about the signs of his declining health. His weight had increased significantly even before my passing. I attribute that to the fact he was working tirelessly and under stress about my wellbeing where he was not getting the proper amounts of sleep.

As a basic requirement for the insurances, Rufus needed to have a physical examination performed. It was a blessing in disguise because he immediately learned that his blood pressure was extremely high. He met with a registered nurse at one of the local public schools who in no uncertain terms told him he was a walking time bomb. She was not going to approve the underwriting of the two policies he wanted with that diagnosis. It was a stark indication of his life expectancy – two numbers on her blood pressure monitor. What's notable is had he succumbed with a heart attack, our friends and family would have attributed it to grief.

Then the nurse suggested a home remedy that could effectively reduce his blood pressure quickly over a significantly short period of time. But the nurse admonished him additionally when she insisted that he become more physically active. She told him to go to the grocery store, purchase a bag of garlic, purée 2 or 3 cloves in a food processor with water, strain the liquid, and drink twice daily and see her in a week's time.

Rufus followed her instructions to the letter with the exception of the main ingredient. Instead of a bag of garlic, he mistakenly bought a bag of .... It would be funnier if I continued this story from another perspective. Again, the following actually happened and is nothing short of hilarious.

Feeling very proud of himself, Rufus told his best friend about his predicament while Milton was driving home from his office as the Virgin Islands Director of Personnel and the suggested remedy by the school nurse. Milton incredulously listened as Rufus described the side effect as an initial painful urination that tapered off attributing it to his arteries and veins clearing up. Milton quipped as he asked,

"Is that what they taught you in medical school Dred?"

Rufus continued to testify about how much better he was feeling. What he was experiencing was merely superficial and nothing to do with the remedy. So I compelled Milton to intervened where I was able to get him to make a detour on his way home in hopes that he would stop by the house and set Rufus straight.

Upon his arrival Rufus proceeded to show Milton his garlic stash in the refrigerator when he uncontrollably began to laugh.

"That's ginger Dred!" Milton cited in between laughing breaths as my poor baby stood with the refrigerator door opened looking dumbfounded.

I wish I knew how to tell him earlier. But that was the purpose of Milton's presence and repudiation of what Rufus truly thought was true. Rufus acquiesced to Milton culinary expertise because he cooks for his family from time to time, otherwise Rufus would have challenged his claim – it's just what they do. They keep a running one-up-man's scorecard. All Rufus could say to save face was,

"That's why it tasted like ginger beer."

What happened next can only happen in a small island community.

My Guys were traveling for another weekend of normalcy to visit my mother and sisters in Puerto Rico. Perched above the scores of airline passengers, in the distance one of the TSA agent recognized Rufus and began to laugh. A sole voice laughing in the distance echoing within the confined facility. It was his classmate Darlene. Like a periscope Rufus identified her and their eyes met when he immediately deduced that he was the punchline she was enjoying. When he finally got through security, Darlene confirmed what he already knew.... Milton told her.

After purchasing garlic for the first time and actually double checking the grocery receipt for reassurance, for the next week he unenthusiastically drank the homemade potion and was able to reduce his numbers to get the necessary insurances. He also understood why garlic is a repellent to vampires.

◆ ◆ ◆

I wanted to check off all of the boxes, no matter how challenging that may sound. What makes it more difficult is compatibility changes with maturity; younger people tend to know what they want in a partner and older people definitely know what they don't want in relationships. It would be a lot easier if someone on St. Thomas was available because he knew more people there. In actuality, I had a lot more friends than he locally and I was an island transplant. And for some reason, all of those local relationships he had in the past all ended precariously. After spending twenty-five years with someone, if you don't know what their habits and tendencies are, then all that time has been wasted.

I remember around the same time Rufus was doting over the break-up of Miss Credit Card, I was also getting over a recent break-up in Puerto Rico. I didn't reveal much about that relationship although the one and only time I showed him the neighborhood where my ex lived, Rufus would razz me about how long and far I had to drive to include paying tolls to get a kiss. I broke that relationship because he hadn't any goals for the future. His warehouse was sparsely populated and still is. I realize now that it really wasn't his fault - he never had been exposed to anything that fostered his imagination to dream.

Rufus and I were both unknowingly yearning for companionship as evidenced in our warehouses at the same time. The both of us also thought a new relationship so soon may be considered a rebound. So mutually there was no sense of urgency with us to get into a new relationship. We actually compared stories after our breakups where it was determined that I actually saw him once a few years earlier in our lives. I wasn't very clear about the details back then when we spoke, but now I recall with clarity.

I was visiting my Uncle on St. Thomas and my cousin Anna took me out on the town on a Saturday evening to a club called Studio 54. I described the looping road in the area I later learned to be Upper Contant where the club was across from the Virgin Island's Hotel lobby where a band was playing at the hotel's Bar and Lounge. Rufus told me in no uncertain terms that back then, although Studio 54 was the hippest club on the island, everyone was across the street at the Bar and Lounge until the band finished at 1am. Then and only then the crowd would venture across the road. He continued to explain saying unequivocally if there was a band playing in the lounge on Monday, Wednesday, Thursday, or Saturday nights between 1985 and the summer of 1989, he was the bass player on the stage. I told him then that I remember exactly where he stood on the stage because he was noticeably taller than the other members and he concurred. Additionally, I told him that even though I was single at the time, I would never have been interested in a musician because I had my judgmental and preconceived notions of band groupies back then. He told me that I would have probably had to stand in line because that period in his life he mostly chose to remain single. Additionally, I would have had to go through Priscilla who kept everyone interested in her bass player at bay.

He continued to explain how introverted he was initially on stage. The fear of messing up kept him musically on point. He simply stood like a mannequin with only his fingers on the fretboard and over the pick-ups moving. Then with the four evenings a week frequency of consistent playing came the confidence and personality that seasoned musicians outwardly exude as they groove on stage. He explained how he evolved from just peddling the root notes in the chords to find the sub-melody in the music realizing that since he wasn't allowed to sing, his fingers could. Priscilla even created his on stage persona whenever she introduced him she would say,

"And last but not least, in the back, the tall, dark, guy on the bass that never smiles..." and he would scowl on cue.

Just like every relationship – whether romantic, business, or social – Rufus expressed that the band when through its growing pains as the members turned over because of different disputes. There were mostly good times as they practiced weekly learning new songs and choreographing movements on stage so the players won't appear static. Like in the performance of Tina Turner's *Private Dancer*. Rufus described the choreographed performance that was themed to be reminiscent from the scene from Casablanca when Humphrey Bogart said,

"Of all the gin joints in all the towns in all of the world, she walks in to mine."

The song always began the set where the band began with the bass playing the staccato intro as the two male singers struck poses like mannequins. Then Priscilla at her leisure walks in through seated audience singing,

"Well the men come in these places, and the men are all the same,
You don't look at their faces, and you don't ask their names."

Upon her arrival to the stage, she flirts with both mannequins as if to suggests which one she desires most.

"You don't think of them as human, you don't think of them at all,
You keep your mind on the money, keeping your eyes on the wall."

Then she chooses one and the mannequin comes alive to dance the chorus as she sings,

"I'm your private dancer, a dancer for money, I'll do want you want me to do,
I'm your private dancer, a dancer for money, and any old music will do."

Then as the second verse began, the mannequin froze and she danced with the other singer during the second chorus.

When he described that performance to me back then, I remembered it vaguely. But now with access to our Warehouses as I reminisce, it feels like I am back in the club. This new sense of awareness now enables me to compare what he told me and what I actually experienced when I was there. In essence, he also saw me as he played while peering at the audience, but his vantage of me was blinded from the stage lights. This new perspective also allows me to clarify some of the discrepancies in the details in his story. Back then I observed that there were only two singers – Priscilla and the guy who I later learned was her husband Warren and Rufus' best man at our wedding in Puerto Rico. At the time we had that conversation, Rufus submitted that if there were only two singers on the stage, I had to be present after mid 1986.

Later in our reminiscence, he recounted the hilarious manner in which the other singer was fired. I've heard that story a couple of times from both him and Priscilla where he mostly began stating that Priscilla always told him she thought Rufus was going to be the first member of the band to be fired because of his aloofness during the practice sessions.

As only he could, he began to describe the times when they practiced nightly at the Charlotte Amalie High School before landing the contract at the hotel where the musicians and the singers practiced in different rooms at the high school. Rufus explained that he was the wild card because nobody knew who he was; all of the other members derived from the high school where they practiced with the exception of Rufus and the keyboardist who hailed from St. Croix and was an elementary school music teacher. Both of them always got into it whenever there were conflicts with the chord progression in the songs they practice. During the heated arguments the band always voted collectively about who was correct or what sound better where Rufus always lost because they kept reminding him that the keyboardist acquired a Bachelor of Arts degree in Music from the local University. Rufus in the end submitted that music was not a democratic process when many times he would retort that the keyboardist didn't know what the hell he was doing hiding behind four synthesizers. And to further get his jabs in, Rufus told me that he told the guy that he had a BS [Bull Shit] degree in Music.

So when the singers practiced, in addition to learning the leads for their particular songs, they also practiced the harmonies and choreography. What was unique about some of the harmonies they sung was at times Priscilla incorporated counterpoint. [Without being too technical, we have all heard harmonies sung to melodies of songs. In arranging counterpoint for voices, while the harmony follows the lead as two notes, the counterpoint is established at the fifth of the lead where that vocal line jumps about the scale creating their own chords.] At time they sounded like five singers and musical explosions to the ears. And what was most fascinating was Priscilla did all of the vocal arrangements and she too had no music degree – just and amazing ear.

Then Rufus commenced to described the comical termination of the other singer was reminiscent from a scene from the 1993 movie *The Five Heartbeats.* He described that during one of the live performances at the hotel, Warren maintained his choreography while edging closer to Rufus who was at his left to report that the other singer was not singing – he was only 'mouthing' at his microphone. Unable to really hear because of the amplified sounds from the instruments and the acoustic drums Rufus yelled,

"What!"

Warren continued singing backup while dancing and waited for the opportunity when he spun away from his microphone towards Rufus and repeated more colorfully,

"That son-of-a-bitch ain't singing." Then he returned to his microphone.

From Priscilla's periphery, she knew something was amiss and he told her what he had deduced because the harmony he heard from the stage monitors in front of them was missing a voicing.

In addition to being the bassist, Rufus was also the sound engineer. The PA mixing console was at his left and out of the view of the audience because it was strategically hidden behind the right channel house speakers. Rufus walked over to Warren to tell that he was going to mute his channel and it was confirmed. At the end of the song Priscilla tapped the microphone of the other singer and it was audible when after she said,

"Ladies and gentlemen, we're experiencing a little technical difficulties and we will be right back."

Five minutes later the band returned to the stage with one less singer.

◆ ◆ ◆

On the other hand, my circumstance wasn't as colorful at that time. I love dancing on weekends mostly to Salsa music during Happy Hours. I met a guy that I thought was the one until I realized he had no goals and I knew my future didn't include him.

Rufus' meaningful relationships were of the long distant variety where the most recent before I came into his life told him that she still wanted more space. It doesn't make sense because it's not supposed to.

So as The Laws of Attraction suggest, like energies attract. Our cases of personal despair were a form of synergy that inevitably caused the chain reaction of circumstances to manifest and materialize. For reasons that still escapes me, everything that transpired afterwards still remains a mystery where we both definitively were unable to solve our own questions of compatibility.

So exactly why did my cousin on St. Thomas feel the need to invite me at the last minute to the dinner party Rufus was hosting at the Chart House restaurant still remain unanswered. Only divine intervention can explain what happened to us where two broken hearts were able to meet and mend. If she hadn't invited me, this would be a completely different story with different characters probably told by someone else.

CHAPTER FIVE

"I am now wondering whether she was chosen randomly or whether the yet to be understood wonders of the universe inexorably detected the inherent possibility of compatibility."

THE EXAMPLE OF ME UTILIZING my gifts of Total Recall where I was able to remember details about someone I peripherally viewed at a distance in a night club Bar Lounge in my distant past who later became my husband of twenty-five years is nothing short of serendipitous, to say the least. So what if I can again search my Warehouse and find someone from my subconscious past and it yield similar results? That would simply be kismet.

So as I pondered the limitless possibilities – sorta like flipping through volumes of pages of my subconsciousness or like the fast-forwarding of a video on a television DVR. I finally came upon moments I had to work on St. Croix around the last years of my employment at Marshall and Sterling Insurance, the parent company of Theodore Tunick. I remember two distinct occasions when my work week was extended into the weekend. Once by a scheduled upgrade to our computer server and the other time when my return flight was canceled due to inclement weather. Back then even though I had the freedom to work at home, my job also required that I visit all three branches on the islands regularly, including the office on St. John.

Whenever I travelled and had the opportunity to overnight on St. Croix, I used to communicate with My Guys in a very unique way.

In downtown Christiansted on the boardwalk, there was a live video cameras stream. It was there to entice mainlanders especially in the winter time when it showed the tropical picturesque view of commerce to remind of a warmer alternative to visit. Rufus was able to capture the live video link and integrate it into our home control system. So before video chat on our cellphone was 'a thing', we would have one-way video chats with my image on any of the six television screens in our home. I did it at the Cruz Bay dock on St. John too. There were also several places on St. Thomas to tap into, but since we lived there that would have been kinda creepy.

We even did it back in 2005. Kevin was in kindergarten and Rufus insisted that I travel with him to Denver to a Tradeshow. I told him that I refused to stay in those "crummy" hotel like he had the previous two times he went on his own. Crummy was his definition of checking into one building in the cold and his room was in another. Crummy was they did not make up the room during his stay. He was new in the industry and was watching his bottom line. But what did he expect when he paid $39.00 per night.

I was also concerned about Kevin missing school so we flew my mother over and I had one of my girlfriends take him to school daily. We had one-way video chats with him every morning. The difference then was Kevin and my mother stood by the security camera by our parked cars and I got to see him dressed for school on Rufus' phone while I spoke to them on mine. Oh yeah, I made the reservations at Denver's historically oldest hotel The Brown Palace Hotel and Spa.

Anyway, what caught my attention in my warehouse was the duality of the situation during those two particular weekends on St. Croix. The first instance when I was unable to fly home, my coworkers invited me for dinner when it rained and we dined at The Buccaneer Hotel's restaurant where I stayed. The other time we had dinner at another restaurant by the name of Gertrude. Those evenings initially were insignificant, but as the details are now revealed in UHD clarity, I recall casually observing the presence of a stunningly dress woman having dinner with a group of friends. I remember how the male counterparts at our table - who were either married or romantically engaged - had momentary lapses of judgement when they made it overtly obvious that they were staring. What made that initial sighting noteworthy was she again appeared at the second restaurant and garnered similar attention. Coincidentally there was another facet that now causes me to pause and ponder as I recall. The similarity in the demographics of their dinner party and ours drew my attention to the fact that both the lady and myself were the only African Americans in our otherwise large group of friends.

On both occasions she was impeccably dressed and I dually remember being momentarily awestruck by her presence myself. I also distinctly recall that whenever she excused herself to the lady's room, she became a distraction as I noticed how all of the men in the restaurant all followed her with their eyes. That kind of attention she garnered those evenings were synonymous to celebrity sightings.

Even though we never formally met, my subconscious only recalls the impressions that were made in my consciousness and I can now reevaluate briefly what was experienced. But as I review both encounters in detail – unlike the hundreds of thousands of people that I briefly observed in my life – she has now become an enigma in my Warehouse. I am now wondering whether she was chosen randomly or whether the yet to be understood wonders of the universe inexorably detected the inherent possibility of compatibility. And as a result, the mere thought of her inexplicably allows me to teleport to her location instantly at the speed of light. At the moment I can't really explain, but somehow I am now able to sense her energy from back in the restaurants as it lay dormant in my Warehouse. And with that information, I am able to hone in towards her like finding frequencies on a car radio.

Consequently, I also assumed that she was in a happy relationship. But as fate often has it, an intuitive feeling suggested – correction – compelled me with the notion that it wouldn't hurt to briefly explore the possibility of otherwise. To my chagrin, I immediately was able to ascertain that she was no longer living on St. Croix – in fact she was presently residing in Florida. Had she relocated recently?

Additionally, after a week of intermittent eavesdropping, it appeared that she had been there for more than a year and she hadn't been back to St. Croix in about that same period of time. And most importantly, I was able to learn the fact that she was presently single.

She resided in a sprawling intercostal apartment with floor to ceiling windows overlooking the waterway and was in deep thought. Meditation seemed to be her means of centering herself during her afternoons alone. Those moments of silencing her mind allowed a clear path to her deepest thoughts and was her way of dissipating the unwanted contents in her proverbial Warehouse. Then I came to the realization that she was consciously aware of her thought processes. That kind of insight immediately intrigued me. She truly was not a novice when it came to the subject of the subconscious mind. And as I perused her surroundings, I took notice that her personal reading library was more extensive than mine and the topics ran the gamut.

She considered herself as a work in progress and enjoyed the benefits of understanding the sub primal level of her inner being always striving to comprehend what was going on within herself metaphysically. All the while I kept wondering why she was on that personal quest of self-discovery. She was wound very tightly and could actually benefit from a few knots being loosen.

I was now considering whether she could be the one. Then something unusual happened that I never would have considered otherwise. I was faced with the following dichotomy.

If I was alive and was able to similarly observe another moment in her life peripherally - you know - like I did when I saw Rufus at a distance playing the bass on stage or if she was a character on television in a reality show, I honestly think I would have turned the channel. The same way I had my preconceived notions about musicians and groupies. I would have instantly thought that she had it all together and she was on the Reality Show to overcompensate trying to build her brand superficially with her appearance. I would have even determined that she would have been high maintenance. But now I realize that's unfair; that assessment was now the furthest possibility from my consciousness.

You see, during my life my affinity to be judgmental clouded my idea of people's sincerity in some of their decisions and caused me to wonder about the integrity of their intentions. My narrow minded notions at that time simply suggest that mature consenting adults were either in relationships, between relationships or emotionally problematic if they weren't in a relationship. So a single beautiful woman would immediately default to the between relationship category. And if that status was prolonged for an inordinate period of time, the status would scream problematic. I would conclude they seemingly were unable to be happy and found unfulfilled comfort in being alone.

My purely unscientific survey and analysis was initially based on the experiences of my fraternal twin sisters. Even though they both were married – where my shorter sister was twice wed - I often wondered about their choices of dates after they divorced. I classified them in my unscientific second category. The information that further formulated my theory was perceived from my then skewed points of view; skewed from my not knowing or from my limited evidence and facts. Two sisters do not make a focus group.

Maturity later and my passing now rendered those notions of mine as ignorant and totally off based. Any person who knows they are being judged will generally highlight their positive attributes for consideration and would keep hidden what information they deemed sacred. But again, back then I could only superficially see what was revealed with my small flashlight and having not been invited into the proverbial Warehouses of those for further insight, I realize now that many times I have unfairly judged.

In Afterlife, my perceptions are no longer skewed because what I now see is one's illuminessence in the form of their unfiltered light spectrum. As I described briefly earlier, light is simply electromagnetic radiation where its spectrum is divided into bands of wavelengths that are seen and unseen.

Everyone is capable of visualizing light-essence when they get pass the superficial. The problem is most of the time that's all that is seen. When you truly love someone it is at times expressed sentimentally when you may say something like 'you are the light of my life.' That's the way I will forever feel about Kevin as long as I remain in his consciousness. I have felt that way about him even before the time he was born. Unfiltered, unbiased love.

I also feel that way about Rufus. But should he fall in love again, that energy I still feel from him now will inexorably wane and will be a sign of how the forces of the universe reconciles.

Unfortunately, most men are generally poor candidates to recognize this facet of another individual's being. Why? Because most can't get past the physical. So I have to keep that in mind if I am able to perform the virtually impossible and if this relationship is pursued. On the other hand, some women often at times fall into the same category of failure but for other reasons. They obviously see the same thing as men, but preconceived notions are now factored like biases and prejudices which again are unwarranted.

Notions like "she thinks she's cute" or "she thinks that she is better than us" clouds their evaluation. I even overheard her telling a girlfriend of a near incident in the lady's room when she was between relationships. A group of African American women saw her matting her face from perspiring and re-applying her makeup. They began their diatribe to intimidate expecting the same sheepish reaction of instant retreat they often get when they did similarly to their Caucasian counterparts. Her narrowed eyes reflected theirs in the mirror and they realized her resolve when they immediately and instinctively left.

She then pivoted her story to when her mother threatened her with beatings if she allowed her siblings to be harmed in school and she did nothing about it. So if her sister told her that a girl in school was bullying her, she would open a can of whoop-ass. If her brother complained similarly, some guy would get his ass kicked.

So imagine this for a moment. Suppose you are able to see the true essence in someone that you've never met, similarly like you do when you see a baby. That is the illuminessence that I now see and is of the understanding that everyone is capable of - not only in Afterlife.

Illuminessence can also be a double edged sword. When that sense of awareness is achieved, you unknowingly at first become the center of attention like a magnet that attracts everything and everyone. It begs to be repeated – like an innocent baby in a room organically gets your attention unless there are several babies in the same room. And if you are not aware, magnanimity becomes your lure. You unwittingly evoke empathy and wisdom to those in your presence if only they are willing to hear beyond what they see. People tend to say you have "It." But if you are not aware, that altruistic persona that is pure at times becomes convoluted when ego is invited.

Many stories of rises and falls from grace have been witnessed and written about politicians, clergy, and celebrities who all had 'it' and failed miserably to do the right thing with it. In essence, everyone has 'it'.

With all that said, I am now able to unveil the secrets of the living. The notions I've had when I was alive that would have suggested she must be problematic if she is single is total folly. With my new sense of enlightenment, her superficial appearance now is discounted as I am able to evaluate the underlying situations and circumstances yet to be revealed. Only the unforeseeable future would determine whether she would be right for anyone she may desire to share her life with – whether for fleeting moments or for the rest of her life. I was particularly concerned about the latter for My Guys sake. But her unforeseeable past could only be realized if she told someone about herself in my omnipotence. And with all of the powers of perception I possessed, although her warehouse was revealed, I didn't know any of the stories behind its contents.

Even though I could not read minds, I am able to perceive the mind as energy. As a result, I was able to discern that her thought frequency was similar to Rufus' which on the visceral surface suggested compatibility. But I also needed to know whether she was also going to be good for my son too.

Incorporating offsprings in relationships can be a red flag particularly if one has a child and the other doesn't – not to mention if both have children with a disparity in ages. The fact that she has a son who age is similar to Kevin further suggests that something worthwhile was there.

I was going to need some background and that meant that I needed to have her tell her story again to a friend. This was going to take some time and until then, I was going to be very patient and figure out her routine. I knew that I had to get it right. So I stuck around. The weeks that followed I learned a lot more and after a month had passed, I was absolutely sure.

CHAPTER SIX

"Her life's story was so intriguing I stopped checking off the lists of qualities I had and simply listened. Some of our similarities in her stories were eerily uncanny."

S HE IS THE OLDEST OF SIX SIBLINGS from a small town in north Florida and even though she spoke with a clear American accent to her colleagues and friends in North Miami at the Pilates studio where she worked, whenever she spoke to her "Momma" on the phone, her southern country-girl accent could not be escaped.

Her parents were married for a half century where her mother is the missionary and her father is the pastor of the small church. He lovingly referred to her as "Daughter" and his "Sleeping Beauty" instead of by her name. He taught her to drive his Ford F-250 at the extraordinary age of twelve which suggests she was statuesque in her adolescence gifted with long legs. From time to time he allowed her to clandestinely wear makeup reminding her to remove it before entering the house after her return from school.

She lamented about the lost opportunities she's had where her mother shot down many of her childhood dreams and aspirations because it ran counter to religious tenets that were taught on more days and evenings than most other houses of worship. She confidently suggested that her life's trajectory could have been different if she was allowed to showcase the potential of her world class sprinter speed. She described a moment when her son ran track when she humbled some of the brash members in a short sprint while wearing heels. But as a teenager, she only wore dresses and her Momma didn't allow her participation on the track and field team because of her thinking that it was not proper for a young lady to show so much of her legs.

Additionally, she explained that even though that she attended a predominantly White secondary school, she could have also been the Gabriel Union in her own version of the teen movie *Bring It* as the head cheerleader with her charismatic personality. But again, she also was prohibited by her mother for similar reasons. Her defiance led her to the drum major team where her siblings actually kept each other's secret.

In her formative years she spent hours reading any and everything she could get her hands on. And at their family church weekly services she played the drums and camouflaged the latest Judy Blume novels between the pages of the holy books because their services were so long. And when she was called upon by her father to recite scripture or sing songs – between playing the drums – she was always ready for prime time delivering the verses often at times harmonizing hymns with her sister. And their biggest act of defiance was being able to watch the Soul Train where the devil's music was played and danced to while her mother was grocery shopping.

During the few times she has returned home she preferred to stay at the church's guest room because it gave her a sense of peace. It was where she went to recharge her emotional batteries when her life and the world fell out of balance.

Her mother was continuously concerned about her emotional welfare and hoped that she would find the kind of joy and happiness she complains to her about often saying, "Your father doesn't listen to me." After fifty years of marriage he definitely heard it all.

She is a single mother of a son who is coincidentally two days older than Kevin. That was intriguing particularly because there was some perspective there when I actually imagined both of us possibly being in different hospitals around the same time. I now wanted to hear more about her child raising philosophies.

She has been divorced from her husband for the past eight years. Ironically they were married around the same time Rufus and I were having been separated after a trial reconciliation with counseling off and on for the past five years inclusive being married for eighteen years. Although couple's therapy was sought during their separation, the relationship became somewhat tumultuous after its dissolution.

Early in her marriage she was carefree and hadn't any notion of having children because she told her husband that she practically raised all of her siblings until her high school graduation. She modeled for a stint and after she was separated, her employment history ran the gamut. She is presently a fitness instructor and was about to move from Miami to Fort Lauderdale to be closer to the new Pilates studio she was about to open with her former client and present business partner and the new private school her son will be attending in the fall as a high school freshman.

It was a very long time since she last traveled to St. Croix where her most recent relationship was with a practicing doctor. She described how he became overly possessive and very insecure when others gave her compliments. The mere gesture of being approached to be offered assistance in stores were preludes to arguments. And after he suggested that she relocate to St. Croix and be his office secretary, it was a convenient reason to dissolve their engagement to the point they remained cordially estranged.

I was fortunate to be present in her Warehouse on those weekend afternoons at her apartment when she opened up to a girlfriend stating that she had no regrets about her present circumstances. She recapped her life stating how she was married young and was carefree in the early nineties. Close to the turn of the century her husband pressed her to have a child when she finally relented and had what she considered was the most wonderful pregnancy only to attract a staph infection during the delivery and her daughter died two days after. As a result, her life was forever changed.

She described the deep depression she endured even through her subsequent pregnancy a year later after they delivered a beautiful healthy son. She lovingly refers to him as 'Her Heart' by evidence now on her phone whenever he calls. But after the death of her first child, their marriage was never the same. After soul searching, counseling, and therapy, she and her husband separated. She admitted that their attempts to reconciliation was fruitless because the emotional bond was gone. He underestimated her resolve assuming that after leaving she would soon come to her senses and return with their child since she was unemployed at the time. She showed tenacity and determination where temporary public assistance allowed her to start anew working several odd jobs - at one time three simultaneously - having moved in with her younger sister until she was able to be on her own.

She strategically chose to at times live within walking distance to the best school districts for the benefit of her son to attend. She explained that after losing jobs because it conflicted with her son's pick up schedule, she asked the universe for a reprieve. She explained that at one school she found an angel in the form of his teacher who would take her son home when she worked too far to pick him up on time. And another angel just happened to live in her apartment complex. That neighbor she allowed unfettered access and would wake up her son and get him ready for school and at times cook for both when they returned. And when her divorce was final, her ex-husband was awarded weekend custody until the age of majority.

She was confidently aware of her attractiveness, being reminded of it every day by obvious stares and unwelcomed cat calls. She dreamed of a life of leisure and all her necessities taken care of by evidence of the message board hanging in her bedroom with several clippings of magazines. The same awareness she had when she meditated to rearrange her proverbial Warehouse. Because of her avid reading she was also aware of The Laws of Attraction.

In all of the stories of Aladdin, The Genie in the Lamp is a metaphor for The Laws of Attraction when it grants all of his wishes. But in real life, you must be prepared to receive those blessing because if you aren't, it may overwhelm you. So as a result of her dreams of leisure, The Laws of Attraction granted those wishes too.

She was once offered a lucrative opportunity for employment and a new start in Denver, but that was thwarted when her ex-husband threatened to sue her if she were to take their son away seeing that he had become a lawyer. So she had to let that opportunity past.

Her universal request was again answered where she attracted the attention of men of significant wealth where she was treated very well. Lavished with gifts, private plane and first class trips to New York, Denver, and Las Vegas to the trendy restaurants, Broadway shows, mountains and casinos were now her reality on weekends. During that time, she was always aware of what happened to her son.

Her first relationship ended when that suitor yelled at him and worst - was giving her son paternal advice. She immediately saw the disconnect where her son and his father already had a great relationship and another father figure would be detrimental to his impressionable mind.

That relationship dissolved naturally when she made the conscious decision to no longer have her son interact with any one she was romantically involved with.

After that episode, her subsequent relationships were like deja vu. She had known from their inception whether or not they would last or for how long. And she always made her intentions very clear. Those affairs eventually became strained after development when they insisted upon more of her time than the weekends offered.

Even though the weekend fairytale that her life had become inexorably granted the wishes she yearned, subconsciously she longed for more. There were so many conflicting issues that always seemed to threatened the balance she sought. All of her suitors were significantly older – which she knew made them feel youthful – but her biblical upbringing was an influence in the proverbial scale that weighed the fact they weren't equally yoked. In the end she came to the realization that although the conveniences that were provided with the various levels of wealth they afforded for the lifestyle she enjoyed, still it didn't make her feel at peace.

She explained that she always felt like she was on display with them: having to dress a certain way, having to look a certain way. She always had to look her best. She explained at times it became belaboring like work.

At one dinner date she described how between the courses of the meals, she had to learn the placement and position of the silverware to queue the servers. And at another dinner party she was chided for picking up after herself being reminded that the servants were there for that. Ultimately she abhorred the way the housekeepers looked at her when she was at their homes. Invariably, every time a wedding date was imminent, the perpetual fairytale that her life had become, eventually ran its course when the proverbial clock struck midnight.

She reminisced about the extremes of life experiences she had participated. From the first and only time she was married during her lunch hour at the justice of the peace while working at Barnett Bank in North Florida, to the gorgeous wedding dress fitting she had in Aspen Colorado for the professionally planned winter wedding describing the white mink hat chosen instead of a veil and crown that was later canceled due to her change of heart. Now more recently having her ex-husband threatened to file a restraining order on her fiancé when he opened a practice in Miami and would show up at the pool area by the apartment that he owned, but refused to cash her rent checks after they had broken up. That's why she was in the process of moving again.

All of her relationships slowly came to precipitous endings when she became engaged – particularly when it involved her son. Even the business relationship with the pop star Shakira. It's not what you're thinking. Shakira thought she was an amazing personal trainer and wanted her to relocate to the private island in the Bahamas with her son, but she graciously declined. On the other hand, her fiancé's having never met her son, all had suggestions for him to be enrolled in the best boarding schools after they were married. As a result, the threat of being sued for custody always loomed.

Her therapists deduced what she had already knew; her son always came first; before everyone – even before herself. And even though her heart still yearned for love, she made the conscious decision to remain celibate over the past year and began the slow process of finding herself through meditation in her pursuit of inner peace.

The Attraction she now sought could be summed up with one word; she just wanted Peace and in whatever form it entails. Poetically she stated that at times she "welcomed death for the simple opportunity to sleep."

The world's distractions were actually being removed primarily by not having a television to convolute her Warehouse and having a very few select friends. She also learned to holistically make new requests for the ends and the means with the faith she knew will eventually materialize. She also wished for her ex-husband to have what she has been enjoying with her son - a great relationship.

All the opportunities she prudently turned down and the sacrifices she has made were bearing fruit. Her son was an A student and his future was going to be as bright as the illuminessence he has been in her life. She was going to be an entrepreneur in a few months. To that end, she rid herself of negative energy thus remaining cordial toward her ex-husband to the point where she even agreed to annual vacations during spring breaks where she simply insisted on separate accommodations for herself.

◆ ◆ ◆

What a testimonial I thought initially. Her life's story was so intriguing I stopped checking off the lists of qualities I had and simply listened. Some of our similarities in her stories were eerily uncanny. Like the fact that Rufus and I were both officially married by a Justice of the Peace during our lunch hour also. Record Scratch ....??? Please allow me to clarify.

Our wedding in Puerto Rico that I will later describe was thoroughly enjoyed and an unintentional ruse because the female pastor failed to secure the necessary marriage license after all the time we met with her for counseling before our wedding. In actuality, she admitted that ours was the first she had officiated. In hindsight she was more concerned about the wedding not being the kind of spectacle others had become. She instructed us to notify our guests against flash photography during the ceremony and it was her choice of 'San Antonio Voluntary instead of the traditional Bridal Chorus - which reminds me at the rehearsal when my mother-in-law asked me,

"I thought you was going to walk down the aisle to Here Comes the Bride."

The pastor stated that song was too secular.

Anyway, we were officially married six weeks after on St. Thomas. Weeks prior the pastor called to unequivocally remind us that we were not legally married and she actually said,

"You guys are living in sin."

Rufus took control of the situation because it became overwhelming as I often pondered and later suggested to him,

"...what would my mother think?" because no one else actually knew.

Rufus suggested that we get married in St. Thomas - adding that hundreds of tourists do it annually at the Family Court. So a couple of weeks later while Rufus worked for his cousin as the Electrical Foreman/Estimator/Office Manager at the island's biggest electrical contracting firm, he requested extra time for lunch. His cousin inquired why and Rufus simply expressed that he was going to get married, setting up what he knew was going to be a priceless response,

"What the fuck you talking about?" he incredulously began. Then concluded to state, "Wasn't I at your wedding?"

What also was a secret was the fact that no one who attended the wedding in Puerto Rico knew. They were also unaware that the week before the ceremony, Rufus quit his job at the bank. His cousin hired him immediately a week after to be his bookkeeper. So after being granted the addition time off for lunch, Rufus gave him the condensed version of the state of affairs because we had an appointment at the court.

We registered our names and by law there was supposed to be a 10 day waiting period to allow for people with "Cold Feet." What tourists commonly do is register in advance of their vacation. To add insult to injury, for those people who took the institution of marriage lightly, the following actually occurred like from a scene from another romantic comedy that at times was our lives.

The Honorable Judge Meyers required that the consenting adults he was going to marry subject themselves to a brief counseling hoping to never see you again in his court. It mostly was catered to tourists. He even suggested that some decisions to marry are made under duress or when the parties were too inebriated to remember what happened the night before. He then began by reminding us how serious the institution of marriage is and how too many enter it lightly and with their eyes closed.

I could not help it but I began laughing. Yes, I began laughing first … then Rufus. The Honorable Judge was about to sternly lecture us directly by making us his case in point. We apologized for our foolhardy reaction and briefly explained that we had taken marriage counseling and were in fact 'ceremoniously' married in Puerto Rico last month amongst 75 family members and friends.

After the explanation about the snafu, the judge instructed his clerk to pre-date our application 10 days and executed the license in our presence along with my girlfriend and landlady Jackie – Cleo's wife; foregoing the clause 'with the power vested in me I now pronounce you …. yada yada yada….'

For the several years that followed, every time we saw the Honorable Judge Meyers: at the supermarkets, on the airplane, and especially at the annual Chamber of Commerce Balls, our eyes would meet and there would be the usual nod, smile and giggle.

♦ ♦ ♦

So as she poured her soul out to her Jamaican girlfriend at the studio and her apartment, to an elderly Jewish client at their monthly lunches, and to a concerned ailing real estate male companion in New York over the phone about her circumstances during those subsequent afternoons over a period of two months while I just happened to be eavesdropping, I became certain of one thing. If they were to ever meet they would absolutely complement each other.

She was stoic at times, Rufus was light and from a sub primal level, he was at times day and she conversely was night. But a supernova would surely result should their true essence of their existence was allowed to shine.

In public she would always put her best face forward - always ready for primetime - so to speak. And on the weekends she cocooned herself with books and learn about life's wonderments in times past. She meditated regularly which was another way I could garner information and gain insight about herself. She remained a voracious reader having read what appeared to be infinite volumes that once were catalogue similarly like how Rufus has his music, videos and audio books.

She had to give away most because she felt strongly against the disposal of books and had once actually dumpster dived for a complete set of books that were discarded. She is also a proud carrying member of a library card. She's read everything from Marcus Aurelius to The Hero's Journey by Joseph Campbell. And I overheard her commenting that one of her favorite books includes a whimsical story where the Big Bad Wolf testifies that Little Red Riding Hood lied about him.

Rufus similarly had also become a recluse. When he traveled to visit my family those subsequent months after my passing - especially when there were three-day weekends - he hid his depression well. On the surface, his behavior appeared normal. But it was all a show of strength and resolve that he maintained for the public.

Everything felt tenuous not knowing whether she was ready to get into another relationship until I overheard her telling her Jamaican friend what she had been expressing to the universe. She read her affirmation aloud to her:

"*I want to be loved - not superficially - and appreciated for who I am. I want my opinions considered and not discounted because of my gender, nor assumed to be naive because I am at times considerably younger.*"

And because of her religious background, she wanted to be equally yoked. She unapologetically stated that the one word that totally encapsulates her is vast.

She also knew that her family was concerned. She told her mother that after her son graduated from high school, maybe then she'd again fall in love with someone; she edited that message when she told her girlfriend that she might even move in with a gay friend if all else fails just for appearances. That was her four-year plan. Her mother quipped reminding her that at that point she would be 50 years old and she would be a lonely old maid living in a house filled with lots of dogs that would eventually eat her after she dies.

CHAPTER SEVEN

*"I knew with all certainty - not that I wanted to marry that man,
but I simply knew I was going to marry him. It was crystal clear
and there was no ambiguity."*

A
LL OF HER CLIENTS WERE EQUALLY ENAMORED with her because I overheard them saying how much of an amazing instructor she was. Unknowingly, they too were attracted to her illuminessence because they were without preconceived judgement. They loved being in her presence and she equally loved gaining from their wisdom and experience. Mostly she represented that symbol of youthful vigor and disposition as they worked hard during the hour workouts and private sessions to maintain their appearances as they strived to stay in shape. Her intention always was to safely tone, shape, realigned and strengthened their anatomies. Although she kept her age her trade secret where most of her clients thought they were considerably older than she, those who were actually younger all mistakenly thought she was.

She sought the advice of her elders as far as prolonged relationships were concerned and reciprocated when they sought her youthful points of view. She knew about the powers of perception and persuasion by evidence of the crop top apparel she purposely wore daily to display her signature toned abdominals and arms. And if she didn't wear the yoga pants daily that hid her shapely legs, they all would accuse her of fitness heresy for holding out on them. But if they knew that at 4:30am in the morning she endures a grueling half hour regimen of exercises to maintain her figure, they would think twice about any insurrection.

Strangely enough, she was different because she was never concerned about her weight being very conscious of what she ate.

Vegetables were her mainstay like broccoli, asparagus and lots of spinach. And whenever the urge for protein was too much she'd satisfy herself with an occasional steak.

What she was mostly concerned – but seldom kept her awake at night – was whether she would be able to fit into her classic dresses in her wardrobe. That was the only benchmark she used instead of scales or buying new clothes.

From my perspective, she was an old soul. She loved the classics in the form of the Blues, actresses, dresses, and movies. And from time to time, she'd pick up her biographies of Josephine Baker, Diane von Furstenberg, Coco Chanel and even Muhammad Ali for quick references. And in her leisure she'd break out a small combination 19-inch television with DVD player to watch the box sets of Andy Griffith and Sanford and Son from in her closet.

Just like I would have assume, her clients all thought that she had it all together with her magnanimity being able to discuss and counsel anyone who cared to listen. I was present when after her last class in the morning, three of her clients stuck around to chat. She walked in on the tail end of their discussion about how they were all totally enthralled with her. The older Caucasian said,

"I keep telling my husband how incredibly beautiful she is..." continuing to comment about her poise, the way she dresses, and her skin.

"I have been all around the world and seen beautiful people from all over but ... look at her. She is the most beautiful African American woman I have ever seen," a Jewish client added.

"I called her Black Barbie" the Venezuelan chimed in.

She became visibly paralyzed. She knew what the world sees, but to hear it from women she really loves and respects made her feel very uncomfortable where she immediately began to perspire in the areas of her body where her shaven follicles were overwhelmed to the point she had to go to the restroom.

Upon her return, the Venezuelan stuck around to now express her appreciation. She was an expatriate from the Hugo Chavez administration days that travels monthly to and from her economically depressed country. In confidence she told her how she has been working out all her life and for the past eight years as her age nears sixty, she has never felt nor looked better since she has been her trainer. How she is continuously inspired when she works out and always looks forward to the next day. The Venezuelan too assumed that at the moment of her conversation she was romantically involved until learning differently from the soon to be business partner. Instead of being judgmental, she told her blatantly that with what she had going on – without the emphasis on her superficially – it was a shame that she was single.

◆ ◆ ◆

For all intents and purposes, she seemed too good to be true. Judgement without all the information are how hasty decisions are made. The one thing that I took from the many perspectives and points of view I was able to gather – she was very fascinating to say the least. I have enjoyed reading stories from various authors who all described their coming of age. She was three years my junior and possibly had more life experiences than me and my girlfriends: the death of a child, a divorce, and was definitely deserving of the weekend fairytales she had now grown wary of. It seems that she was now creating a new life trajectory and had simpler goals for herself. She actually had a 4-year plan which simply involve getting her son across the adolescent finish line and into college. Afterwards, her intentions were to concentrate on her own eternal happiness. It was obvious that she would need a partner to compliment her as she forged forward in her new business venture.

Like me, before my diagnosis I had just resigned from my job of 23 years and was about to embark on a new entrepreneurial venture called Interpretation & Translation Services. I found that locally the Latino community spoke Spanish but could not write it very well. From time to time I would receive calls at my job and at home requesting that I translate something or provide a translated transcript for legal purposes. The funniest requests were when I had the opportunity to work with defendants who would from time to time tell their court appointed lawyers, "*No speakey no Ingles*" when they actually knew how to speak English.

I had already secured the domain and trade name, business license, stationary and business cards that Kevin helped me designed. Our house was going to be paid off in six months and it was going to afford us a life of leisure on our terms. In hindsight I can submit now that the only lesson to be learned from my passing was life is short and now is always the right time to move on.

She also started purchasing domain names after securing the first for her new studio's website and a few others for the future endeavors she had in mind. She even procured her first laptop and some photography equipment when one of her clients suggested that she could do well creating an online presence for extra money as a trainer.

At one point in our marriage Rufus had an idea where I would be in front of the camera as he produced a home cooking show from our kitchen after I was a helper on the local PBS station culinary program. Afterwards he told me that I had more personality than Julia Childs, but I did not have the interest and I digress.

He prophesied the notion of being a videographer a decade ago. And when he came to visit his mother before the family cruise, he purchased a new Sony 4K Camcorder for $2,500.00 to add to his electronic collection since he no longer needed my approval.

She now had thoughts of building up her brand in front of the camera with a website in conjunction to producing workout videos. So organically things were beginning to materialize on their own.

But ultimately a major problem still existed. With all this time invested so far, how was I going to get Rufus to meet her? The chances of them meeting on their own were none - forget about slim. And on a slightly obscure existential level, that is possibly the exact thing the 'angel' that brought Rufus and I together probably thought before we serendipitously met. They definitely do not have anyone in common like my cousin Anna was in being instrumental initially when I met Rufus. But then again, there was me. And I am here, now.

◆ ◆ ◆

Everyone in love or anyone who have spent a significant amount of time with their love ones can look back and recall the moment it all began because of its significance. All those wonderful experiences and stories where they indescribably have no idea about the circumstances that has forever change their lives keeps us wondering in hindsight, why were we so fortunate. The simple answer is The Laws of Attraction. And unbeknownst to us it summons accomplices to play vital roles in granting life's wishes.

Rufus was a wonderful partner until the end of my life and from everything that I had recently learned, I knew without ambiguity she was sincere and he would make her happy too. I was beginning to get excited. And as I recall the circumstances under which Rufus and I met, we really didn't have anyone in common directly. Which begs to question whether blind dates are actually chanced meetings. The Laws of Attraction is the manifestation of like thoughts turned into action.

I know before I met Rufus, I was distraught having recently ended a short lived relationship when I lived in Puerto Rico. I also knew that I dreaded coming to St. Thomas when I was younger because my grandmother dragged me along with her to visit her adopted son around Carnival time. For clarification, I didn't hate St. Thomas; I hated the long ferry ride through the rough seas which took hours and made many people seasick. So only on very limited occasions I saw that side of my family.

So was it kismet when I was chosen to be the liaison for Metmor Insurance in the Virgin Islands after the territory was devastated by Hurricane Hugo in September 1989? Consider the following: I was chosen – not because of the quantity and severity of insurance claims, nor because my employer thought it was absolutely necessary for me to be away from my home for extended periods of time for the unforeseeable future. Or was it because I spoke bilingually. Ultimately, I was chosen because I was one of the few unmarried employees in the company at the age of 22 and bilingual. So frankly, I had no choice. And I wasn't looking forward to working in a storm ravaged territory for the unforeseeable future either.

At the same time my grandmother's adopted son Uncle Miguel, was a counter agent for Liat Caribbean Airlines, and he just so happened to recognize me when I arrived at the airport in St. Thomas to report to work. We chatted for what seemed like a brief reunion until I was able to hail a cab to my company's apartment that was leased for a year. I remember that period was before cell phones and instant messaging. The popular personal communication device at that period were beepers and phone pagers.

Almost two months had passed after the hurricane devastation and the island's electricity and communications services were slowly being restored. So I naturally gave my uncle my contact information at the office on St. Thomas. The following evening, I was invited by my cousin Anna to Rufus' dinner gathering at the Chart House restaurant. I later learned that Anna and Rufus were coworkers at the local branch of Banco Popular de

Puerto Rico and I was invited so I won't be in the apartment alone that Friday evening. It was going to be an after work happy hour type affair over cocktails and dinner.

Years later I learned from Rufus that he was a bit perturbed at the last minute invitations when Anna notified him in the afternoon after the bank closed that she had invited me. He said the guest list kept increasing – from three, to four, to six. Rufus said he initially only invited Anna and her boyfriend Glenwood, that's it. Then Anna invited her sister Nicole, Nicole then invited her high school girlfriend Tara. And finally Anna invited me. He later quipped that it seemed like she was making sure all of the available seating were occupied in his car.

As Rufus likes to tell the story, he explained that his 2 door coupe was designed to hold 5 passengers – but 4 comfortably because his long legs rendered the seat behind him useless. That evening I was picked up last and I squeezed myself in on the driver's side and I sat uncomfortably behind him. He explained later to me that he was a little peeved after I was invited because he immediately thought and hoped that I wasn't too overweight to fit in his car and further indicated that evening was the most people ever to occupy his car which was otherwise a 2-seater.

During dinner I spoke mainly with my cousins and I was skeptical about Rufus' relationship status because it was apparent that he was without a date although the party of six had four females. My judgmental views were quickly dispelled early when I was able to discern otherwise.

He was such a gracious host where everyone was engaged in conversations and I was thoroughly enjoying the festivity. At one point Rufus stated that the gathering represented a state of normalcy as the island's economy and commerce activities were slowly being restored. I was able to discern immediately that he frequented the Chart House when the manager welcomed him back. Rufus proceeded to tell us a story about how he met the previous manager who was a Caucasian from California and was responsible for the local guy having this position.

Initially he and some of the employees came by the bank to cash their pay checks and needed approval because they were drawn upon a mainland bank. Rufus expedited the approval of the checks because he recognized them from the restaurant and told the manager in the future to come to his desk first before going to the bank queue. A few weeks later, the manager recognized Rufus playing at another hotel on a Friday night and was surprised that he was a musician remarking how much he loved being in the islands and the band was amazing.

The next time Rufus went to the Chart House, the manager told him that his money was no good at the restaurant; he only asked that he adequately tip the server. Rufus was being reserved with his story, but now being able to access the contents of his Warehouse, I was able to visualize that at that moment Ms. Credit Card was his date.

The manager later extended the same privileges to Rufus' subordinates which included all of the tellers and the bank's messenger. So for their birthdays they were rewarded with an intimate dinner by the ocean in the evening with their significant other. One young teller complained to Rufus that her boyfriend's only idea of a dinner date was taking her to McDonald's and the movies. He told her not to take no for an answer and quickly showed her how to calculate 15% of the bill for the tip since there weren't cellphone APPs back then for that. She returned the next day to work to report it was the best date she had to that point in her life.

When that manager was transferred back to the mainland, he was replaced by a local employee who was instructed to maintain the privileges he had implemented.

That's a perfect example of how 'one good deed deserves another.' The inverse is also true when Rufus continued to describe another series of events when he was asked what did he do before working at the bank. He then began to tell us about another series of events that he navigated when he briefly worked for the local government at the Department of Human Services Headstart Program and how he wound up at the bank.

He began recounting the story stating his supervisor was a Caucasian female from Alabama who felt justified to tell him "he wasn't going to amount to anything in life." That comment was prompted when she observed him studying on the job during a break period. She was taken aback when he immediately quit. He said he was twenty-two at that time.

After a brief hiatus from working, he was introduced to Priscilla when she decided to form another band after returning from New York. At the same time, he took the placement test for Banco Popular and scored very high because as he recalled it was too easy. As a result, he had a dilemma. The bank required that all new employees attend their Teller School in Puerto Rico for 6-weeks. That would conflict with the new band schedule. As a result, an interim bassist was hired to play the weeknights while Rufus played on the weekends traveling to Puerto Rico on Sundays and returning the Friday afternoons.

He was hired as a teller with a base monthly salary so low back then it was laughable. Another teller from St. Lucia was training to work in one of the two branches on St. Croix who was Rufus' hotel roommate while in Puerto Rico and was also in the training classes who later became Kevin's Godfather. I met him the following Carnival season in 1990 when Rufus introduced him saying,

"He has a superlative for a first name that sounds like a last name and a last name that is definitely a first name, Maxentius John."

As of late, they would reminisce about how far they have come in their lives where he's currently a Shop Steward for Southwest Airlines and still is incredulous about their initial paltry wage at the bank.

Six months later at the bank Rufus stated that he became the branch's Head Teller. That was around the time that Anna was hired fresh out of college as a Service Representative and she too had to attend Teller School in Puerto Rico. He loved telling the following story.

As a result of the frequent turnover of employees and being promoted to the Head Teller by default, he was not duly compensated. He informed his supervisor that if he was not given a raise by the week's end, he was going to leave all of the cash lockers in the vault unlocked because as far as he was concerned the Human Resources department in Puerto Rico had him classified as a Teller.

They tested his resolve. So after the bank closed on Friday, Rufus received all of the excess cash from the tellers and duly accounted for the denominations and left the cash lockers and the vault door opened and told the assistant manager that he was about to leave. He was summoned into the conference room by the branch manager who was a Puerto Rican transplant. Rufus explained that he sat in the room for over thirty minutes from which he knew was a power play on their behalf.

When the manager entered he was nonchalant in his demeanor and disposition sitting across from him. Rufus imitated his Puerto Rican accent when he began sayin,

"Rufu, is everything alright?"

Rufus expressed that he stared back annoyed because of how long he was kept waiting and simply shook his head in the affirmative. The manager reiterated,

"Are you sure?"

Rufus continued to show his disdain.

"Are you sure nothing is wrong?" the manager persisted.

"Stop the crap" Rufus began. "I told you guys my intentions on Monday. I am not asking for anything that I don't deserve."

After the manager realized that there was a shift in the room, there was a pause. Rufus then continued to state,

"I am going to be perfectly clear. I am not quitting; I just want to be properly compensated. I didn't ask for all the extra cash in the bank. And I already know that since the other teller gave me their excess cash, they have already gone home." He then reminded the manager the following,

"You know I don't need this crap; I make more money playing music in the evenings where I work less days and less hours."

What's telling was a few months earlier Rufus had another meeting with the manager when he applied for a car loan to finance his first new car being held at the dealership. The manager told him that his loan would be approved for a 'more economical' car like a Toyota Tercel because his salary didn't substantiate its repayment of the Madza 626LX. That's when Rufus first apprised him of his moonlighting gig. Rufus told him "thanks but no thanks" and proceeded to reiterate that under no circumstances was he going to pay for a car that he did not like nor want.

The next day he went to Chase Manhattan Bank that held the note of his student loan because they had a record of his repayment history and would be amenable to extending him the credit – not to mention the loan was going to be secured by the automobile as collateral. The loan officer was also a groupie on weekends in the audience at the Bar and Lounge and was fully aware of his moonlighting activities in the evenings. All she required was a letter from Priscilla stipulating how much she paid Rufus. Priscilla did her better coming into the bank the following day and provided all the assurances Chase Manhattan required.

The next day he rolled up to the bank in his new car on Friday. At the end of the business day, the manager asked him for a ride to the airport in the late afternoon where he goes home to Puerto Rico and returns on the first flight on Mondays.

So with everything full circle in the conference room, the manager did what was right. On a note pad he wrote a directive to the Human Resources essentially quadrupling is current salary and faxed it to Puerto Rico. After confirming its receipt via the phone with a brief call, he showed Rufus what he wrote and asked,

"Is everything okay?"

"I'm good" Rufus replied.

Approximately one year later Rufus explained he was promoted to the Operations Assistant Manager and later the Operations Manager where he was told that no one in the 95-year history of the bank has ascended so quickly. There were still turnover issues regarding maintaining tellers so when he required replacements, he decided against the Puerto Rican options because of the language barrier and requested Maxentius be transferred on St. Thomas for several months until he could get several new employees trained and up to speed. Max lived at the Windward Passage Hotel which was conveniently adjacent to the bank on the waterfront. He later told Rufus that as a result of his directives, he was able to pay off all of his personal debts as a result of the additional per diem he received for every day he worked on St. Thomas.

Which now leads me back to the comment made by the Nutrition Manager at the Dept. of Human Services from Alabama to Rufus. Several months had passed after he quit that previous job when their eyes inauspiciously met. She just happened to wind up at the Bar and Lounge and was in the audience when he saw her from the stage. Later in the set when the band members were introduced, Priscilla cited the usual announcement of her Tall, Dark, Bass Player that never smiles that evening. And for the very first time his scold was not manufactured as he glared in her direction.

Then next time their eyes met was in the bank. She was at one of the tellers where she wanted a check drawn on a mainland bank cashed for emergency purposes. The teller informed her that the check had to be deposited when the funds would be available in 21-days. The teller saw the urgency of her request and brought it to Rufus' attention. In an instant, the moment she told him that he wasn't going to amount to anything came immediately to mind as he verified the name on the check. He then stared in her direction to convey that he hadn't forgotten what she last told him and the stare remained until her facial expression recognized the disdain she was receiving. And because the teller was between them and she was generally out of his view, Rufus initialed the check to be cashed because he knew where to find her if the check was returned for insufficient funds. After she realized that Rufus had approved her check, from his periphery he saw when she mouthed the words "thank you" but he did not acknowledge her gratitude. He even wished that the check would later bounce so he could personally pursue its collection and have the opportunity to express what he really wanted to say when he quit.

Now as I retell that story for the first time, it is surreal because it was told from the perspective from his Warehouse and I realize that Ms. Alabama was also present at the Chart House that evening causing him to recount that particular story.

And as I earlier described about one's illuminessence, back then I saw glimpses of his magnanimity. On that initial evening when we met, I mainly conversed with my cousins and most of the times relegated myself as a wall fly just sitting and listening. There were no preconceived notions because I didn't know him. And as far as I was concerned, Rufus simply shined. At the end of the evening, I distinctly remember being driven back to my apartment first due to the proximity to the restaurant.

Upon my return that evening I knew with all certainty - not that I wanted to marry that man, but I simply knew I was going to marry him. It was crystal clear and there was no ambiguity. I subconsciously put my thoughts and aspirations out to the universe. I was so sure of myself, I immediately called my mother. She was the first to hear my affirmation. And with the universe duly informed, Rufus didn't have a chance quite frankly.

Those few hours spent over cocktails and dinner left an indelible impression when he was such a gentleman. That evening I dreamt about the possibilities with him in my future and I was glad to dispel my notion where I initially thought that he was engaged or otherwise spoken for. Those judgmental tendencies resided way before my sisters' divorces. But again it was only my immaturity making assumptions when I wondered briefly why he wasn't in a relationship. And if I had allowed those unsubstantiated thoughts and ideas to fester and convolute what had been granted by the universe, again this would have been another story that wouldn't have been told or by someone else.

Two days later on Sunday the party of friends increased when along with my cousins and Rufus, my uncle and aunt, their neighbors and son were on a ferry to spend the day on the island of St. John. I immediately thought it was going to be a long journey like when I traveled to St. Thomas with my granny, but after 15-minutes I was really relieved. We toured the island via a hired safari and wound up at the beautiful Trunk Bay until the late afternoon.

First and foremost, I thought the beaches in Puerto Rico were nice until I saw how naturally beautiful St. John's were. White sands and the clear water was a perfect canvas for my bikini bathing suit. Quite frankly I wasn't sure that Rufus was going to be invited, but I was extremely pleased when I saw him. Later he told me that he brought along his electronic chess game to play by himself in case he became bored. Instead we were observed strolling along the entire length of the beach as we began to get to know each other.

I really thought the following work week would continue similarly with more citings from him because I knew how I felt and I was certain he felt similarly. But after Monday without hearing from him, I thought that he had a busy day. And quite frankly, I did not know whether the circumstances at his home were restored. But I didn't hear anything on Tuesday and Wednesday.

During my lunch hour on Thursday I was about to call him when I was informed by the secretary that a Mr. Turnbull was on the other line. Rufus explained that where he lived the power was not restored yet and he wanted to take me out before I returned to Puerto Rico. I was relieved. I told him that my wardrobe did not include anything casual so not to hold it against me. We went out that evening to the Marriott Frenchman's Reef Hotel. Then we went out again that Saturday to his Kenny G concert I described earlier.

The following weekend he flew over to meet my family. My sisters were excited to meet him after hearing all the details about how we met. You have to remember, back then I could only describe him to them because I had no pictures. And if I had taken his picture, it would have taken several days for the film to be developed.

I remember how I thought for a moment that he was not coming as I waited for him at the airport arrival area. His flight arrived and he wasn't there. He wasn't on the following American Eagle flight either. I cried silently thinking that he had a change of heart and he was too good to be true. I allowed my mind to wander where I could hear my girlfriends and coworkers now remarking,

"*Niña, él es como todos los otros chicos*" [Girl, he's just like the other guys.]

I have heard their laments and complaints when their relationships dissolved. And to make a musical reference, Rufus never appeared like the Rick James lyric in the song *Fire and Desire*,

"*Love them and leave them. That's what I used to do ... Use them and Abuse them.*"

Additionally, there was no way to contact him back then because there weren't cellphones and only he had a pager from the bank. And ultimately, I was too embarrassed to go home fearing what my family would think and say. So I sat in a fetal position on a low lying wall in the new dress and shoes I bought earlier in the week as I composed myself and gathered my thoughts.

It was fate that kept me at the airport when he appeared with the passengers on the last flight from St. Thomas as I still held on to hope. He saw that I was crying and quickly apologized and explained that there was an issue at the bank which caused him to miss his flight and was on standby thereafter.

That's when he met everyone at my home where my mother, my sisters and I lived in the upper level of a three-bedroom house and my granny and uncle lived below on the lower level. Later that evening I drove him to his hotel and I guess I remained longer than I should have because my mother called and the phone rang in his room.

"Christine, get your butt home!" my mother could be heard on the phone even with the receiver close to my ear.

"But mom, we aren't doing anything" I cited trying to appease.

"I don't care ... you don't know that man!" she concluded.

One week later it was Thanksgiving and I was home with my family celebrating the holiday in the late afternoon when 'angels' recruited by the Laws of Attraction played a joke on me. Rufus told me his mother returned to the islands to visit and they were supposed to have dinner at his uncle's. He said it was his mother's idea when he did the following.

He drove to the airport and caught the next flight to Puerto Rico. He caught a cab and provided turn-by-turn directions from memory to my house. His intention was to call me from the street so I could open the padlocked carport. But on this instance – which never happened before – the padlock was opened. Rufus simply walked into the carport and towards the kitchen's screen door. At that very same moment I was about to get ice cream from the freezer when I saw him.

"Aaaaaaaahhhhhhh!" I screamed and ran into my grandmother's room. Then I snuck out the front door and ran upstairs to make myself a little more presentable.

When I returned my granny already had him seated with Thanksgiving dinner on his plate. Upon my proper introduction, I asked him how he got to the house to which he stated that he memorized the direction. Then in attempt to be accommodating, we all could not find the television remote control because I wanted to turn the channel to the football game. We finally gave up when I was about to serve Rufus ice cream when I found the remote in the freezer.

Essentially, that's how our relationship began. He did try to derail the inevitable when he suggested that we date for a few years before getting married. He specifically mentioned five or six years when I unequivocally stated,

"Not with me you won't."

So as the earth made a complete revolution around the sun one year later, my affirmation came true. On November 3rd, 1990 – exactly one year to the day after we met – we were 'ceremonially' married in San Juan at a Moravian Church nestles on the side of a highway named for the 19th-Century abolitionist Roman Baldorioty de Castro. He was the historical equivalent to the Virgin Islands Moses 'Buddhoe' Gottlieb on St. Croix.

The year leading up to that fateful day was the kind of courtship of a romantic comedy. Full disclosure alert again. I couldn't believe that Rufus threw my mother under the bus at my second memorial service on St. Thomas. A week earlier he was too distraught to say anything at the service in Puerto Rico – only thanking everyone for their presence. Before the second memorial service began, Rufus thanked Anna for inviting me to the dinner stating that the past twenty-five years were mostly the best of times. Later Milton read the eulogy that Rufus prepared and he lightened the spirit of the congregation by telling everyone at the church how we met.

He recounted that when he came to Puerto Rico for the first time to meet my family, my mother didn't like him. I knew that he said it to provide levity to the solemn occasion. He suggested that only my shorter sister and my grandmother took an immediate affinity towards him. That sister liked him immediately because of his dark complexed skin; my granny probably saw the potential for great grandchildren in the making.

He conveyed what I told him early in our relationship that my mother worked at the Credit Bureau and how she performed a background check on him specifically to see if he had children or bad credit. Rufus reciprocated confessing that he did similarly. He explained that we were spending a weekend in San Juan and he got a glimpse at my checkbook and saw it was from Banco Popular and memorized my account number. Since he was the Operations Manager at the time, he accessed the computer system and was able to see my account information.

During our engagement he loved to rib me about how I always added an inch or three whenever I had to record my vital statistics where my height on legal documents were concerned. I never gave it a second thought. I was 5ft 2 inches, but my height police officer of a fiancé at the time would 'height-hate' stating that "for the record, I was 5ft with half inch slippers on." Anyway, way back then I compensated by wearing 3 and 4 inch heels when we dated.

We were always spectacles whenever we were out on the town in San Juan seeing that the male populace was generally diminutive and the disparity in our height was immediately noticed. Consequently, we had that same effect when we were on his home turf on St. Thomas. Years later a co-worker on St. Thomas accused me of coming to the island and taking away one of the tall eligible men from the local women.

The months leading up to our wedding were a blur having to travel intensively on bi-weekly Fridays after our jobs to Puerto Rico to primarily visit my family, attend marriage counseling - which was a requirement of the pastor - periodic wedding dress fittings because it was being tailored in a boutique in Old San Juan, and to go dancing in our favorite club in Isla Verde El San Juan Hotel and Casino.

I remember asking him to support me in my quest to lose weight before the wedding. I made the mistake of telling him that the ladies at the boutique told me if I lost 2lbs, I will be able to fit into my wedding gown. And if I lost 5lbs, I would be able to sit down. He was so horrible eating snacks in my presence all the time.

Then on that happiest of days, I remember feeling like I imagined Princess Diana did nine years earlier when she walked down the aisle at St. Paul's Cathedral to Jeremiah Clarke's 'San Antonio Voluntary.' Our wedding ceremony was presided by an English speaking female pastor. It was the only criterion Rufus insisted upon since we were getting married in Puerto Rico stating that he wasn't going to recite anything he did not understand.

The case can be made that only fate knows why people generally meet for reasons as mundane as passengers on a coast to coast flight, teammates in a pick-up game, lifelong childhood friends or life partners. Two people that were arbitrarily picked to participate to help at a training seminar, later are having cocktails at a pub and wind up in the others hotel suite. It happens every day. The result can be the beginning of a beautiful relationship or the beginning of infidelity providing their needs are not being met at home.

From my unique perspective, Rufus and the lady I briefly saw in the St. Croix restaurant were both emanating the same frequency of emotional distress although the appearance they both presented to the world suggested something entirely different. Both had no one in common, but now uncommonly they both had me. Now I knew why Rufus again was emanating signals of lost and despair, but why was her frequency similar? The Laws of Attraction states that like thoughts will seek and find like thoughts. Was she distraught over a recent end to a relationship? Did someone close to her recently pass too? I spent the following days and weeks trying to ascertain why.

Then in early May I learned that she continues to mourn the loss of her daughter 16 years passed on the anniversary of her death. She commemorates her annually in solitude as she goes through the keepsakes from that very short period of life that are kept in a wooden pine chest her father made for her. At that point I came to the new realization that my mother will continue to mourn me similarly.

CHAPTER EIGHT

*"I had successfully gotten him to go back to work on an intermittent schedule,
I now had to figure under what circumstances I would have to get Rufus
closer to her and allow the Laws of Attraction to do the rest."*

A FTER I PASSED AWAY ON JANUARY 20, 2015, Rufus decided to take the rest of the year off. Financially he could. A year before we had paid off all our debts in by mid-2014 to include the final payment on our 20-year mortgage. It was his plan to seclude himself in obscurity and every now and again address service calls from his clients. He purposely did not seek new business because he didn't have the mental capacity. Otherwise if he didn't have to take Kevin to and from school and the occasional grocery shopping, not even the neighbors would have known that he existed. So if there was any chance for me getting them together, he had to get his butt out of the house. To paraphrase one of our favorite comedian Robin Harris where in a joke he suggested that some people stay at home and claim they are looking for a job expecting that when they hear a knock at their door, the knocker replies, "Job."

With that ridiculously stupid reference I can't believe I remembered as a preface, nobody is going to knock on his front door and say "potential girlfriend" either. So in order for Rufus to meet her, he had to get off his proverbial ass and go back to work. He had to get back into his routine; he needed to get back into the game.

So in my quest to get these two lost souls to meet, I began the process of influencing the following circumstances and manipulated decisions that provided the kinds of situations and opportunities in my attempt for them to meet. Again, the following actually happened and from my perspective, it was a test run. I wasn't quite sure how I was going to achieve anything, but it was all a learning process.

Later in the month of May, out of the blue Rufus got a call to return to work. Back in February when he notified most of his clients that he was taking a leave of absence, he further explained that if anything was going to impact any of his ongoing projects, he would do what's necessary to keep it on track. Then his favorite clients on St. John, Tony and Randy called and out of the blue they decided to upgrade the 80-inch TV in their screening room.

They are extraordinary Interior Designers in New York with a who's who clientele to include a recent presidential candidate. Their design concepts can be viewed in the notable periodicals and they have cameo appearances on interior design based television programming. Their vacation home on St. John was featured in Architectural Digest and is called Solenberg that actually has an interactive 3D website so that potential short term renters could take a virtual tour.

Rufus loves working for them because of their non-assuming personalities. He said they are unlike no other client he had. First of all, the project was the biggest home he has worked on to date. They are meticulous in the manner they approach their designs making sure that your visual senses are always engage – even while you lay on your back looking up at the ceilings. When he first described the house to me after two years of going to St. John on the barge daily and the project was nearing its completion, Rufus cited the following,

"No painters made any money working on the house because none of the surfaces on the five level compound are painted. All of the walls – interior and exterior – are either stone, tiled, or wood."

They actually came by our home to see exactly what Rufus does when they said that all of the electronics should be scaled back.

Every now and again when they were on island, they would cook lunch for the crew. I met them several times when Rufus was excited about another milestone achievement in his scope of the project. Even my taller sister met them when she commented about how handsome she thought Randy was when he replied,

"You do know that I am gay, right?"

Rufus said it was actually pleasurable traveling on the barge daily to work for them. He and I even spent a weekend there when the project neared completion where he made sure that everything worked. I remember how I really enjoyed waking up with my toes in the pool with my coffee in hand looking at the sun rise behind Tortola.

They asked Rufus to come over because they were considering having the 80-inch television in their Screening Room upgraded. Rufus said that they corrected him when he initially called the room a theater. They were haggling over the upgrade and wanted recommendations. Rufus explained that initially they didn't even want televisions, now they have ten. And now for some reason Randy can't understand, Tony wanted a television bigger than the 80 inch. I loved them both then, but now I had to play one against the other. Tony wanted the upgrade and Randy thought everything was fine as is. Rufus came over and started showing them the options as far as size and cost.

They asked him what was the biggest available television. He told them about a Panasonic 150-inch plasma at the cost of $500,000.00. He explained that he saw it at one of the electronic trade shows. And at that cost an installation team will travel from Japan and install it. The cost was prohibitive and he even had a picture of it where he actually stood next to it for a sense of scale and was reminded how hot the screen was. It would suck the cool out of an air conditioned room and act as a radiator. He then began to use masking tape on the wall so they would have an idea of how big the screen was going to be.

During the home installation process, Rufus use black-painted plywood cut to different TV screen sizes so that they could decide before actual purchases. That day he now searched his supplier's website on his tablet and suggested a 160-inch fixed screen and a 4K projector from another supplier at a cost of less than 10 percent of the Panasonic TV. They agreed. It was customary to request a partial payment to satisfy his supplier's cost and request the balance after completion. They prepaid the entire proposal amount immediately and said they would return when it was completed.

Later in the afternoon Rufus called Milton and told him the details of his new project. Milton actually hated these kinda calls because many times it involved manual labor like helping him lift something, but he was also handsomely compensated. Every major piece of furniture and appliance in our home Milton helped Rufus bring down those steep twenty-six steps. I remember the time they both watched me sideways in

1999 after I purchased one of the biggest stainless steel refrigerators at the time in Brandsmart USA and they needed the help of our neighbor to get it into the house. Two years later after Milton got married and bought their home, Rufus took him to Brandsmart USA to get appliances and he bought the same model but smaller because of lifting nightmares.

Coincidentally, the 80-inch television Rufus was going to replace Milton actually helped him hang. So when Rufus called Milton, he had flashbacks in his warehouse. At the same time Rufus knew how to goat his friend when he explained it was going to be a 160-inch screen without qualifying it as a projection screen. But in the end, he was capable to do the installation alone when he suggested that the project was a 'sympathy job' seeing that he was already paid in full. And when that project was completed, Randy and Tony returned to celebrate making lunch for Rufus where he posted pictures of his pre meal salad on Facebook and later taunted my mother about what she was eating at the moment.

After the project's completion, Rufus felt compelled to take my family on a Western Caribbean cruise. It was about the time of year when we usually got away annually. He took care of all of their reservations and they had a wonderful time. The thought of Ms. Coral Gables possibly derailing what I was meticulously developing at the time made me pause as I am now recapping.

Around the same time, he contacted his graduation class secretary Amazia and told her he had finally made up his mind and to add his and my mother's name to the list for their class reunion Alaskan Cruise. The reunion was being planned to commemorate 35 years from high school in July 2016 and he intended to have my mother go along to replace me. He was also researching a basketball summer camp a year ahead to coincide for Kevin for the time he was in Alaska.

◆ ◆ ◆

Simultaneously at that time she had finally moved to Fort Lauderdale and was working hard to open the studio with her new partner. She was flying to health and fitness summits to acquaint herself with various Pilates apparatuses. She had the clarity of mind in her past to instinctively forego similar opportunities to go into business on her own.

She intuitively declined several times because the investors were former suitors who she assumed the arrangements would not be strictly business.

Now in between scheduling the various trades for the design build out at the strip mall that her partner's husband owned, she began to get nagged about putting herself back out on the dating scene. Those enticements were entirely of my influence and subliminal exertion. I was in her partner's subconscious mulling her along. But she didn't take her partner on. What they actually did was begin to take professional dance lessons together in the evenings to further bond. They had only known each other prior as trainer and client. Now their relationship was evolving into business partners and friends.

For a New York Minute – after all, I am from Manhattan – I even wondered about the possibility of Rufus taking a Pilates class when the new studio opened. It would be normal. But I quickly dispel those thoughts. He didn't even know anything about Pilates as I take a quick look in his warehouse. Furthermore, he didn't even like using the Bowflex I had in our gym at home. Not to mention, I remember a conversation she had about feeling trepidation when training older men privately and was very careful about not putting herself in precarious situations like always using valet services so she wouldn't have to be followed into parking lots. It was another form of personal security she consciously undertook. And to this point, a potential Pilates class would also be an odd request for Rufus. The peculiar thing about the unknown forces of the cosmos are they cannot be forced; they systematically and organically work everything out.

So after I had successfully gotten him to go back to work on an intermittent schedule, I now had to figure under what circumstances I would have to get Rufus closer to her and allow the Laws of Attraction to do the rest.

Upon his return from the cruise with my family, circumstances were already set into motion for my attempt at destiny. Another client on St. John was so pleased with how Rufus automated his roll up shutters he now decided to include a full blown lighting integration in the renovation. Because of how much it cost to build and complete Randy and Tony's vacation home, they told Rufus that they would never again do another project in the islands because of its isolation and logistical nightmare commenting that things were easier in Russia. But one of their Manhattan clients bought his wife a vacation home on St. John and The Guys were commissioned for the renovation. They recommended that the entire construction crew be hired including Rufus. The project was a renovation and new construction. That's where Rufus was for Christmas when he bought me the Microsoft Surface. And to get an idea of the scope of that job, Rufus said that they repaved the public road leading to the house.

The problem was in order for Rufus to procure, sell. and install this new panelized lighting system, it required that he become certified with the electronic protocols of the lighting modules by the manufacturer. In other words, this was not simply changing light switches and dimmers like the old system was designed. Potentially it could be a fire hazard if you failed to do as specified. So with that kind of exposure, he would have to spend several hours online calculating lighting loads and take the certification test. The other option was to go to the manufacturer for an on hand training in Utah or North Carolina. Coincidentally and quite conveniently, there was a third option. At the end of the week there was a condensed training seminar scheduled for the first week in August in downtown Miami. All that was necessary for him was to simply show up, spend 8hrs, take a test, and wallah.

At the same time at my subliminal behest, her business partner continued to pester her about her social life. Currently her social interactions were more consistent to a hermit. The few times she did go out she would reveal to her date that she has been celibate as a litmus test to see whether their intentions were more than fleeting. It was comical quite frankly because those allusions were my attempt to derail any development of further interest. At the same time, I continued to work my magic behind the scenes. Additionally, I have to keep reiterating that the previous statement and following actually happened.

Her business partner commandeered one of her credit cards and signed her up to the same obscurely named dating service Zoosk that Rufus was also a member. Now think about it. How often has anyone taken your credit card and used it in that manner? Zoosk was uniquely important because of the way their site works. There's an interactive verification process - not the email auto reply concept. Additionally, their site also works with your GPS location. So the stage was set. Events were in motion. The puzzle pieces were all on the table, and now fate had to put it all together.

◆ ◆ ◆

With the opportunity to grow his business revealing itself, he signed up for the training seminar on Tuesday August 4th via email and duly received his confirmation to check into the hotel at a discounted rate. And after almost giving up because he was getting frustrated, he was able to secure the last seat on a Spirit Airlines flight to Fort Lauderdale two days later on Thursday to attend the training seminar that Friday.

That was very significant seeing that American Airlines by default would have been the airline of choice because they flew direct flights from St. Thomas into Miami International Airport. That was the airline he chose because of the miles he had accumulated and he loved hanging out in their Admirals Club before returning home. But all of their three daily flights were fully booked. If he had decided to attend the training seminar a week earlier, undoubtedly a seat or few on the flights to Miami would have been available. So as a result, the short notice reservations he made online on Spirit was extremely crucial - in fact it was absolutely key. In order for everything to work, he simply had to fly into Fort Lauderdale International Airport opposed to Miami International. So despite all the jokes about Spirit Airlines and all of their additional fees, he was booked. It was the major catalyst in making everything work together - I will explain later. And to tickled my spirit with a little case of levity, two days later I watched something I have never seen over the hundreds of times we've flown as he was uncomfortably sandwiched in the middle seat between two obese passengers.

CHAPTER NINE

"The more I considered my miscalculation, I immediately realized that it could possibly derail everything I had orchestrated if they actually were able to meet or communicate."

I T WAS FRIDAY August 7, 2015 in the early morning where Rufus was meandering from his hotel to the training seminar held in downtown Miami at the Hyatt that started at 8am. Even though the rates were discounted for the out of town attendees, he instead decided to book the weekend at the EB Hotel close to Miami International Airport because it was one of our favorites. A month and a half earlier after the Western Caribbean cruise with my family, Rufus decided to extend their vacation one day longer. He rented Infiniti's biggest SUV and they went to Sawgrass Mills to shop. Although there were scores of four-star hotel closer to the Fort Lauderdale airport where they were departing from, they overnight at the EB Hotel to experience what we had enjoyed several times before by booking separate suites.

After arriving yesterday evening, as he drove from Fort Lauderdale International Airport to Miami in his car rental, on the 595 West expressway he saw a billboard advertisement where Jill Scott was performing Live in Concert at the Seminole Hard Rock Casino Hotel on Saturday August 8th at 8pm. As he drove he contemplated whether or not he would be able to attend. He figured that he would spend all day on Friday in training, on Saturday he would hang out with his sisters and purchase school clothes for Kevin at Sawgrass Mills, then later he would attend the Jill Scott concert in the evening, and return back home on Sunday. It was a full weekend.

So there it was - the stage was set. Over five months of surveillance and meticulous planning, and I was extremely pleased to realize that she hadn't deviated much from her routine. The only major difference was she had recently moved from Bal Harbor to Fort Lauderdale.

She went out on a few dates with a young doctor in residence where he was at least fifteen years her junior where he actually thought that he was older than her. I actually became nervous at the possibility that she only had affinities towards doctors. With that new revelation. I recalled that her most recent fiancé was also a doctor from the mainland but practiced on St. Croix. He was more than fifteen years her senior. He even opened a practice in Florida to be closer to her before they broke up. Although he was well established, his circle of friends saw her only as 'the weekend girlfriend.' Their discussions amongst friends were generally of medicine and made for mundane conversation as they discounted her intellectual participation.

Rufus on the other hand was the exact age of her ex-husband – six years older - so that compatibility would be immediately noted. But he was now in Miami for the weekend with a very narrow possibility of meeting amongst the several hundreds of thousands of people and twenty miles of separation. It was like trying to get two strangers to meet in a football stadium. How was I going to bridge that gap? I calmed myself and allowed the forces of the cosmos to do its thing.

In their combined warehouses I also failed to see a very important detail despite my ability to see and hear everything. My exuberance prohibited me from discerning what otherwise was not overtly obvious but may definitely factor into the equation. The more I considered my miscalculation I immediately realized that it could possibly derail everything I had orchestrated if they actually were able to meet or communicate.

How could I have missed this. It was as plain as night and day. But now my tendency to be non-judgmental clouded my judgment. I shudder at the thought that everything I have done thus far could all be for naught.

◆ ◆ ◆

There weren't any doubts whether he was going to pass the training examination because that's what he came to do. Afterwards Rufus returned to the EB Hotel to enjoy the suite's creature comforts: the modern decor, the two 50-inch flat panel TVs simultaneously playing ESPN in the

Bedroom and Livingroom. He walked to the nearby Miami Subs leaving both televisions on and ordered a sandwich and duly returned to the Livingroom's long modern sectional sofa where he sat and ate the sandwich while watching Around the Horn.

After eating, his juvenility kicked in when he started to toggle the privacy blinds that was sandwiched between two huge tempered glass wall panels that separated the bedroom from the shower slowly watching it go up......... and down....... up....... and down.......... up......... and down.......

Then he was prompted to take the Sleep Number Bed through the paces like an amusement park ride manipulating the remote to cause the mattress to inflate and deflate several times. I observed the big kid in him at play.

After he had enough, he decided at that moment to purchase one so he went online on his phone and ordered a king sized mattress for his bed at home as a birthday gift later in the month for himself. He also began to take notes of the room's design sketching mental plans in his mind. The subsequent days later at home, he actually fabricated two wall mounted bedside tables and purchased matching lamps locally from Silk Greenery to complete the look. He built wooden shrouds around the TVs in his living and master bedroom. He stained everything dark oak similar to the EB's color scheme. Then later completed everything with the purchase of similarly colored curtains to tie everything together. He was amazing like that. Kevin later ribbed him telling anyone who would listen that his dad installed curtains in his bedroom where there are no windows. But again, I am getting ahead of myself.

He then called his best friend Milton to shoot the breeze. They had their own way of greeting each other on the phone that sounds endearingly tribal-listic.

      "YO-OW!" Milton began

      "YO-OW!" Rufus echoed

      "Wa deman sayin' mehn?"   [*What's going on man?*]

      "I ahright. I had dat trainin today."   [*I had the training today.*]

      "Soyo back on-de Rock?"   [*So are you back on island?*]

"Nah... ah still here in Miami"   [*No, I'm still here in Miami*]

"Oh yeah.... I remember yo tellin' me 'bout deh trainin."

"Yeah mehn ... all deh."   [*Yeah man, all day.*]

"I 'pose to go to Vegas fo ah credit union meetin' nex week."

[*I'm supposed to go to Las Vegas for a credit union meeting next week*]

"So de credit union kyan hol de meeting on-de rock?"

[*So the credit union can't hold their meeting on islands?*]

"Alla de udda credit union board members comin from de US Dred."

[*All of the other credit union board members are coming from the US.*]

"So anunda junket, eh?"   [*So another junket, right?*]

"Yo-no I kyan confirm wa-you sayin' ova de phone."

[*You know I can't confirm what you are saying over the phone.*]

Do you see what I had to contend with for the past twenty-five years? It was really bad in the beginning - like listening to a different language but only catching a few arbitrary real words in between. But when Rufus slowed his phrasing, what sounded like Calypso began to sound like English. And what's crazy is the fact that they can turn it off and on.

After hanging up, he remained sitting on the closed toilet seat in the water closet as if he was hiding from himself. He proceeded to open the Dating App and began thumbing his way around his phone. At the same time, she was winding down in her apartment after her ex-husband picked up her son for the weekend.

In all actuality, he had no intention that evening of chatting. After the experience with Ms. Coral Gables, he did not want anything to interrupt his perfectly planned Saturday. For the moment, he simply wanted to sleep and recharge himself for the tight schedule of back to school shopping, family time, and Jill Scott. So he began going through the motion of reading profiles which over the previous months had become a noble pastime.

Reading profiles made him feel hopeful knowing that he wasn't the only one seeking a relationship. And at the same time, many of the membership provided too much information prefacing by stating, "Thanks for reading my profile ..." where a biography of sorts followed. Additionally, others cut through the chase and were suggestively promiscuous. And a significant amount was overly desperate. He also found some of the profiles to be mundane to very witty and whimsical like:

"*You must love dogs...*" - 'suppose one had an allergic reactions or predispositions' he suggested to himself.

"*You must love my kids...*" - 'Suppose your kids were a terror like Bebe's Kids?'

"*No games, no one night stand.*" - 'What do you say yes to?' he concluded.

"*No little kids, No Drama, No Baby Mama's.*" - 'That's a lot of resentment going on there.' he thought.

"*Looking for a travel partner.*" - 'That seems to be a thing.' He remembered seeing that a few times.

"*You have to have a relationship with your dentist...*" - 'Now that was simply hilarious - there was no snappy comeback from that comment.'

Some profiles even had Non-Disclosure Clauses prohibiting the use of their names, pictures, comments and likeness. They undoubtedly were practicing lawyers or watched too many court shows on television he thought. He also was pleasantly surprised after learning the definition of a Sapiosexual when a few women used that term in describing themselves. Having never heard the term before and ignorantly assumed it was another recognized sexual orientation, he looked up the definition and immediately realized that the term aptly described himself. Later he realized that he was so out of his element when people at times suspected they were being Catfished if he avoided subsequent video chat requests. But the one he found to be the most original was from a lady whose background he deduced to be in Human Resources where she cleverly referred to her dating prospects as applicants in her interview process.

He thumbed through scores of other profiles similarly like I did five months earlier when I scan through in my brightly lit warehouse but much slower when he came upon one. As with all of the others he had seen so far, he briefly looked at her profile pic and his eyes veered to her very brief Storyline. It was simple and poignant. To him it actually stood out without including preferences, suggestions or litmus requirements. Simply put, it just made a statement. It was totally different and unique than the others he had read thus far because it was unassuming. It read that way because it was humbly written by a concerned friend that simply stated,

"I recently completed a Motorcycle Certification course."

His interest was piqued briefly because he coincidentally completed a certification himself. The statement was enough to make him pause for a moment and do what he thought he wasn't going to do that evening. All of the other profiles suggested that you check off items on their list to garner attention like, being a dog lover or the cryptic manner one requested a Baby Daddy in her "*You must love my kids*" statement. He thought that her accomplishment was worthy of celebratory well wishes so he clicked on the Message Tab and wrote the following,

"*Hey there, congrats on your motorcycle certification. I guess your bike is way bigger than you are.*" as he imagined her straddling a Harley Davidson at a traffic light keeping it erect. He had no expectation of a response and continued thumbing.

Truth be told, less than 10 percent of women respond to Direct Messages on Dating Site because they are empowered because of the reality of the social dynamic of being semi-anonymous or they are otherwise engaged in a chat. Oppose to over 80 percent of the men replied to any message they received and at time maintain multiple chats.

Now this dating App Direct Messaging system was tantamount to dial-up speed in the internet age. The Flintstones woodpecker could have dictated and deliver messages faster than the way this App was set up.

When you sent a message to a person via the App's messaging system, their phone or tablet buzzes alerting them of an incoming direct message. And in order to view the message, you had to first open the App, click on the message tab in the recipient's profile page, then you are able to read the messages. The problem was that it took about 30 second to a minute delay between message sent and message received. It was somewhat arduous because the site administrators seemed to be monitoring the correspondences of the non-membership for the possibility of personal information being passed like telephone numbers and email addresses. Non-members could send messages but could not receive. If a non-member received a reply or an unsolicited message, they would have to pay the membership fee to be able to correspond. And if you decide to give the person any personal information like your phone number or email to bypass the dating service, they already had your money. So as members of the site, you had to reopen the message tab every time you were notified to refresh and see the new messages.

During the months when I surveilled her, I recognized the great lengths she consciously put herself through in her pilgrimage towards the peace she continuously seeks: the elimination of a visible-broadcast television, the deleting of personal contacts she otherwise no longer wanted to be associated with, diligently requesting unsolicited direct marketing mailers to remove her email from their database, and purposely disabling all of her notifications settings on her phone. In other words, the only way she would instantly know if she received an email or text, she had to be looking at her phone. She loathes distractions and thought that people spent too much idle time on their mobile devices.

Unbeknownst to her, earlier in the afternoon while back to school shopping, her son handled her phone because the battery in his died. Since their recent move, he spent a lot of his time messaging and chatting with his friends from their old neighborhood. He downloaded the messaging App on his mother's phone that required the notification setting to be changed and thought nothing about it when queried to accept the changes to the phone. It was done so innocently and it was another puzzle piece that was also necessary. From her point of view it simply appeared that he was on his own phone. So when her phone buzzed from Rufus' direct message, she found it very peculiar and was compelled to find out why.

The puzzle pieces were beginning to come together. Normally it would have gone unnoticed but she picked up her phone anyway and saw that it was from the dating App. She was still incredulous wondering why the phone buzzed. After reading the message she immediately thought that it was different. It was unusual and equally unassuming compared to most of the messages she had received which generally complimented her on her three profile pictures. Additionally, it also felt different because it suggested that he actually read her profile even though it wasn't much of a message. From Rufus' point of view, it was the reason he felt compelled to comment. It was totally contrary to most of the other profiles he had perused on the site because it was reserved in its tone.

After a moment of hesitation, she navigated to his profile picture and immediately noticed that there wasn't any. It only had the site's default shadowed silhouette of a male and void of any pixelated information.

"That's weird." she actually said audibly and I garnered that she was now considering that Rufus must not be too serious if he had not posted pictures to his profile.

She had dabbled with the site after her business partner notified her. And she even got upset after what she thought was going to be a one-month membership that turned out to be three. Subsequently, Rufus' three month's turned out to be six. So she also knew that he had to be a member in order for him to receive any messages. If it wasn't for the mere fact that his remark was sincere and congratulatory, she would have otherwise definitely ignored the message. Moments later she replied,

"Thanks, but I don't have a motorcycle."

That was one of the circumstances I was very concerned about. I actually held my proverbial breath. Not because she replied, but I really thought Rufus was going to say something corny like he did months earlier when he was at home and could only communicate with members in the Caribbean. The lady was from Jamaica and Rufus actually wrote,

"AWah gwan? [Translates to "What's going on?"]

Back then I immediately thought,

"*Really? Are you kidding me?*" That was awfully bad. He must have gotten that line from a Jamaican movie. His 'macking' skills (urban definition – talking and/or flirting) were deplorable. Was I going to have to dictate his conversations too?

But what I was mostly concerned about was whether she had an affinity towards dating Black men. From what I was able to finally gather and discern, all of her relationships in her past were with suitors whose persuasion where different than her own - including her ex-husband who is Caucasian. I never sensed that she was prejudice against men of her same race because that particular topic never arose - although her estranged sister exclusively preferred dating outside of her race based on what I was also able to gather. But after delving into her warehouse quickly when I nervously became concerned that my oversight may derail everything I had already set into motion, I learned that she went to a predominantly Caucasian primary and secondary schools. Most of the guys that had crushes on her in her adolescence although she was prohibited from dating were White because that was the environment and neighborhood where she grew up. After leaving home and arriving in Atlanta to stay with a cousin for a stint was the first time she became aware of her limited social circle of friends. In other words, she was exposed to many African Americans. And later, she recalled being treated like an outsider in Atlanta because of her interracial marriage. That's why she felt more comfortable when they moved to the most cosmopolitan area in Florida, South Beach where she lived with her husband initially after leaving Atlanta.

I too remember when some of my clients on St. Thomas met me for the first time accused me of speaking white or were just incredulous when they met me for the first time having earlier only known me over the phone. I never had that problem when I lived in Puerto Rico. After Rufus and I were married, I had his framed picture on my desk. As a result, everybody's refrain became congratulatory as if I had my "Black Card" re-validated when coworkers and clients commented,

"You are married to the Bassman?" That picture inexorably gave me acceptance although I wasn't seeking it. The first person that made that comment, prompted me to call Rufus and ask,

"I didn't know that you were the Bassman?"

He corrected me stating, "No, the Bassmon."

Anyway, I do not understand how or why she did not see Rufus' pictures in his profile because I was 100% certain that he had pictures posted - three to be exact. As a matter of fact, a lady after briefly chatting with him and further realizing that he was too far to pursue suggested that he should use the moniker Chocolate Charmer after seeing his pictures. Before then, he hadn't created a screen name; he simply used the site's default Zoosk Member 54321. The only thing I could offer to why she was unable to see his profile pictures was my anxiety had built up the necessary energy to precipitously keep the appearance of his profile picture files hidden from her view for the moment. After all, it was all electronic information and I know I had manipulated it before. I don't know how I did it this time but I assumed it simply worked with the strength of my will.

He was still thumbing other profiles when he was notified by the App and saw that she had responded. He went back to her profile and saw that her picture had a VERIFIED label which represents that one of the administrators of the dating site was granted permission of a live view of their members via their reverse cameras on their cell phone or tablet in real time where they would compare your face to the uploaded pictures and deem it authentic. After reading her message he replied,

Chocolate Charmer
"That's cool anyway.

While the moment that allowed for her message transmission to go through, she too had no intention of a prolong conversation because she had Pilates classes in the morning. And since his profile didn't say much of anything - only the vital statistics of age, height, etc., she was about to continue what she was doing when something else caught her eye. She saw he was from the Virgin Islands. "That's uncanny" she thought, so she was compelled to type the following for clarification.

Coco
"So where are you from?"

From his experience on the site, many of his correspondences ended quickly after the other person learned that he was not local. These women weren't looking for pen pals - they weren't teenagers - they wanted one-nighters, companionship, and the holy grail - husbands. As a result, he decided to immediately disclose where he was from so he would not prolong what he considered was inevitably going to be a short conversation anyway stating,

Chocolate Charmer
"I'm just here for the weekend. I am going back to the Virgin Islands on Sunday."

Her familiarity with the Virgin Islands piqued her curiosity after she read it, but he still didn't specify which island. So she contributed the following,

Coco
"Really? I have been to St. Croix many times."

Chocolate Charmer
"That's cool, I am from St. Thomas."

Coco
"I have also vacationed on St. Thomas once."

Chocolate Charmer
"Really? Where did you stay?"

Coco
"I don't remember the name of the hotel, but I really had a good time."

Chocolate Charmer
"St. Thomas is a beautiful place. I must admit I take it for granted"

Coco
"Are you here visiting family?"

Chocolate Charmer
"As a matter of fact, I flew up for business yesterday and I am going to do a little back to school shopping tomorrow."

The mention of back to school shopping was something that's not regularly discussed on dating sites so that also caused her to explore his profile some more. A lot of people are skittish and self-conscious about posting pictures. At least he filled out the usual vital statistics of age, height and built, that are generally subjective until it can be verified by a face to face first date. The other thing noteworthy that stood out to her was the mention of him being Widowed. That made sense about the back to school shopping.

Being an avid reader, to her language is very important and the choices of words truly have implications. So the term 'Widow' held more of an emotional significance than stating that one was Single or Divorced. 'Never Been Married' was a proverbial red flag for anyone over the age of forty for obvious reasons: forty years and never been in a significant relationship suggests that you were a 'playa'. He was 51. He could have stated that he was Single and still be truthful, but that would suggest later if a conversation developed that his marriage was of no consequence. Their chat continued for at least another 10 minutes with all the delays that allowed me to add all of these potential caveats when he asked,

Chocolate Charmer
"Would you like to have lunch with me tomorrow?"

There was the usually pause in response so he quickly took the opportunity to follow up his message with another hoping that both messages could be compiled as one when he added,

Chocolate Charmer
"On my way from the airport yesterday I saw a billboard showing Jill Scott was performing at the Hard Rock. I was thinking about going. I know we don't know each other but, would you like to go?"

The pause from her side ensued. He figured that if she had replied he would have seen her notification by now after they had created a cadence in responses. He laid his phone down on the vanity and continued to wash up in preparation for bed. Another five-minutes past and there was still no reply. He sighed and wrote the following.

Chocolate Charmer

"I really enjoyed chatting with you and I apologize for being presumptuous. For what it's worth, I normally don't give out my phone number but for some reason I am feeling compelled to. My name is Rufus and my number is 340-555-1212. I truly hope that I didn't spook you. Good night."

CHAPTER TEN

"After getting to know her during those months, I witnessed her
resolution and the selfless manner she provided for her son. I
also saw how her influence could foster a cohesive relationship
with My Guys."

O N SATURDAY MORNING WHEN HE AWOKE, normally he would check his phone for the time and see whether there were any pressing emails. But this time he was also hoping there was a message notification from the dating app. There weren't any. He then opened up the App to the dating site and saw that her pictures in her profile were removed. Just the moniker Coco and her vitals remained. He closed his phone and actually said aloud, "I guess I spooked her....aw well." and when on about his day.

Later after breakfast that morning he was on the highway enjoying the growl of the Chevrolet Camaro as he maneuvered the labyrinth of the I-95 and the 595 expressway on his way towards Sawgrass Mills Outlet Mall. At times he clocked 100 mph when the conditions were right. He always considered car rentals as the best way to test drive choice vehicles. And over the past quarter century we have test driven our share of a wide variety.

I remember the first car rental we driven as a couple was a Mustang GT convertible back in 1990. It was our first extended trip together that also served the purpose of meeting my future mother-in-law for the first time in West Palm Beach in the summer. It was also the last time he allowed me to pack luggage for extended travels because I really over-packed. I am not kidding. He was of the attitude, "If I have to carry everything – I might as well not carry anything that's unnecessary." At that point, I packed like Milton and I didn't even know him. The trunk space in the Mustang was so small it only allowed for his camcorder case and we drove that poor car to his mother's home with a pile of mostly my luggage in the small back seat and on my lap. I repacked and left most of my clothes and shoes at her house and we headed to the Turnpike on our way to Orlando.

I remember how he commemorated our trip with a linear stop-frame motion animation video. A profile picture of the Mustang with the top down, oversized caricatures of our heads frolicking around. He drew the highway highlights from Miami to Orlando and slowly moved the taped background to make it appear as if the car was moving. He added a soundtrack of the collaboration Secret Garden by Quincy Jones with Barry White, Al B Sure, El DeBarge and James Ingram because we heard it several times during our drive on the turnpike.

Now today was going to be the first time he was going to purchase school uniforms for Kevin on his own who had been staying in Puerto Rico at my mom's since the cruise. He texted pictures of the different styles of pants and polo shirts to my son to choose from for his sophomore uniform. He also purchased king sized bedding to coordinate with the colors of the EB Hotel suite.

◆ ◆ ◆

There was a stark contrast in the comparison of activities surrounding her that Saturday afternoon. It was her off weekend from doing the laundry in the lower level coin operated laundromat. If I also had to contend with her going back and forth between floors with her laundry basket, frankly I am not certain what was going to happen. So to my delight, she was more subdued and static. She was deserving of the down time from her Saturday morning exercise classes and the long week of teaching proper forms to include the lengthening and strengthening of bodies at her new Pilates studio.

Recently settled from her latest move into a new apartment and was at home enjoying a bottle of wine, a periodical and the personal concert of sorts in solitude. She listened to her inspirational Divas on Pandora: A compilation of poetic empowering melodies sang by the female stylings of Erykah Badu, Lauryn Hill, Nina Simone, India Arie and Jill Scott to name a few. Her son was going to be away at his father's for another 24 hours and for the remainder of the time she had left alone in the weekend, she was going to enjoy the monotony that she now appreciated as peace.

This sense of tranquility was a contrast from the jet setting weekend lifestyle she once enjoyed but never really gotten used to. Like the time she explained that she had copied the Fantasy Football betting sheet of another fiancé's friend in Las Vegas and she won $30,000.00 when the winnings were tossed all over the bed. Peace from playing the part of someone else's trophy and arm candy, to now working six mornings weekly.

It was a stark change from when she was an employee when her schedule was more flexible. Now she was the business – not only a partner. And it did not bode well for casual time. As a result, it had been quite a while since she was involved in a meaningful relationship. And without exception, anyone brave enough to ask her out were deliberately confronted by her direct pointed notions to see whether or not they were worthy of her companionship and attention.

I have even seen a few potential prospects shot down like a target and go down in flames. I have witnessed some leaving their courage behind after saying juvenile stuff like,

"If I was a cop, I would give you a ticket because you have FINE written all over you?"

Lately she was more annoyed at their lack of manners and blatant disrespect that seemingly suggest their environment was the blame. And if thoughtfulness and manners were qualities of the past, it was all the same.

Additionally, I never considered that Rufus was out of her league. Coincidentally, the 2010 romantic comedy *She's Out of My League* was one of our favorites where the protagonist was a low esteemed TSA agent who by simply doing his job caught the attention of a gorgeous traveler who made the conscious decision to no longer date individuals who may later be unfaithful to her. In other words, she wanted a safe relationship. He almost blew it when his friends and family kept reminding him that 'she was out of his league.' In the end, he got the girl and in addition to continuing his job as a TSA agent, he acquired his pilot's license to fly single engine aircrafts to nearby cities. Hmmm …. Pilot's license.

By comparison, her son was always and remained priority one. All of her relationships after her divorce ended because her suitors had their own ideas of what they wanted for her son. Could her life have been different? Absolutely. Would it conflict with her universal request for her son to have a great relationship with his father? Absolutely. Would she have the kind of peace that she sought in the end? Absolutely not. Unless court summons and custody hearings were something she also wanted in the future.

After getting to know her during those months, I witnessed her resolution and the selfless manner she provided for her son. I also saw how her influence could foster a cohesive relationship with My Guys.

So with that in mind, I was no longer concerned for Rufus - skin color withstanding. He had seen this movie before even though at times he would pigheadedly make statements to me like, "He thinks he's the smartest guy he knew." We all draw from our life experiences to overcome uncomfortable situations. How you dealt with those circumstances separates you from those who instinctively think they are not deserving of more. This reminds me of another series of events that actually changed Rufus' resolve forever.

After Rufus had the meeting with his first client when he started his own business, before my eyes I witnessed how his confidence grew. That afternoon in 2003, I left work early to celebrate with him landing his first project at the local Greenhouse restaurant overlooking the island's harbor on the waterfront before picking up Kevin at daycare. Over early dinner he explained how scared he was while he sat across from the Philadelphia Mogul's desk as they negotiated the options to electronically integrate his vacation home being constructed. He explained that he was there a half hour early for the meeting and his heart was beating faster as the witching hour neared. He added that he was only able to calm his breathing immediately after he saw the nicely framed huge photograph of his client shaking the hand of the President of the United States at the time - George W. Bush hanging in view behind the desk. The picture was strategically hung in place to intimidate. Little did his client know how much disdain Rufus had for George W Bush's politics at the time. An unapologetic C student was currently running the country. And the fact a year before the most powerful man in the world was almost taken out by a pretzel? Rufus said he was unimpressed. In hindsight if his client was shaking the hand of the Vice President Dick Cheney – who shot his attorney by accident while quail hunting - again I would be telling another story. In reality that was impossible because Cheney shot his friend three years later. And the way Rufus always makes visual references, The Philadelphia Mogul has an uncanny resemblance to Dick Cheney ten years his junior. Over dinner he said that he actually respected his father George H.W. Bush because he was a good president in his opinion.

Rufus explained that the shift in confidence occurred unnoticed. That first project taught him everything he needed to know about interpersonal business relationships. Before he worked for his cousin helping him become the biggest electrical contracting firm in the Virgin Islands. Although he was very much appreciated, Rufus quit because in the end, he was disrespected dispelling that lifelong notions that "blood is thicker than water."

The Philadelphia Mogul taught him about the importance of being timely. He would brow beat the subcontractors who were often late for the monthly progress meetings saying, "I had to travel here from Pennsylvania and I'm on time." From that day the local lexicon "island time" no longer referred to Rufus.

Or the time the contractor told the Philadelphia mogul that they were going to submit a change order for the error made by the concrete subcontractor for pouring the bedroom and patio floor surfaces the same height. Mr. Philadelphia reply was,

"I build skyscrapers for a living. Frankly I don't care how many times you pour the slabs ... I'm only going to pay for it once."

One time Rufus felt his wrath when his interior designer from the mainland began instructing him about the changes that were not in the agreement and Rufus performed and submitted that request for payment. In no uncertain terms, his client told him that he was going to pay for something he did not approve. Rufus was angry, but it was also a very expensive lesson learned.

Then the tables were turned when Rufus told his client that in addition to wiring your home for what were agreed, the industry recommends that it should be pre-wired for future eventualities. His client simply said no. So less than a year after completion, the client learned that his caretaker was enjoying his swimming pool more than he does even after leaving explicit instructions to not use the pool. He asked Rufus to install cameras. Rufus reminded him about his decision to forego the pre-wiring and told him that he did it anyway because he already paid for the bulk cabling. He showed him the cost to just install cameras versus what it would have cost him to remove some of the existing cabling, add cables, and re-pull, terminate and reconnect the system through the embedded conduits making certain that the disparity in the costs – although subjective – was justified. The Philadelphia Mogul told him,

"In business I negotiate to win and today you have taught me a lesson."

In the years that followed Mr. Philadelphia turned Rufus on to some of his local friends and clients which invariably grew his business with one after the other high net worth customers. One customer even told him the following,

"Because we have homes in this part of the island, we tend to pay a lot more for basic services than we would otherwise pay for (the same services) on the mainland. But since you were highly recommended (by the Philadelphia Mogul), I won't question your invoices."

Rufus told me that he never took their confidence in him for granted.

Rufus had a standing invitation to stay downtown in Mr. Philadelphia's Hilton managed hotel and another hotel property he had in Delaware. Later when I was sick we took him up on it and spent four days where me and his secretary became friends because she was a cancer survivor. He told us what sites we had to visit especially with Kevin while in Philadelphia: The Liberty Bell, the Franklin Museum, etc. even meeting us in the evening in his tuxedo on his way to a gala to give us free passes. We watch our first Major League Baseball game in his seats at the Phillies stadium and had access to his Yankees seats if we wanted to go when we returned to Aunt Debbie's in New Jersey.

He told us to have lunch in the biggest sport bar outside the three stadiums that we later found out was owned by Mr. Philadelphia and his partners. But the experience I remember most was when he recommended that we have dinner at a trendy Mexican restaurant.

The line was long and the evening was cool. We waited our turn to get to the hostess. When Rufus asked whether there were reservations for the Turnbulls, we were told that the restaurant didn't take reservations. Moments later the owner apologized saying she was expecting us. We were escorted into a crowded dining area where a table seating for four was vacant. We later learned that the building where the restaurant was housed belonged to Mr. Philadelphia.

During those years Rufus became very comfortable being very candid with Mr. Philadelphia later realizing he was thirteen years younger and they could talk more freely since their business relationship was over and they actually became friends. One time he visited and traveled without his chef when Rufus chided him when he was seen eating from a Chef Boyardee can remarking,

"Gourmet dining at its best."

Or the time Rufus told him every time he visited, he seemed to have a new girlfriend. He added that his last girlfriend who was instrumental in picking the kitchen cabinetry locally didn't even get to see it installed. Or another time Rufus came home with what initially looked like a bazooka but was a huge set of plans to renovate the penthouse of Mr. Philadelphia when his contractor was already applying for the necessary paperwork for Rufus to legitimately work in Philadelphia as a licensed low voltage contractor.

Or when his latest girlfriend who had two teen daughters hogging the Great Room television and he called crying for help. He told Rufus this is college bowl weekend and my girlfriend is in the Master Bedroom watching Hallmark, her daughters are watching MTV in the Great Room because they don't want to watch TV in any of the three guest rooms – he was going crazy. Rufus simply started to laugh and continue to tell me that he led him into the theater and put on the game. Mr. Philadelphia thought he could only watch movies in the theater when he incredulously asked,

"Do you mean after all these years I could have watched my games here?"

But the story he used to tell the most was the time when he met the actress Sela Ward.

Rufus had recently upgraded the theater integrating the lights and putting cover art on a graphical user interface. It was going to be a Christmas gift for Mr. Philadelphia. He told Rufus,

"You're a small business. If is easier than what I had to do in the past to access my movies, send my secretary an invoice."

Right on cue before his eyes Rufus destroyed the movie catalog binder by tearing the pages.

"What the fuck are you doing?" the Philadelphia Mogul began then continued. "I want to watch movies later."

Rufus began the orientation of the new control system that catalogued all the movies and integrated lighting and A/C when during the presentation Mr. Philadelphia interrupted to ask,

"Do you know Sela Ward?"

"The actress?" Rufus inquired

"Yeah, she's in the kitchen right now. "

"Get the fuck outta here." Rufus exclaimed.

"I'm serious, come let me introduce you."

The two of them are causing me to curse more than I would like to.

They walked to the kitchen and there she was with her husband and Mr. Philadelphia's girlfriend at that moment. Rufus told me that before he could be introduced, he began ranting like a groupie saying,

"I loved you in the episode of Frasier when you were the supermodel he met on the airplane and his family didn't think that you existed and...." Then he paused in mid-sentence as his audience of four incredulously stared at him seemingly dumbfounded. Rufus flipped it when he stated what he knew they were probably thinking,

"What? A tall Black guy can't like Frasier?"

They all laughed. Luckily he showed restraint this time because a captive audience of four is more people at any time who have ever laughed at his jokes. Instead he continued to explain saying,

"That supermodel episode is my favorite and as a matter of fact, I have it on a DVR system at home and I can even watch it here on my phone," and proceeded to demonstrate.

After selling his vacation home on St. Thomas, Rufus and Mr. Philadelphia remained friends. I only met him that one time when we were in Philadelphia. He was gracious enough to call Rufus when he learned about my passing. And Rufus continues to follow the lessons he has learned from that relationship. As a result, his confidence grew to the point where he unequivocally states that no one can intimidate him. That was business; this also was going to be business of the heart.

◆ ◆ ◆

During the afternoon the music compilation continued to stream from her iPhone to a Bose Bluetooth wireless speaker. Every time a Jill Scott song played, a subliminal seed was planted in her consciousness. In fact, she had actually forgotten about chatting with him last night. After reading the Jill Scott invitation an evening ago – and hearing a Jill Scott song - a mind/body association was made. The uncanny truth is I overheard her telling her Jamaican girlfriend that she wanted to go to the Jill Scott concert a week before. That was the catalyst to everything I had already put into motion: the training seminar, Spirit Airlines, everything. And when she saw the invitation, the coincidence was overwhelming.

But as the afternoon transitioned into early sunset, the rotation of subliminal songs was intentionally more frequent which triggered her to recalled the last direct message she read earlier in the morning before removing her profile pictures. It was again gracious and apologetic for something that was not of his doing. She felt a little guilty and decided to check out his 'not too serious picture-less profile again. This time his photographs were visible along with his vital statistics. I was relieved that she was now perusing his two other pictures. She also saw that his photos were also authenticated with the VERIFIED status.

I always thought Rufus to be very handsome although he always thought otherwise of himself. That humble attribute actually made him more attractive to me. Consequently, over another conversation with her Jamaican girlfriend I overheard her saying that she was not really attracted to the "pretty boys." Her high school sweetheart wasn't particularly handsome even though she wasn't allowed to date because of her religious upbringing. But she said that poor soul had enough confidence to sit in their parlor while her mother loomed like a hawk always in view even before open concept living was a thing. Her mother continuously made suggestions of the homely offspring potential if anyone copulated with him. He was two years older and later went into the military where he wrote her letters weekly and request leave to take her to the prom where after building up so much good will, they were actually allowed. She admitted that she had every intention of marrying him, but her mother's comments bringing home ugly grandkids made her think differently. I actually thought, first the dog eating remark and now the potentially homely grandchildren comment? If this social experiment worked out, her mother is going to be a tough audience.

After reviewing his last message again, she thought it was inconsequential - after all - he wasn't local and was leaving the next day anyway. And although her last meaningful relationship was of the long distance variety, it absolutely would not be in her best interest now that people depend on her six days a week.

I sensed at that time the moment was fleeting and I had to try something. After all, I was able to get them to initially communicate. That was a major accomplishment. But it definitely wasn't time to celebrate. The only thread that connected her to any thought to him was un-reeling off its spool. So I used my eternal influence to selectively queue more Jill Scott songs and have them streamed to her phone more frequently.

Again in hindsight, if he had traveled on American Airline, this story would not have gotten this far. They may have briefly chatted and that would have been it. But for the error in the Live Salsa DVD and the bag of mesquite, I had to cover all bases like I also did with his flying lesson. I had to stay a step ahead. I knew he would not have failed to notice that Jill Scott billboard on the 595 West ramp from the airport because that is his type of music. And up to this point it was the main puzzle piece.

♦ ♦ ♦

Later in the afternoon Rufus hung out at his mother's house. While there his sister Lena expressed her preference of the new Ford Mustang and got into their customary argument being contrary about mundane topics. Quite possibly if Rufus was driving a Chevrolet Vega his sister would have said she preferred the Ford Pinto. Due to her medical conditions she can no longer enjoy the indulgence of Ponche Kuba liqueurs so her appetite for arguments and gossip now feeds her.

He took both his niece and sister for a spin in his rental Camaro on Biscayne Boulevard and made the engine growl when the traffic allowed. When they returned he still was considering whether he was going to see Jill Scott having yet to make up his mind. As the hours passed it became more unlikely.

Around 6pm he said his goodbyes and decided to go to the closest Red Lobster to his hotel to have dinner. He had just declined having dinner at his mother's because he always did by default. His sister stopped offering him food all together. His reasoning was while he was on the mainland, he preferred dining at venues that weren't on St. Thomas. Only when his mother prepared the local Johnny Cakes and Pates he would keep his credit card and cash in his pocket. His rationale was that nobody in the islands made Johnny Cakes and Pates as well as she did - thus having something to eat on the mainland that he could no longer get locally.

I remember that on the morning of our wedding, my mother-in-law made Johnny Cakes for my family for the first time. We all collectively loved it so much and couldn't believe that something with simple ingredients could be so delicious.

The longer we were together, Rufus no longer was concerned about people's feelings when it came to his diet. He treated my mother similarly when we were in Puerto Rico. My family never stopped offering and many times my mother and granny felt affronted and took it very personally.

◆ ◆ ◆

As another Jill Scott song played, in her mind's eye I could see that she thought about him again. She began to wondered whether he was her new affirmation for peace and happiness she'd asked of the universe. Life was rapidly becoming overwhelming with the new opportunity afforded to her. She now had a second priority which was to give all her energies to her new joint venture in hopes that everything would be successful in the competitive world of Pilates in South Florida.

People tend to become jaded and quickly bored after they have gotten over something new. Many people had that attitude with casual relationships and they definitely had it with fitness clubs in South Florida. They were always looking for the next new thing. The changing fitness trends were now Spinning and Hot Yoga. By simply opening her studio by default designate it as a new thing. Her style of Pilates was not the classical that is commonly taught to ballet and ballroom dancers. She used her athletic background after sustaining an injury and rehabilitated herself on the various apparatuses and in the process developed her own method calling it Athletic Pilates.

Well known athletes like Kobe Bryant, Tom Brady and LeBron James are not very well known for using Reformers. It was initially designed for rehabilitation and now can strengthen the most ignored smaller muscles. Her concept was to tailor new workout sequences daily so the process won't quickly become stale like many of the franchised studios in the area.

Many of the Pilates studios simply were established for wives and girlfriends to do something in the mornings and most weren't profitable by evidence that they weren't even open when others were. And to add insult to the industry, many of those studios would cancel classes if a quorum of clients were not present. It is commonly practiced as the norm and when she was an employee she adhered to it. Now as an owner she flipped the script. Two people or more at her studio was deemed a class; one-person present got a private lesson to work on their form.

She genuinely just wanted to do what it took to become established and soon after become profitable. But another relationship would definitely be a major distraction and would require a lot of her precious free time. Additionally, she was done traveling because she now had a business to run and a partnership to satisfy.

She spent the last year in therapy sessions learning things she had already known. Additionally, although it was an inordinate amount of time since she'd been in a meaningful relationship, she weighed whether it was prudent to complicate things now.

That was an opening for the negative thoughts to continue reminding herself again that she had been down that road before. She began building up mental barriers with the few attributes that she had briefly learned about him: He was tall - 'he probably was a cluts' recalling an earlier awkward date in her life. He is a widower - 'he probably is an emotional mess with baggage.' She remembered how long it took for her to get to terms with the loss of her daughter. Not to mention the expectation of having to travel to the islands again now that she was working six days a week. It was already a major sacrifice when she worked five days.

I immediately began to sense that she was also harboring trust issues and had become very selective with who she considered were her confidants. Many wanted to be her friend because of how she looked and how she carried herself. They too were cognizant of the incessant cat calls and stares she received. They also incorrectly assumed that she welcomed the attention in hopes that their insecurities would be bolstered by simply being in her association.

It was a high stakes game of social networking that quite simply scared her especially when she overheard some of her client's testimonials.

She had witnessed subtle emotional abuses of clients and friends where they had become replaceable by someone younger and/or more attractive women even after enduring the plastic surgeries. As a result, some of her private workouts were emotional therapy sessions where they would lay on the reformer bed and vent. Some knew how to play the game very well establishing and securing their worth where they allowed the infidelities as long as they were financially cared for. Her ailing male Jewish friend in New York loves to remind her how stupid she was repeatedly stating,

"You keep leaving them before you were married.... You could have been financially set."

But that kind of deceitfulness made her very uncomfortable.

She also learned that most men of privilege generally lacked the necessary confidence to romantically pursue relationships and primarily led with their wallets to make them appear more socially desirable. At one social event she overheard one guy referring to himself as a 'Zillionaire'. In many cases that would be sufficient and most times it was. That's why they drove Rolls, Bentleys, Porches, and Maseratis. And if they were caught away from their cars, they wore Rolexes and Bulgari's while they walked. Fortunately for me and my self-serving motives, she had been down that road before and chose to get out of the cars and she also knew what time it was.

Then came the moment of truth. It wasn't a concern but in her scrutiny of his less than lack luster profile, under Race, instead of using the default option of African American, Rufus clicked Other and wrote the word Black. Rufus never referred to himself as an African American. For as long as I have known him, the sentence, "I am an African American" never rolled off his tongue. He held a high consciousness about himself after he told me of the privilege he considered it was to have attended an elective class in the 11th Grade in high school taught by the late Dr. Lesmore Emanuel. He explained that Dr. Emanuel told the students he would get into trouble if they told anyone in the school's administration or their parents what he was teaching in class.

The class was officially called African and Caribbean History where he clandestinely also taught Evolution. The students became aware and familiar with the theories of tarsius spectrum and the different stages of prehistoric man from homoerectus to homosapiens. And coincidentally they learned about the renowned paleoanthropologist Dr. Louis Leakey way before Richard Pryor told the rest of the world in comedy that the earliest remains of man were identified as African.

He taught them a more laudable historic depiction of Christopher Columbus. He suggests that Columbus kept annoying Queen Isabella when she gave him the three worst ships in the armada – The Nina, The Pinta, and The Santa Maria – in addition to emptying the prisons for his crew in hope that they fall of the edge of the world since until a little more than 500 years ago it was considered flat.

Rufus expressed that the class was very instrumental in his emotional development where he used to feel inferior based on the amount of melanin on his skin being teased and ridiculed by his lighter complexed peers especially in elementary school.

He also told me about a neighborhood light skinned black girl actually repeated to him what her father – who was her same complexion – had told her mother – who was also similarly shaded,

"If you ain't White, you ain't right."

She repeated that mantra like it was her pledge of allegiance. Her father soon after left his wife with four kids for other whiter pastures.

Those social issues he had to navigate as a child were very complicating until he told me that everything as far as race was resolved later that school year in February 1980. He attended a student conference in the dead of winter in Washington DC. For two months on a weekly basis, four hundred students at a time participated in and became members of the Presidential Classroom for Young Americans as high school seniors. Rufus was chosen by his principal as a junior. During the week he saw the Nation's Capital at work visiting the White House, the CIA building in Langley, the State Department, the Capitol Building, and the Kennedy Center. Every student was also afforded a one-on-one personal meeting with their congressmen who at the time was Dr. Melvin H. Evans. But the most indelible impressions that stayed with him was the comment made by a fellow African American student he befriended from Kentucky by the name of Rochelle Garner who simply told him how beautiful his skin was to her. They became pen pals and thirty-five years later are still Facebook friends when he recently reminded her of what she said. Rufus told me that in the class taught by Dr. Emanuel, he learned self-respect.

On the other hand, she politically and consciously refers to African Americans as Brown people and all the various shades that are entailed associating her son as light brown. Her mother is of American Indian Heritage and her father was Dark Brown like Rufus. And at times she jokingly refers to her son as a Halfrican pointing at similarly curly haired kids in the mall as his cousins.

She never really had to really address the subject – only that one stint in Atlanta when she felt the disdain from people who she didn't know but looked like her. And after all, initially naive she later realized the animosity came from the fact that her husband in her early twenties was Caucasian.

Today her circle of friends are multicultural mostly Jewish, Latin descent and Caucasian. Consequently, almost everything that I have learned about her for the past several months she had been recounting in confidence to her Dark Brown Jamaican girlfriend.

So the subject of Race never was consciously a factor whenever she made decisions of the heart. She unapologetically admitted to not particularly making it easy for anyone. Confidence was most endearing and appealing to her. Her ex-husband was relentless in his pursuit of her in the early nineties and quite frankly wore her down. And the relationships that followed served their purpose as life's lessons that turned out to be moments of discovery and personal growth.

And in the end, for the past decade fitness had become her life. That's where her clan reside. From the time she taught mat Pilates at the local community college where mostly Asians attended as an elective and considered it to be the best form of exercise they had experienced in America until now. The disturbing truth that she coped with and hoped to be contrary, was the fact that very few African Americans in South Florida were health conscious and could be found in Pilates Studios. And the few that come into her studio, she goes out the way to make them feel at ease.

CHAPTER ELEVEN

"If I knew how, I'd slap him upside the head like Patrick Swayze did in the movie Ghost."

I T WAS THE EARLY EVENING and Rufus was in Hialeah sitting at the bar after placing his order of Surf-n-Turf and ordered a cocktail as he waited. He looked around the restaurant and became a little nostalgic as he observed families and couples in their gaiety.

We had dined at Red Lobster scores of times over the years. The last time we were in Orlando with my mother a year ago. I remember when the waiter gave Kevin a kiddie menu and he was affronted. He decided to order crab and lobster to prove to the server he wasn't juvenile. Those memories were all coming back to him.

I remember the time the three of us were in Tampa for a week where I insisted that we go to the Olive Garden for a change of pace. I reminded Rufus how much he loved the pasta at Olive Garden in New Jersey when he actually told me that I had to have been married to someone else. He insisted remembering eating there and definitely not enjoying it. Anyway, I didn't relent; I put my foot down so he came around.

We went to the Olive Garden on the second evening of the vacation to as he put it, 'to get it over with.' Rufus and Kevin began smiling and giggling as we walked into the restaurant and the obvious reasons were few. First, we were the only ones in the restaurant and it wasn't early. That was a time before social media reviews made or break your business. We were led to a table and had succumb to the second obvious reason.

Dining experiences are all about your senses - not only your sense of taste. The best entree served in that restaurant that day would have been unpleasant because the carpeting reeked with odors from what My Guys suggested was from the day the restaurant opened. It appeared like the rug was never cleaned. When the waiter came to take our order, we excuse ourselves.

Then of late we discovered an up and coming franchise in Gaithersburg Virginia when Rufus was at another training seminar and we parlayed it into a vacation when we visited the National Archives in Washington DC to see The Declaration of Independence. We were walking along a lake and over small pedestrian bridges by our hotel, when as Rufus describes it, the smoky odor of hickory and mesquite summoned him like a genie-like smoke caricature cartoon of a finger guiding us into the Copper Canyon Grill. It instantly became our favorite restaurant - Red Lobster was kicked down a few notches. He loved the salmon salad where the entire salad was served chopped and slightly warmed by the added permeated smoke from the grill. We later discovered there was another location in Orlando and we dined there every time we visited the theme parks. Then we later found another location in Boca Raton. He even took Milton there for dinner once when they were having physical examinations at the Cleveland Clinic in Westin.

So while he sat on the corner stool he was overcome with melancholy and instructed the bartender to change his order to take out. Ten minutes later he was back in the Camaro growling.

◆ ◆ ◆

There wasn't much of anything else in his profile for her to nitpick as she remembered. Another reason why less is more. Unlike many of the women on dating sites with litmus tests and checklists. If he had a profile of high standards, she generally would have surgically dissected him with the soundtrack of Erykah Badu's *Tyrone* appropriately cued in the background saying,

"Every time I asked you for some cash, you turn around and ask me for some ass..."

So it was unnoticed when I skipped that song and made sure it didn't replay.

When India Arie's *I am not my Hair* played, it reminded her of the permanent damage she had done to her mane when she kept appearances relaxing her hair. She was now cutting off the damaged ends periodically and treating it naturally hoping that it would regrow healthy like it was before they both weren't being stressed. She now was camouflaging it with hair pieces and weaves to thicken its appearance over the past year that wound up with a uniquely curly exotic look. And when another Jill Scott song played, the universe spoke to her through the music.

You see the Jill Scott billboard and the subsequent invitation was a passive method of hypnosis. Still trying to rationalize, she suggested to herself that there wouldn't be anything in common or familiar between them. He's widowed. That's the last thing she needed at the moment was an emotional wreck. But she also considered herself as a work in progress – and in one of her writings – she referred to herself as a broken tune.

Then she remembered the preface to the recent conversation she had with her Venezuelan client at her studio. She was a talk show host in her country before she had to flee and presently a motivational speaker and life coach in the South Florida Latino community. She continued to suggest that over several years of interviews on radio and television, she had come to her own personal conclusion that widowed men are great life partners – especially if he was married for a prolonged period of time. Then on cue, the following song by Jill Scott played.

https://www.youtube.com/watch?v=zjd-JA9XlJE

Jill Scott
"Back Together"

Pieces of me, were scattered...Blowing in the cold
In different directions...hmm. Truth, truth, truth be told
Oh, then I looked into your eyes, everything felt like it could be alright
You went and put me back together, Back together .... again

Going through heartache... You know I think I lost my mind for a time
And couldn't get better....... Couldn't get no better
No matter, no matter how.... hard I tried
Then I, I looked into your eyes, and everything felt like it could be alright
You went and put me back together,
You went and put me back together,
Back together again ... Somebody sang

Put me back together again
Somebody sing...hey...hey, hey, hey, hey yeah
Put me back together again
Surely did...oh!

122

Now I'm walking in the sunshine
And everything feels so right
You went and put me right back together
Put me right back together
Baby look at what you did
Oh, ay
You did it

Back together again
Back together again
Back together ooo, again
And I feel like I'm walking on air, baby
Thank You

♦ ♦ ♦

Less than five minutes after leaving the restaurant with his takeout on the passenger front seat, he was heading back toward the hotel listening to NPR when his phone rang. The phone was paired to the car's audio system and he glanced at the unfamiliar number that appeared on the center console screen. His first instinct is to always ignore and let it go to voicemail for the following reasons: if the contact name did not show and especially when driving on the mainland. At this moment in time If I was present I would have screamed "Are you fucking kidding me?"

Disclosure Alert. In our 25-year relationship I can count the amount of times on one hand when I cursed in Rufus' presence. The first time was four years into our marriage when we were going through the process of purchasing our home. The realtor wanted us to either purchase the horrendous furniture in the house or allow her to bring prospective buyers in our home after closing who may or may not have been interested in buying the crap. I told her that after we close the first thing I was going to do is have the locks changed. She told me I was being unreasonable... so I told her,

"Then you can put the fucking furniture in your own house!"

And now after everything I have done - right down to being "DJ Afterwife" - skipping inappropriate songs to keep her head in the game of life, he has to think whether he was going to simply touch a screen on the audio display? Seriously? Are you kidding me? At the moment I didn't even care about Florida's mobile device distraction law. If I knew how, I'd slap him upside the head like Patrick Swayze did in the movie *Ghost*, but it would probably would have made things worse by causing an accident, so I digress again.

After all the metaphysical maneuvering I had to do. The puzzle was complete. The pieces were all in place. And most importantly, she was on the other end of the call that had already rang four times despite her better instincts. She was cold calling someone she did not know nor seen and was in the process of being dissed. She might have well dialed someone else arbitrarily in the football stadium. But after everything I have done, it was the sincerity of his last direct message and the inclusion of his phone number that prompted this defining moment in time.

"Hello?" Rufus answered

"Hi, is this Rufus?" her voice asked.

"Yes?" Rufus replied

"This is Coco from the dating site; we chatted last night." She explained.

"Oh yeah .... I hope that I wasn't too forward last night when I asked you out ... I know how that could have appeared seeing that we don't even know each other." He apologized again.

"Actually I fell asleep and when I read your last message today in the afternoon. I didn't want you to think it was something else that caused me not to reply."

While he drove his mind was recounting the previous evening events. His skepticism briefly kicked in as he whimsically mentioned,

"I checked your profile this morning and I saw that you had removed your pictures." Rufus recounted.

"I did" she replied softly giggling "I was receiving too many weird messages from the members." she continued to explain.

While they continued to talk, a couple of things slowly began to develop. To him - her voice was beautiful and clear - similar to my New York accent. She even has been told that her voice sounded like 'pillow talk.' Additionally, he smiled at the thought that if he could raise one eyebrow without closing the other eye while driving, he would have tried. He quickly recapped in his mind, *"She fell asleep, woke up, read too many weird messages - including this afternoon - and removed her profile pics."*

Hmmm he thought knowing that he didn't see her pictures in the morning concluding again, "*Oh well.*"

Now, there was a reason why I transcribed that short dialogue between Rufus and Milton. That's how they normally speak to each other. It took me a while to really get to understand it. She probably heard,

"Oh yea ....Ah hope dat ah wasn't too farwad las nite wen ah ask you out ... Ah know how dat cudda appear seeing dat we don't even know each udder."

And at the same time I use to just nod my head and kept insisting initially for him to speak more slowly. So in her defense, I knew exactly what she was going through. His voice is very deep with a not so strong Caribbean accent, but it was distinctive. He always switched his accent on and off based on his audience. It has been modified over the years together with him where he made a concerted effort to speak more clearly to me so that I could understand what he was saying without having to repeat because that annoyed him. And from my point of view I was witnessing another case of deja vu.

In essence, she was unable to totally understand what he was saying. That wasn't good. At the same time, she quickly recounted a disastrous, but very comical short lived encounter with a European guy she met post marriage at a cocktail bar who was strikingly handsome. As customary, she wasn't particularly enamored with his looks, but she was totally enthralled with his accent even though she could not fully understand what he was saying. For all she knew he was spewing the typical compliments she had grown accustomed to from men when they were mostly annoying. Now these commonly unwelcome comments sounded like music in a foreign accent – or so she thought. These chanced meetings during her lunch break were unengaging until they finally decided to go out on a date. He was incredulous thinking that she was one of those progressive American women and kept repeating what she thought was the same compliment.

When she finally was able to establish what he was trying to communicate – the fact that he thought that she was so cool to agree to go out with him after he continuously stated he was married. SCREECH!!! Cue the stylus scratched across the record's phonograph. She bolted and vowed that would never happen to her again. Consequently, with that immediately in her mind, she asked Rufus to speak more clearly so she would be able to understand.

Rufus immediately remembered the remedy to our language barrier and took the opportunity and pulled into the parking lot of the Univision Television station and commenced to speak slower and in short sentences with his undivided attention.

What she thought would have been a short 'I just wanted to let you know that there weren't any hard feelings' kinda call, instead wound up being engaging. It was engaging because the conversation was never about her 'superficial' due to the fact that he had briefly forgotten what her profile pic looked like. But again, her removing the pictures was a subliminal decision that I compelled her to do similarly like how he felt compelled to leave his phone number 24 hours earlier. And as a result, they just spoke as if they were innocent childhood friend meeting at the playground for the very first time.

She learned about what he did for a living and the reason he was in Miami for the weekend while he became impressed by her recent milestones of opening a Pilates Studio. He actually said,

"That's an exercise thing, right?"

She corrected him and elaborated that it was a form of workout she had developed.

The conversation was interrupted by the security guard at Univision as it was explained that he was unauthorized to park in their lot. So he drove to a nearby 7/11 and stayed in the car idling as they resumed their conversation.

His phone showed forty minutes had quickly transpired. Before they hung up, he asked her what was her real name. She jokingly replied,

"What makes you think Coco isn't my real name?"

"The same reason Chocolate Charmer isn't mine."

Then he explained that a lady he had briefly chatted with suggested that moniker instead of the site's generic name Zoosk Member followed by a number string.

"My name is Stephanie," she began. "To be quite honest, had I noticed that your name was Chocolate Charmer, I definitely wouldn't have answered your message yesterday."

After a few more seconds of pleasantries Rufus wound up the conversation by saying,

"I really enjoyed talking to you. Would you mind if from time to time I call - if only to say hi and ask how was your day?"

"I'd like that very much." She replied.

♦ ♦ ♦

I was able to get her to respond to his initial message on the dating App where she otherwise wouldn't have – which was a major coup. Twenty-four hours later as a result of my musical prodding, she again followed up with a phone call that she thought would have otherwise been brief. And although I can swear that I never cheated during exams while in school and college, I was now behind the scenes slipping the answers to Rufus where to this point he was passing her test.

To those that believe in the existential but don't have any rational explanation, what I was able to accomplish so far is what the angels do for the living. As I see her laying on her side in bed with both eyes opened in her darkened bedroom, many things were going through her mind's eye. She tried to recall the last time she had ever spoken to anyone for the first time without being complimented to paralysis. And at the same time, although she was about to retire for the evening, something else kept her up later than usual. Could he be the one? Her expectations were uncertain for the moment and maybe in the morning it would be fleeting.

I'd like to suggest that they were not unlike most creatures on earth – both lonely and were growing tired of being alone. I also realized that in addition to not seeing his pictures yesterday I may have unknowingly prohibited her from seeing his moniker, but it's all in the same. Unassuming is the word that comes to mind that defines how they 'talked by fate and not by sight.' He thought her profile statement was unassuming and she thought he was equally unassuming for not posting pictures but later had. In the end, they both put their cares aside and simply did what felt unassumingly right.

So as each new sunrise begins a new day, another page in their storied life begins a new chapter to be written. Being able to bear witness to the confluence of events that brought them to this point simply renders a sigh. And as I compare the similarities of happenstances when Rufus and

I met a quarter century ago no longer begs to question why. Because those two days in August - up until I told their story - would have remained a great wonder and another one of the universe's vast secrets. And for the moment, it will now be entirely up to them to see how far they intend to pursue this friendship and whether outside forces are allowed to intervene.

CHAPTER TWELVE

I
N THE SUBSEQUENT DAYS AND WEEKS that followed, their friendship blossomed despite all of the technology available to him. He tried googling everything about Pilates and Stephanie and was disappointed when he came up empty. After all, she only provided a first name which may or may not could have been true. But to his satisfaction, she responded to his online dating comment. And the subsequent dialog was prolonged because of the Virgin Islands reference. On the following day, she called with the intention to merely recompense to the unanswered gracious invitation he left. It wasn't warranted, but she thought it simply felt right.

Twenty-four hours later, both hadn't communicated any further where two different narratives were being developed: she still concerned whether he was the manifestation of the hopes and dreams that she had requested from the universe. He simply enjoyed the conversation had if only for those moments. What she was going to soon learn that he was a man of his word.

On Monday before leaving to go to work on St. John. Rufus forwarded a text message simply saying,

"Good morning and have a nice day."

And as a result, she was first to call him later in the afternoon. He was at the local Home Depot in St. Thomas when he recognized her number. For the next 10 minutes, he was the only person in the store wearing a cell phone and a ridiculous smile on his face.

The following is the actual transcript of the text messages between Rufus and Stephanie. I found their conversation to be exactly like I would have expected ... unassumingly innocent. No superficial references were discussed as I suggested earlier liken it to when two childhood friends getting to know each other. You have to remember that Rufus had only a fleeting glimpse of what she looked like when he saw one of her three profile pictures before he initially messaged her on Friday at the EB Hotel. Afterwards, she removed her pics the following day. But again I must reiterate that having surveilled her during the past months and learning her tendencies from her conversations, I knew she would be more amenable towards him if he was at a visual disadvantage. And although their subsequent weekend dialogs were on the phone, the added bonus was when she heard the nocturnal creatures like crickets and frogs in his background when he hid downstairs away from Kevin reminded her of the evenings where she grew up.

...Actual Transcript from Rufus cell phone...

August 9, 2015

Rufus

Hi Stephanie, I just want you to know that I was pleasantly surprised when you called and I really enjoyed our conversation. ....it would have been better over lunch or dinner, but I don't mind the baby steps. Is it okay to call you on the weekends just to compare our week?

Stephanie
That would be really nice.
Sweet dreams ;-))

August 10, 2015

Stephanie
Good day. How are you?

Rufus

I'm having a great day so far. ...I'm on St. John working in a very beautiful house adding more electronics.
How about yourself?

August 11, 2015

Rufus

Good Afternoon, yesterday you sent me a message inquiring about my wellbeing. I'm not sure whether you sent it in error because you didn't reply to responses. .... but your message was a pleasant surprise otherwise

Stephanie
Of course I did not send the message in error ;-))
How are you today? Working? I had a pretty slow day at the studio, but very
energizing. I am now tutoring with my son. I hope that your son is doing well.

Rufus

I'm working at home today. My son has been at his grandmother and aunts in Puerto Rico since final exams and basically had the kind of summer away from me as accustomed. I have been over to hang out twice a month....to make sure they are not abusing him.

Stephanie

Got it. So he spends summers with his grandparents. That's nice. That gives you a lot of time to work and play. Cool.

Rufus

Work is a necessary evil I truly enjoy, but play has been few and very far between. When I am in Puerto Rico my sister-in-law has been taking me to the Salsa Clubs and Concerts (I truly love Latin Music) ...I am even taking private lessons over there.

https://vimeo.com/334328150

Stephanie

That's so cool.
I took private salsa lessons for a while.

Rufus

Hmmmm.... (Eyebrows Raised)

Stephanie

Well put them down (eyebrows) I wasn't very good at it.
I'm going to try bachata next. Slower more sensual.

Rufus

(Smiling).... I agree. I love that about Latin Music

August 12, 2015

Rufus

Good morning, I'm on my way to St. John for the day. I reread your "...wasn't very good at it comment." and I am still smiling. Have a great day

Stephanie

lol! Just read your message. Super busy day. Are you back from St. John?

Rufus

I got home around 5pm. ...I'm finishing up some projects at home.

August 13, 2015

Rufus

Good morning. ...this is becoming a habit that I was accustomed. ... (saying Good Morning to someone), on my way to St. John again... [texting you on the 30-minute vehicle barge ride]. Have an amazing day Stephanie

Stephanie

Well Good morning. I'm happy I get the pleasure of receiving your morning greetings ;-))

https://vimeo.com/334193246

VLOG from STEPHANIE

"Good morning ... How are you ... hmmm ... I'm just getting to work and I am still sitting in my car and I thought I'd say ..., Hi .... Hi Rufus TurnBool (that's how she pronounced it initially) ... (giggles)... How are you.... I just want to wish you an AMAZING day today ...and umm, I hope everything goes your way...bye.

Aug 14, 2015

Rufus

Good morning, I'm on my way to Puerto Rico for the weekend. My son was supposed to return today, but my mother-in-law asked me to replace her kitchen sink so the both of us are returning on Sunday. (Free Labor. .... I'm not complaining. ...she pays with FOOD)

Stephanie

Hi. I've just finished work. I'm sitting on my balcony eating a coconut Popsicle. Awesome, right?

How's your son? It's really nice of you to help out your mother-in-law. Is it hot there?

I was in Puerto Rico about two years ago and I got to visit the oldest cemetery there and a really amazing Catholic Church. It's an interesting place. The people drive like maniacs though. I've never seen driving like that before. Lol!

Rufus

Yep, you've been to Puerto Rico. Over the past months we have been reminiscing to my in-laws about their sister/daughter. She was an awful driver in Puerto Rico when we dated; she drove me around the island WITHOUT breaks.... actually stopping her car in curbside and driving in the breakdown lanes on the highway. My son was in disbelief ....my only explanation was I tolerated it because I was in love. She became a conscientious driver after our son was born. .... before she was Gangster.

My son gave me a big hug at the airport which made me feel great even though we speak several times a week. I am doing the things for my in-laws that I used to "beat around the bush " .... which is generally home maintenance. My two sister-in-law's are divorced and when I am asked to fix something in their apartments, I always joke saying "if you were still married to so-and-so it would be fixed" or " you won't have to wait until I come over.

Stephanie

Lol! I love that story. It must be hard on Mom, losing a daughter. And you and your son. I know it's just a thing not quite understood.
Oh my...that's a lot of women in your life. You better teach your son how to help you soon ;-))
It's good you don't live there, you'd be working after hours all the time.
There's nothing like the love of your child. It just feels differently. Maybe without condition.

Rufus

25yrs of memories leaves an indelible impression on one's life. They remind me that they loved our relationship.

Stephanie

Wow! Beautifully said, dear Sir.

Rufus

Last week when we spoke on the phone, something you said stuck in my mind. The fact that you too have a 14-year-old son and he's your priority and you are concentrating on his education, should we really be getting into a relationship?

Stephanie

Is that " should I be really getting into a relationship?"

Rufus

I have not met you, but I like your spirit. .... I too can't wait to kick my son outta the house. ... (I say that in jest), but I have made a promise to myself to raise my son in the manner in which my wife and I had discussed to provide all the options for him to make the best decisions for his future

Stephanie

I'm confused about what you wrote... Please explain. Are you saying you should not be getting into a relationship? Or I?

Rufus

Without meeting you I REALLY like the vibe you exude. ...and I am willing to pursue a relationship at the pace that is comfortable to us both......if you are so inclined. I'm even planning to visit Miami next month for a football game with my son. ...contingent on his grades. ....and maybe we can have lunch or dinner this time

Stephanie

I'm enjoying our exchanges for sure.

Of course... You'd want to meet me, as we are a distance apart ;-))

That sound great. I'll send more pictures to give you an idea of whom you are speaking.

Stephanie

I took my pictures off the site and all of my information.

Rufus

The distance is actually a good thing. ...it can give us Pause if we have doubts, but I am the kinda guy that have not given my partner reasons to despair. My Zoosk subscription actually expire Today so I too am about to remove my pics. ....and my birthday is next Saturday. .... hint hint. BTW, what's ur last name?

Stephanie

Stephanie Brock. What's yours?

Rufus

Rufus Turnbull, I'm on Facebook. I wasn't into Social media, but I got tired of repeating myself when people asked me 'how I was doing? "....so they can see How I am doing.

Stephanie

That's a strong name! I'm not on Facebook. I've always been super private.

Rufus

I always hated my name. I was the butt of Name Jokes waaaay back in elementary school. ..." ...when you build a house, you have to build the Roof First...." Then on TV, 9 times out of 10 if a character's name is Rufus, most likely it is a dog. I began to feel better about my name when I discovered Rufus and Chaka Khan. What do you mean by Strong name?

Stephanie

Turnbull sounds like a strong Native American name. What does it mean? I like it!!

'STRONG LIKE BULL' Lol!

Rufus

There's maybe something to that. ...my parents were born on Tortola British Virgin Islands. ....to this day, random people that don't know me, simply look at me and say, "You are a Turnbull. .... or Fahie (mom's maiden name) .... it's uncanny. My mother and father divorced when I was 4, and we haven't had a relationship since. ...my mother is my Girl. ...she gives me what I call 'Blood Pressure Test Typed Hugs' every time I see her

Stephanie

That's so cool that you have an amazing relationship with your mother. My parents have been together for 47 years. Same house I grew up in. My father's a pastor. I grew up super-duper strict. It didn't bother me though, I'm a home type being anyway ;-)) I guess boring, good girl type. Church is the reason I had problems moving my hips in salsa ;-))

Rufus

Lol....the salsa comment made me laugh .... it's easier than you think.

Stephanie

Funny It is.......I am over it now

Rufus

Okay. .... what's your favorite musical group?

Stephanie

I like all kinds of music; it depends on my mood. Erykah Badu, Bob Dylan.
Pink Floyd
Classical piano
Gospel etc.

Rufus

Eclectic. ...I have a neighbor (white guy) that have been trying to get me into Pink Floyd. .... now I have to give it another try. ...my taste in music runs the gamut, back in the 80's and 90s I played in a local band....

Stephanie

Pink Floyd is amazing. What did you play? What instrument...I mean.

Rufus

I still play the bass

Stephanie

Bass is always my favorite. At concerts I focus on the bass. If I could play, I'd chose the bass.

Rufus

You are NOT just saying that. ...lol. Bass it the 'coolest' instrument in my opinion.... it's easy to learn if you approach it correctly. I posted a YouTube video of our group back in 1987......if you are interested

Stephanie
My favorite Pink Floyd Song
Check out this video on YouTube:
https://www.youtube.com/watch?v=IXdNnw99-Ic

Rufus

Okay. ...definitely

Stephanie

I'm not kidding. It's like an obsession sometimes. I literally focus on bass at the theater. Lol!

Send me your YouTube please. I may not respond right back, I'm going to cook dinner for my son.

Rufus

Smiling. …. Okay let me find the link………Watch "Priscilla & Company Valentine's Day Special 1987.flv" https://www.youtube.com/watch?v=5cZ_vQH8XbQ&t=319s It was an hour TV special we produced and only 24 minutes got transferred before the old VHS tape got chewed up. And I had Hair then

Stephanie

I have 2 words! "Oh Sheila!!!" That is bad-ass! What a great group you all were. And you had some serious moves for a bass player. Bass just usually stand there revealing the COOL! Thank you for sharing that ;-)) On my way to bed now. Sweet dreams.

Stephanie

Ok… One more thing. That must be sooooo super cool for your son to see.

Rufus

Glad you enjoyed it, it was the best time of my life for 5yrs …2nd to being married for 25. ….as for my son. …SMH…He is a tough audience - not easily impressed.

August 16, 2015

Rufus Turnbull

Good morning, I enjoyed our correspondence. …I awoke a bit congested; been a while since I have been sick. …I tend to be a Big Baby when I get sick

Stephanie Brock

Hi. I'm sorry to hear that you are not at your best today. Are you feeling better?

Rufus Turnbull

Very stuffy, my son and I just left the movies and now I am treating everyone to dinner at. …. Nordstrom. ….no kidding. …. restaurant in the department store. Back at my in-laws, how's your weekend been so far?

I'm back on St. Thomas now…, my son loves what I did to his room while he was away. …. tell me about your weekend.

Stephanie Brock

Good morning. I'm still in bed. I'm not feeling my best today. I had a deep
tissue massage yesterday, and now my entire body is achy. I'll take a hot
shower soon. I worked Saturday morning. After that I ate too much, read some
and watched a movie on Netflix ;-)) How did you change your son's room? Are
you feeling all better?

Rufus Turnbull
It was obvious that my son missed me by the big hug I received on Friday at the
airport, then while sleeping at my in-laws, knowing that I was stuffy I did not
turn on the A/C in the room, but it was on when I awoke Saturday....he told me
he turned it on to keep me cool. I am now taking Afrin from last night and I am
a lot better today. ...just a dry cough.... but my voice sounds AMAZING now.

Over the past month I made major changes at home. He had a Bunk Bed system
that over the years he has put stickers and - how shall I say- expressed himself
all over. I threw it out and bought a new adult bunk with mattresses. I also built
a Desk/Chest of Drawers/Bookcase to match his new bed. He called his
grandmother to tell her it looks better than the pictures I texted to them.

Stephanie Brock
That's awesome.
It's wonderful to see them so happy about simple things.

Rufus Turnbull
You love Massages. .... waaaay cool. It may also surprise you but me too. A
month ago I took my in-laws on a cruise from Miami and my sister-in-law
insisted that we all go to the Spa - her treat. - not my son- he's not
interested...

You? over ate? must have been Great!!.... Your pics gave me the impression that
you are athletically thin and you over-ate???.......that's funny.

Stephanie Brock
I don't have massages often. I need to because of the work I do with my
body. It's part of staying healthy for me. I don't like a traditional massage for
relaxing, it has to be medicinal for me. That's cool you enjoy the spa though. I
enjoy the water spas...steam, heated Jacuzzi, infrared saunas etc.

I was very pleased about how their friendship was developing. At
the same time, she was providing cryptic hints about how she felt but

Rufus was as dense as an inclement cloud; it might as well be hovering over his head with lightning and thunder as a thought bubble.

You see, had he not try to analyze the Fink Floyd's song musically as he summarily shunned it rudimentary as a simple song, he failed to see the title of the song, "Wish You Were Here." I realized then that my work is far from over.

Then on August 20th, Rufus awoke with a lot on his mind. It seemed like the inclement cleared – at least the thunder and lighting. After his early morning walk in the fog, he email the following letter.

Stephanie

I will recap: First of all, I am the youngest of ten children born on St. Thomas and on Saturday it will be 52 years my eyes have seen the wonders of life.... hint hint.

I am very active in my high school alumni activities where I preside as our Vice President and my best friend Milton is our President. Truth be told, of the 20 active members, we acquiesce to the female member's directives where we simply go with the flow and sign checks.

I am a self-taught musician from back in the late seventies and as a result have been playing the local nightclub scene from the mid to late eighties. I love most music genres to include the Caribbean reggae and calypso, salsa and meringue, and of course R & B, Jazz, hip hop....and 'some' of the new stuff I hear on the radio and TV. Back in my hay day, I had a mental repertoire of over 100 songs that I could play at the 'drop of a dime.' and could have been the interim bass player for UB40 - but that's another story if you want to hear.

I have taught myself several things over the years that seems to leave indelible impressions on my friends and family: drawing and painting, sewing, carpentry, electronics- just off the top of my head. I dropped out of college in Texas in 1983 because financially it was a struggle and did not want to put any hardship on my family. So I returned home and immediately gain employment for the local government- quit after a year because I felt I was being non-productive. I found another job at a local bank because I needed something to do during the day while I played music 4 evenings weekly.

Reminiscent of a Lifetime TV movie, in September 1989 a Hurricane came and devastated the islands destroying 70 percent of the homes and because most of the low income homes were insured by a mortgage company from Puerto Rico, they sent an agent- my future wife- to St. Thomas to monitor their reconstruction by issuing checks for claims. We were introduced by a mutual friend and actually married on the anniversary of the day we met in Puerto Rico.

I must admit we had a charmed life traveling extensively throughout the Caribbean, mainland US and Canada. Our son was born 10 years after we married and as I reminded him yesterday when he was writing his Autobiography as part of his Summer Reading and Writing assignment, he was on an airplane 18 times before he was one-year-old mostly going to the pediatrician in Puerto Rico - consequently, I was 16 when I first flew.

In 2003 I took a leap of faith and went into business for myself as a Custom Electronic Installer. It has been liberating and terrifying being self-employed in the beginning, but with experience brings familiarity and confidence. It began as seasonal work so there were many leans times financially, but in my business with each new client comes the reward of referrals with a good job done- or specifically, in the house warming parties the guests get to see electronics in homes integrated in ways they haven't seen before and now want similar in their homes.

I can be stoic and stand-offish in my initial appearance to most as a defense mechanism to those I don't want to invite in my inner circle or just not to be bothered. Otherwise, I can be very obnoxiously engaging and funny. I took my in-laws and my son on a cruise a few weeks ago reminiscent of what was our normal activities and they saw a side of me they only heard about. They were surprised that most people on the ship knew my name from my nightly performances in the Karaoke. SLOW YOUR ROLL,,,,,,, I CAN play the bass, BUT I would definitely starve if I made a living singing.... I'm just saying. So what made me such a Karaoke Star that everyone was calling me while I ate or when a guy actually said, "There goes the best F-ing singer on the boat!" as I walked on the pool deck. Lemme just say, I DIDN'T SING THE SONGS....I OWED THE SONGS. (I sang Misses Jones, Prince's Kiss, and Papa Was A Rollin' Stone- [I have an amazin' fake DEEP VOICE]) My introduction on stage was, "My name is Rufus, I am from the Virgin Islands, and I am here to embarrass my son."

Like I expressed to you last week while texting you in Puerto Rico, although we have not met, I thought it was really cool when I read about your motorcycle riding.... MAJOR COOL points. I really like the VIBE you exude in your writing and the brief telephone conversation. One thing we have in common is our love for our sons. Being a single parent is very challenging I have quickly learned and I also had to adjust my work schedule to shorter hours and making up the time *where possible like when we overnight in luxury homes that are on St. John from time to time just to be more productive.*

From time to time I recall what my son told me the evening of my wife's passing in January, "…. Dad, our life was perfect before 2012." - that's when she was diagnosed with breast cancer. (She died as a result of the cancer treatment where the chemo severely weakened her heart two year after being cancer free)

What I now miss most about her were our conversations…. you know…. adult conversation about our day. Also when she insisted from time to time that we watch a CHICK FLICK downstairs in our theater. I told you I get it when you said Breaking Bad is not your type of TV watching experience because she expressed similar sentiments after a few episodes. What I regret most is the fact that she did not taste my cooking and I wish I learned decades ago. What allows me to endure are the words of encouragement from family telling me that we inspired them being married for so long and being the only married couple on both sides of the family. My in-laws remind me that wife repeatedly told them how happy she was.

Stephanie, I truly hope I am not too forward when I say 'I am going to Pursue You Platonically for as long as you are inclined' - for the remaining high school years of our sons- and later romantically if our hearts so desire.

Rufus

Stephanie Brock

Hi, I just read your email. I will respond in length soon. I'm texting so that you know that I did not 'weird- out'. What did happen though is my heart started beating wildly out of nowhere, my body became heated, and I'm sitting a bit dazed right now. None of this (the way my physical being responded to your words) makes sense to me, which is probably a good thing. …being that I try to make sense out of everything. I won't ruin this with the common "thanks for sharing". All that you wrote means so much more than that. Please send your email. I want to put it in my new computer; I am not able to transfer it from my phone.

Rufus Turnbull

I'm just being honest with my feelings. After losing someone you loved for such a long time makes you reflect. Like I said earlier about distance being a major barrier, it can be a good thing if there's uncertainty. But if my words made your heart rate increase, I hope to make it secure.

Later Rufus also forwarded a copy of his email to Milton where he commented,

"Dred, you wearing yo emotions on yo sleeves."

Additionally, he forwarded it to his sister Lena as an electronic elixir since she could no longer have her favorite alcoholic liqueur Ponche Kuba.

After leaving her exercise studio and returning home 1pm, Stephanie responded with an email of her own also recapping the highlights of her biography.

Stephanie Brock

I'm Stephanie Brigham-Brock. I'm the oldest of six. Just the opposite of you, being the youngest. Three girls and three boys. My father's a Pastor my whole life. My mother a missionary. I was raised in a very strict household. I could only wear dresses, no jeans, lipstick, or boys. I loved lipstick though. By high school, I learned to wear it to school and have it wiped off before I returned home. I remember once, I forgot to remove it, luckily my father was outside our home washing the car. He saw my red lips, and motioned for me to remove it before my mother saw it. My father was my partner in crime. He is a quiet man and highly intelligent. He speaks only when he has something of importance to say. I have great respect for him. My mother on the other hand is a talker, a true storyteller. She's so funny, but plays serious for the sake of their religion. That's my opinion of course. I love them both very much. As I grow older, I love them more.

As you know my only child is 14 years of age. I was married to his father for 14 years. We were great friends. After we were married for about 7 years, he convinced me to have a child. I had a beautiful pregnancy with our daughter, but she died shortly after birth. After this, our relationship changed completely. We are not sure what happened. But studies show, most marriages end after the death of a child. I had our son soon after my daughter's death. His father and I divorced when he was 4 years old. My son and his father have a beautiful relationship. They spend each weekend together. I'm 46 years old. I love getting older, I just want to make sure I'm living my life to its fullest. And... I don't believe that I am. But, more on that later. I'm going to bed now.

Sweet dreams.

August 20, 2015

Stephanie Brock

Something of Importance: I'm not very religious. Although I was raised this way. I believe in God. And, I consider myself a spiritual person. I try to find the good in all beings and situations.

August 21, 2015

Stephanie Brigham

Good evening. I am so sleepy right now. I have work in the morning.
I just needed to say, I totally agree, that none of us know what truth, universe, or God is.

I think we just choose that which works for us at the time. I choose to believe right now that there is mostly good in the world or it would have been destroyed by now. I choose to believe that what we all seek is love, understanding, and acceptance. What love is, I am not sure. Maybe a feeling, maybe an action, or maybe just the essence of all that is. I think I see love when the wind blows on the trees. I think I see love when the rain feeds the earth, I think I know love when I smile while looking at my son. But the wind doesn't always blow, nor does the rain fall daily, and sometimes my son really pisses me off. So, what do I know? I know I enjoy our communicating. Good night dear Rufus.

August 23, 2015

On August 22nd, Rufus celebrated his birthday providing the finishing touches to the master bedroom transformation of the EB Hotel decor. The following is the email he wrote to recap the day.

Good morning Stephanie

My birthday was great, absolutely. I know I am getting older, and I am appreciating more of the little things that comes with each day. I spoke to the most important people in my life very early: my youngest sister (lovingly refer to her as my Big Head Sister - when she calls, the name that shows up on my phone is Big Head Lena.) who takes care of my mother in Miami. Then my mom called, then my 2nd youngest sister in Fort Lauderdale Linda. My wife was also the oldest of 3 girls and her siblings are 5 years younger and are fraternal twins. The shorter sister-in-law texted me very early at 5:30am to wish 'her favorite brother-in-law' birthday wishes because she was on her way to teach a weekend course at the university

142

and won't be able to call. Then I received your text. Now don't judge me- but I had already begun to rate my birthday wishes and your message jump to the top.

My mother-in-law and the taller sister-in-law called minutes apart and you kinda slipped from 1st to 5th because you texted - so as a result, my moms and sisters were back on top. [I can't believe I am writing this]. Then my niece from my taller sister-in-law wrote the words to Happy Birthday in her text, (she's in college in ATL) with her well wishes ending with, "Thanking you for being like a dad to me." Oh Boy....musical chairs.... she jumped to #3....the moms are still 1 & 2.

I got scores of Facebook well wishes - many from folks I did not know, but after further investigation I saw that they were my wife's friends. I was thanking everyone individually until it got too much so I posted the following, " THANKS AGAIN EVERYONE for the well wishes. This definitely a First for me and I know Kevin will process his 15th birthday next month in the manner that he feels will help him to move forward."

Everything died down for a while, then my Big Head Sister's daughter posted this on Facebook, "The happiest of happy birthday to my uncle Junie! The coolest of the cool and most awesomely awesome uncle! The tech master keeps me on my toes with the latest! Once you meet him you will totally agree on the level of his awesomeness (it's over 9000!) But too bad, he is my uncle first! lol Love you and enjoy it to the fullest!!" Then my other nieces started vying about who was my niece 1st. It was crazy .... she jumped to #2 after my mom. "Did you see how many times she wrote AWESOME?"

Then at 9:39pm you called and you sang Happy Birthday to me - I felt like John F. Kennedy.......and you CAN SING too........sorry for being fickle.... you are back to number 1! I was so happy at that moment that I was smiling for the remainder of the evening and went to sleep earlier than I have in months.... a proverbial Birthday Lullaby.

I was able to finish my projects yesterday so today my son wants to go to church, mainly to see his friends after months of being away and he spends the afternoon at their homes until I pick him up around 8pm............so I can call you before? My son....my favorite person in the world.......and he doesn't know it.

I almost forgot, do you like strawberries?

August 25, 2015

Stephanie Brock

Hi. I just read your email. It's amazing how much I'm smiling or laughing when I read your letters. I didn't read it yesterday because I was a little concerned about my son's school situation. Although now, I realize I should have read it, because your writing makes my heart feel happy. I too Rufus, am so happy that we've continued our communication. And yes...I love strawberries, especially dipped in dark chocolate.

Rufus Turnbull

Just got off the phone with my mother-in-law. She's worried about the storm that definitely will arrive tomorrow. Reminding me to close the shutters.... she is watching the Weather Channel. I assured her that the storm is not as strong as originally forecasted and I received the 8pm advisory as we spoke.

Then she TRIED to make me feel guilty asking if she was going to see Kevin for his birthday. Kevin wanted to surprise her but I told her to repeat "YOU DIDN'T HEAR IT FROM ME" but we are coming the Saturday after his birthday and not to tell his aunts. .... I am really becoming a SOFTY. You should have heard her, ... her voice was breaking saying that she misses him.... I know I got played.

Stephanie Brock

Lol! Shame on you! Giving up the surprise so easily ;-))It's lightning here like crazy. I love storms, and the smell and sound of the rain. I used to wash my hair in the rain when I was younger. I just love being wet like that. I still love being caught in the rain while going for a run.

Stephanie Brock

You and Kevin be safe. Why the name Kevin? Family name?

Rufus Turnbull

It's a name we both liked. We would speak to him while he grew inside her.

Stephanie Brock

So sweet.

Rufus Turnbull

How are the flowers?

Stephanie Brock

What flowers?

Rufus Turnbull

Oh boy. ...I'm really messing up. .... you did receive the strawberries, right?

Stephanie Brock

What strawberries? Nope.

Rufus Turnbull

I'm confused.

Stephanie Brock
What are you confused about?

Rufus Turnbull
The reason I asked you if you liked strawberries is I sent you flowers and Chocolate covered Strawberries. ...I placed the order on Monday and they guaranteed delivery today at your studio.
Your email said that you liked chocolate covered strawberries so I naturally assumed that you received them.

Stephanie Brock
Do you know where my studio is?

Rufus Turnbull
Hold on. ....2831 E Oakland Park Blvd Suite 7?

Stephanie Brock
Yes, I love strawberries, but I was just answering your question.

Rufus Turnbull
And instead of your website telephone number, I provided your cell phone number for the delivery....... I'm bummed

Stephanie Brock
What address did you send it to? I closed my studio on Monday, because it was the first day of school. But no delivery notice or anything at studio on Tuesday.

Rufus Turnbull
2831 E Oakland Park Blvd Suite 7.

Stephanie Brock
Yes, that's the address.

Rufus Turnbull
It was supposed to be delivered today.

Stephanie Brock
Ok...I am smiling so big, even though I didn't get it. My son just walked in and asked...why are you smiling so much!

Rufus Turnbull
You are getting that too from your son. .... lol......I'm actually hiding in my office.

Stephanie Brock

Well, you are a big softy!!! You could have played it better. Lol!!! You are sooooo Sweet!

Rufus Turnbull

I wanted them to be unexpected, for you to have a daunting look as you receive them....and when you saw the Chocolate covered Strawberries, you would have figured it out.

Stephanie Brock

I think that still might happen. I'm now biting my thumb nail, smiling, with an elevated heartbeat.

Rufus Turnbull

I am checking my email history and everything seemed right. I SO wanted this to be a flawless surprise......biting your thumb? .... LOL.

Stephanie Brock

Flawless? No matter what, it's crazy sweet!!!

Rufus Turnbull

I am bummed out, but .... next time. .... the element of surprise is gone.

Stephanie Brock

You must be the most adorable man EVER! I would give you the biggest hug right now.

Rufus Turnbull

Hmmm....ACCEPTED.

Stephanie Brock

;-))

Rufus Turnbull

I just felt the urge when I peruse your IMPRESSIVE website and saw the pic with the flowers. ....and I remembered you telling me that you had Ice Cream for breakfast. .... thus the strawberries.

Stephanie Brock

Please don't be bummed out. I'm going to have the most amazing thoughts about you tonight ;-))

Did you see my video? I had no voice left after filming all day.

Rufus Turnbull

The one this morning? ....is viewing it 5 or 6 times enough?

Stephanie Brock

Lol! No. The workout video on Brockpilates.com

Rufus Turnbull

Where?

Stephanie Brock
On my website. It shows what I do.

Rufus Turnbull
Watching it now. https://www.youtube.com/watch?v=vDOfVYZ542s

Stephanie Brock
Cool.

Rufus Turnbull
Way Cool....how did I miss it.... I was just focusing on my surprise. .... thanks for pointing the video out to me. Anyway I wrote you another 'installation' last night.

Aug 27, 2015

Rufus Turnbull
GOOD MORNING, It's very early as I lay in bed with a ridiculous smile on my face. I am thinking on what could have been if my surprise was flawlessly executed, but I won't dwell on what could have been; I will find out what happened to the flowers and endure.

Now your video greeting yesterday was flawless. I saw the video file in the text queue, but could not immediately view nor listen because my son was with me in the Hummer and the Bluetooth had connected to the car audio system. Then on the barge I still was not able to. (The picture I took yesterday where he was reclined with both of us smiling) I was trying to disconnect the Bluetooth and connect to the headset around my neck. I decided to wait until we got to St. John and send him into the convenient store for our usual chocolate muffins.......then, there you were, with your voice greeting me through the car audio and video on my phone. I felt a warm giddy feeling inside and simply smiled.

As I am still lying here, having just listened to Sade, Seal, and Roberta Flack as the music softly played from the ceiling speakers ....it planted seeds of thoughts in my mind to plan future surprises in only the way I can pull off....

Anyway, the storm is eminent as I hear the wind gusts outside as it travels nearer. I'm thankful it's a weak Tropical Storm and await the blessing in the form of rain.

Stephanie Brock
Rufus, thank you so much for sharing important stories of your life.

August 28, 2015

Rufus Turnbull

GOOD MORNING, I sent you a short email greeting

Stephanie Brock

Hi. I read your email and it prompted me to share something with you. Only my son has seen it.

Now...when you laugh, just remember that I'm not Spanish. Remember I grew up a preacher's daughter, and I did not even hear the 'Devil's' music until I left home. And... I took a few private lessons last Christmas from a Russian ballet professional. Ok...now you may laugh!!!

Rufus Turnbull

WHO ARE YOU KIDDING. ...what did you say. .... if I recall...you weren't very good. ...Are you Kidding me.????. You are AMAZIN. I am being honest. The only difference is the music. Authentic Salsa basically adds another dimension...

Stephanie Brock

The best thing is that I had so much fun! I felt goofy, but free. My teacher was always trying to teach me to let go and trust the man's lead. The videos are hard to see. But they always get low. I think my legs are too long.

Rufus Turnbull

You are too critical.... honestly.... Your legs aren't too long; your dance partner was too short.

Stephanie Brock

Lol! Ok, I'll stop. I know, I need to loosen up, let go. Ok, I'm on the motherf#*%! (Pulp fiction Lol!)

Rufus Turnbull

Exactly, now I have incentive to be a lot better.

Stephanie Brock

Now I do. I'm looking for a class now.

Rufus Turnbull

Great. ...I am actually getting excited, really. The storm hasn't arrived yet, but it's eerily dark outside for this time of the evening. I cut my thumb on a very sharp knife. I told Kevin if I was still playing music in the evening I would have to improvise. Then I told him of a t...

Stephanie Brock

Oh no. Is it a surface cut?

Rufus Turnbull

The cut is a ½ inch perpendicular cut across my thumb. happened right before you texted.

Stephanie Brock

My neighbor just brought over fresh caught dolphin. Any suggestions Island Chef?

Rufus Turnbull

Lol....never had dolphin. ...is the meat similar to Salmon, ...Kevin told me I am getting too creative. ...he prefers my 'boring' salmon. ... .no mushrooms, no sauce.

Stephanie Brock

deep?

Rufus Turnbull

Kinda .... took a while to stop bleeding. ...can't practice my bass tonight fearing it might open

Stephanie Brock

If deeper than 1/2 inch you need to see a Dr. Or if the blood keeps flowing after applying pressure, again see a Dr. Is it still crazy dark out? Good idea, no bass;-))

Rufus Turnbull

Thanks Doctor. ...it's the calm before the storm. We expect a lot of rain and possibly power outages. I hate night time storms. I am programming a new receiver downstairs in the theater.

Stephanie Brock

Have you listened to Esperanza Spalding/Bassist.? I went to see her when she was performing in Miami. She is an amazing performer.

Rufus Turnbull

Yes, I know Esperanza Spalding. ...incredible talent.

Stephanie Brock

When you finish up...explain. What's a receiver? Ok. Sounds like you are speaking a whole different language (the receiver) Hurts my brain. But thanks ;-)) Cool space though.

Rufus Turnbull

Laffing. ...but simply put, if someone is building a house with several televisions, music in several rooms, automated lighting, blinds, shades, or curtains......any low voltage control. ...they would need someone like me. I know you said that you don't have televisions, so I have concluded that you watch Netflix on a tablet or computer. So do you listen to music similarly?

Stephanie Brock

I listen to music on Pandora on the weekends. I just started using Netflix on the weekends. I just discovered Scandal with Kerry Washington. I really like her. But I finished all 4 seasons in a weekend! And I just got my first laptop a few

149

days ago. I just never thought I needed it. I've always just read a lot. I must say I'm enjoying the laptop. Natalee, my friend, just introduced me to Gregory Porter. I can just listen to him and write while listening.

Stephanie Brock

I've read your email twice already. Once this morning around 5:15 or so, and again just now. I usually don't read emails or text in the early morning, as I have my own agenda and I don't want to be sidetracked into someone else's. But, when I see your name come up... (Rufus St. Thomas), I can't wait to open and relish in your words, as you bring a smile to my face. As I place my open hand lightly on my lower abdomen, my gut... I'm super pleased that our paths have bridged.

Rufus Turnbull

I hope your day was gratifying. It's 3:30 and we are bracing for the storm. Concerned in-laws calling to see what's happening over here. Kevin is doing laundry as I edit a Facebook Post I wrote back in March that I thought was funny and can also give you further insight personality wise. By the way, the flowers snafu was my mistake. I failed to respond to a notification from my credit card requesting confirmation about the transaction. I sent you the same floral arrangement today that you should receive, but the chocolate covered strawberries require a 2-day lead time. I reserve the right to send those on a date unbeknownst to you. (I am smiling with my EYES).

Aug 29, 2015

Rufus Turnbull

How was your day?

Stephanie Brock

I'm feeling a bit out of sorts today. I had a pretty busy day at the studio, even though it's still summer. Most of my clients return at the end of September. I feel kind of lonely today, maybe because I'm talking with you. To compensate, I'm eating too many frozen blueberries and dark chocolate chips ;-)) I'm seriously out of control with this new snack lol! Yummy!

Rufus Turnbull

Good morning, to maintain our privacy I edited your video and added Latin Jazz... ONLY people with the link below can view it. I did it this way because the file was too large to send with the email. I will delete it after you view it...

Stephanie Brock

Wow! I enjoyed watching that. The music does make the moves look better. Thank you.

Rufus Turnbull

How many times am I going to say that you are an amazing dancer......hmmm, every time I look at the video. But when you dance to the authentic music and you feel the CLAVE, (that's the 3-2 polyrhythm), with your foundation, you will find yourself feeling like you are floating while dancing. .... I can recommend any song via Rhapsody

Have a great day. ...I have a joke to tell you later.

Rufus Turnbull

You thought I was going to laugh at your video I truly loved it.

BUT I forgot my niece recorded me on the cruise with my phone upside-down, so I had to record my phone with my iPad in the correct orientation. ...and I forgot all about it.

This video is Public because I need my 15 fans to see. .... (I am a NUT) WARNING. ...don't Drink and Watch; you will spit it out https://youtu.be/9sv4ohtBcTE

Stephanie Brock

Ok...you were right! I'm laughing so hard. The tears are rolling down my face. You are too funny! You are the best!!!

Rufus Turnbull

Is it normal to sleep smiling? Well I have been up since 2am on Storm Watch. It's 5am now and the winds have died down and it's quiet outside. I tried to fall asleep but I just laid in bed smiling about a lovely lady that has touched my heart. ......and a DAMN GOOD DANCER. Stephanie, I am competitive as hell. And if my son thinks I embarrassed him dancing in Home Depot last week telling folks, "I'm not with him" I'm going to be practicing Overtime to make sure I am ready for you. You have another wonderful day Sweetheart. ...can I call you that?

Stephanie Brock

Well alright then...I'll practice also. I have some Latin dance DVDs. I'm going to dust them off today.

I haven't located an authentic Latin dance studio in Ft. Lauderdale yet. There are plenty in Miami. I'll keep searching. How's your cut? How long is the storm watch on for? You are so polite, well read, a great writer and communicator, you are an artist (musician, dancer, tech genius), you are a great dad, and a good looking man. And plenty more...I am sure. I am honored to have met you. I just love being in this space with you right now. You can call me Sweetheart whenever you choose to. I'm smiling...again.

Aug 30, 2015

Rufus Turnbull

Good Afternoon Stef, how was the calories you are about to BURN at your next class (the Burger) .... LOL... If you are such a FOODie, on the Tom Joyner Cruise they have signature hamburgers.... It's DaBomb. I actually selected the cruise ship for our recent trip in July because it had those burgers for Kevin- not for the destination- the cruise left Miami - St. Thomas and Puerto Rico was on the itinerary. (not all of Carnival's Cruise ships have that burger restaurant) I had nine for the week- he had 12. I am actually enjoying the house to myself as I get a lot of paperwork done with NPR in the background. Can't wait to talk to you later

Stephanie Brock

"I BURN Calories for a living". ;-)) Doing my ab workout. My business partner thinks that I need to start advertising what I do at my studio with short exercise examples weekly. So I filmed one today with my iPhone. Not sure how I feel about it. I've always had problems promoting myself and I'm crazy private. But, she keeps reminding me that I'm running a business. She also thinks I should do the no makeup/sweaty look like in this video. Definitely not sure about that one! Lol!

Rufus Turnbull

First of all, YOU'RE AMAZING. ... (there goes that word again) ....2nd, your partner is correct, but no make-up is your personal preference- and mine I must admit, but realistically, your partner is correct again. The solution to your privacy concerns is to hire a Stand-In ......hmmm......I'm cheap, and I would definitely need Traction afterwards.

Rufus Turnbull

Bilge Watching. I must admit, I am a media whore. Don't Judge Me. I have all of the 22 James Bonds movies, have the old and new Mission Impossible series. My video library is extensive. My music library is similar, both physical and digital. I used to buy CD's as fast as my favorite artists would produce, but I listen to the TUNEIN APP via my home control system for radio content and I prefer Rhapsody instead of Spotify. Rhapsody is a paid service ...$10/month to actually play any song on demand instantaneously. I have the $15/month which allows for 3 different streams (everyone in the family could simultaneously listen to different music on demand, and save music files on their devices if you don't have Internet. ...like on some airplanes. Access to over 10 million Devil's music.

I am ashamed to admit I am Smaughing....smile - laughing when you tell me you have been recently introduced to something

Stephanie Brock

My son thinks I am so behind the times. He even wants me to get out of the house on weekends. If I had a safe place with great music to go dancing, I'd certainly go. I know I'm an old soul. I used to try to be different, but I've accepted it. I also realize that having a youthful, in the now, spontaneous soul is good for me. Balance is best. I was just speaking to my Mom. She is so afraid I'm going to end up alone with a bunch of little dogs to keep me company. Then I'll die, and all the little dogs will have me for dinner. My mother watches a lot of Lifetime movies. Lol! She reminds me constantly that my son will soon be leaving.

Rufus Turnbull

Laffing. ...that's funny. ...I think our paths were meant to cross, if just for what we have right now. ...as far as the bunch of dogs are concerned, if this keeps up after our sons make us empty-nesters, I hope to make your mom wrong

Stephanie Brock

Just you, making me smile is so big. Besitos Papi

Rufus Turnbull

Hablas poquito también, aye mami......suki suki now

Stephanie Brock

Really? You know I don't understand that. ;-))

Rufus Turnbull

My best friend is in Miami going to the Cleveland Clinic for his annual physical. My insurance was changed so I am now primarily in the Caribbean network, but I used to go to the Cleveland Clinic with him. We both need to have colonoscopies, but I criticize our local doctor as the B and C medical students. I am going to have him ask the clinic the costs because I know it's cheaper up there and request reimbursement. ......another excuse to travel...

Stephanie Brock

Sounds absolutely fabulous!

Rufus Turnbull

Am I keeping you up too late?

Stephanie Brock

Nope. I'm in bed.

Rufus Turnbull

Cool, I am still downstairs. .... it's only drizzling. This Receiver is kicking my butt.... programming wise......now it gets personal. Also even though your dance video is low resolution, I am going to transfer it to my network storage and try to learn your instructor's moves...and then stream the video to the projector. ... (smiling)

Stephanie Brock

I was just going to ask you about the Receiver thing. So no storm yet. Good news.

Rufus Turnbull

It's coming. ...hold on......Question, how many people have you told about me?

Stephanie Brock

Really? You can just watch him and learn? You know... I am seriously thinking about closing for Labor Day, and also the Friday before. And just staying home and watching Netflix and eating pasta

Rufus Turnbull

Labor Day weekend I actually have no plans

Stephanie Brock

Drinking a really good Cabernet.
My best friend thinks I need some 'veg out' time.
I told my two closest friends. Heather and Natalee.

Stephanie Brock

I tell them everything. They're my truth serum. They keep me honest. And they want the very best for me...ALWAYS!

Rufus Turnbull

I told Milton in an email because he has been busy with government work and he left Tennessee today - he was in an insurance conference, now in Weston until Saturday. I told him that I needed perspective. We actually have dinner once a month on the waterfront just to shoot the breeze. I told him that we both have our sons and I will not pressure you into anything that will make you feel uncomfortable.

Stephanie Brock

It's so important to have someone that you can trust, and that loves you enough to tell you the truth. And in turn, you love them enough to know that they want what's best for you.

Rufus Turnbull

Agreed. I basically kept him at ease about the storm while his wife was erratic. But he knows my personality where I can be completely honest with him. He actually said that long distance is a problem for many, but he knows not for me.

Stephanie Brock

You can't pressure me Rufus. We all do just what we want to do. Although sometimes we'd like to say, 'I was forced.' ;-)) Yes, I have my son. Yes, you have Kevin. We love them as we love our very lives. And for me...I like you very much. Sounds weird, since I've not touched you, smelled you, or tasted you. Oh well...I can't help what I feel. I no longer deny myself, my own truth. I go with my flow, my heart. What is meant to go, will go. What is meant to stay, will stay. Thinking I have some form of control, is delusive. I only think of your time to heal.

Rufus Turnbull

My phone service just went out. ...I initially thought you were asleep. I guess the cellular towers are being stressed. I TOO like you very much, ...I am not the kinda guy who is afraid to wear his emotions on his sleeve. At this point in my life I know what turns me On and Off....and I really would love to introduce you to as much Devil's Music as you can stand. .... LOL

Rufus Turnbull
I dozed off and was awoken by something hitting the house. It's very windy outside. The wind is continuous but no rain.

I love your video greetings and I think you are wonderful, really. We are on curfew because of the storm even though the was no damage on St. Thomas, but St. Croix got a direct hit and power outages. After a damage assessment is performed I think the curfew will be lifted for St. Thomas later.

Stephanie, you are constantly on my mind and trying to make sense of it simply show that our spirits were seeking joy.

CHAPTER THIRTEEN

"If a man shows interest, don't make it easy on him."

THEIR COMMUNICATION NEVER WAVERED. Rufus would text a brief greeting of inspiration in the mornings and at times writing something extra to make her smile. Later she would respond and every now and again, she would forward a video testimonial before or after going to her studio while in her car that were poignant, unrehearsed and at times purposely devised to beguile. Later after both cooked dinner and their boys were settled, they found seclusion in their homes and talk until 8pm. In essence, that was their weekdays.

The weekends began with brief salutations in the mornings but the evenings were marathon phone calls lasting several hours. They seemingly had no problem with subjects to discuss. Initially she just allowed Rufus to talk; he openly discussed the grief he was experiencing similarly like he did with his anonymous Facebook friend from China. Although Stephanie was for all intents and purposes 'semi-anonymous', there was undoubtedly an affinity slowly being forged.

At first it wasn't notable because of the distance between them being considerable, at least from Stephanie's point of view. But as the frequency and the consistency in which they communicated continued, the dynamics changed the more she learned about him.

She knew that she was not going to travel to the islands - that was a nonstarter. But she also learned that he had long distance relationships in his past - including one in Miami - and his most recent lasted a quarter century. That was noble and should be congratulated in these modern times. But her natural instincts were to always protect herself emotionally and put up psychological barriers when she questioned, "why should she be so lucky?" Her positive thoughts started to prevail when she actually began to really consider whether Rufus was the proverbial manifestation of that new request for Peace that she asked of the universe. She gave subtle hints that her interest was becoming more than platonic and knew that he was feeling the same way too. And after almost a month of long distance communication, her heart now wanted more.

Her celibacy for a year so far was not a ruse to scare away potential suitors when they were duly informed, in fact it was another means of reorganizing her warehouse. She engaged in fasts and cleansing practices to free her mind and body of the desires that inexorably caused contention in her life three times before. Having been down that road of high expectations with men who did not fully understand that her son came first was emotionally exhausting when those relationships all came to precipitous ends. The thought that one actually considered buying two apartments in close proximity or in the same building where she and her son could live in one and she and him could live nearby in the other still boggles her mind. But those accounts were now in her past and that's exactly where she wanted them to remain. As a result of her new quest for peace, she again has been doing all of the right things. But in her thoughts at night she considered whether this new experience was truly the atonement in her continuing journey. And at the same time she questioned everything even though what she was feeling felt so right. The mere thought gave her a nervous feeling of trepidation. The following day her nervousness was apparent when she forwarded the following video testimonial. [Verbatim from the vlog]
https://vimeo.com/334193573

Stephanie VLOG

"Hi, ... I am, in my car getting ready to leave the studio right now, and I thought about you, and I thought I'd just say Hi......so....... Hi......Umm.........I was also thinking about - you know - the whole storm thing, and hope that everything is umm ... panning out well with that, and you know - fingers crossed [crossing her fingers] that nothing really happens with that ... umm ... and, other than that - you know - I hope you guys are doing well ... and I just wanna say Hi. And umm....... You know I find myself... really thinking about you a lot, and I find myself really wanting to... you know, umm - talk to you and ...Just last night I found myself .... (giggles) ...bla, bla, bla, bla ... I'm so tongue tied right now I don't know what's going on -...Okay, but I find myself wanting to actually ... **see you**.... okay- there it is ...it's out...(giggles), but mostly I *wanna say....... Hi, okay? And umm.............I'm thinking about you ......take care of yourself.... alright?.........Alright.........bye."*

Typically, when Rufus saw her video testimonials he would watch them repeatedly in succession two or three times. After he discovered and viewed this latest video, I actually lost count of how many times he looked at it. I was trying to ascertain what was going on. From my perspective, it was the first time she appeared slightly uneasy and she was definitely tongue tied which suggests some degree of nervousness. Then I realized he was concentrating particularly on two words and the facial expression that resulted from its utterance. It was endearing when she emphasized the words "see you" and was visually relief after. I instantly knew what he was going to do next. And I was going to help him pull it off.

I realized that in all of her relationships in her past, she has always been pursued romantically. From her ex-husband to the doctor on St. Croix and in between. And with the level of sophistication that she has garnered of late, romantic pursuits should predominantly be a male venture. I even overheard her telling her Jamaican girlfriend, "If a man shows interest, don't make it easy on him." She says that confidence is what she relishes most when she first meets someone of the opposite sex.

The situation with Rufus was different. He has a son and is navigating his new reality of being widowed and a single parent. He seems to be doing all of the right things. But although meeting online may suggest one's intent to date, she also considered whether he was emotionally ready for a relationship. Quite frankly, if his circumstances were different - if he was single and didn't have a son to care for regularly - their relationship would have probably dissolved having not met in almost a month.

She continued to recap that when they made contact his son was at his in-laws and they were just getting to know each other. In the process, both of them were traversing new territories. And after learning he was going to return to Florida in almost two months with his son to go to a football game in Miami, her video testimonial was another subtle invitation for him to change his plans.

After Rufus cooked dinner that afternoon, he made the necessary travel arrangements to visit Stephanie the weekend of Labor Day. When she suggested in an earlier text the possibility of closing on the Friday before Labor Day, it was a subtle hint that flew way under his radar. He used to taunt, "I am the smartest person I know." Grief withstanding is the only reason I doubt his slow judgement as I observe from the sidelines. But if this second hint didn't compute, quite frankly I would have to second guess the reasons why I fell in love with him immediately to tell the truth – you know I'm joking.

Consequently, the video link she forwarded earlier of her favorite Pink Floyd song "Wish You Were Here" in their communication was discounted because he thought the chord changes in the beginning were sophomoric and didn't even gave the song a chance and in essence failed to see the message. But the third clue - the Charmed - unlike the others – was up his proverbial alley. It was an A/V hint (Audio/Visual being an A/V technician). Hell, if he didn't get that hint his head really would need examination.

There was a very narrow window to make this happen seeing that Kevin was beginning his new school term very soon and while in school it would be literally impossible and frankly quite selfish. He figured that these last few days before school had to be leverage properly. They would see my family even though my mother didn't think she would see Kevin until the end of September for his birthday. Instead of flying over on Friday, they would travel a day earlier when he discovered that there was a 6:00am flight from San Juan and he could be in Fort Lauderdale by mid-morning. They would have two and a half days together thereafter returning on a 6pm flight back to San Juan and would overnight at my sister's and both would return on Labor Day. It couldn't be more perfect.

Rufus notified Stephanie of his plans that evening and she was ecstatic. She immediately thought about Kevin's welfare and was pleased how Rufus was able to orchestrate everything at that moment's notice. And accordingly for her mental scorecard, he definitely passed her subtle test. The following morning, he received the following precarious text.

Stephanie Brock

I'm crying as I write this. I'm scared. You feel like someone I've always wanted in my life. But, how can that be? How can I now have what I want? My heart had stopped singing. And now there's a little broken tune trying to make itself into a beautiful melody. You are the beautiful melody. I am the broken tune. Nothing that you say can 'weird me out'. I feel you. I see you. But mostly... I feel as if you see me. I smile now, at the thought of touching your hands.

Rufus Turnbull
This weekend will simply be confirmation for both of us.

The next morning, he forwarded the following email.

Stephanie,

I have been very introspective lately - for the reasons that you can assume because of how my life has changed this year. It makes me constantly question about what could have been. I see LIFE as a bunch of Lessons Learned from experiences. And for the 2nd half of my life I have learn to be open with my feelings from a wonderful woman. She would from time to time ask, "How do I look? Do you love me? Do I make you happy? And constantly, "How does my food taste?"

Early in our relationship, my answers were to simply affirm what I thought she wanted to hear. But the longer our relationship progressed, my answers became non-verbal where she would reply something to the effect like, "I needed to hear it or I needed to feel it, a girl always need confirmation." I say all of that to simply say, Stephanie, I LOVE EVERYTHING I HAVE LEARNED ABOUT YOU SO FAR and I was looking for a sign from you to see where you were and I got it when you were tongue-tied in your video greeting when you stated that you wanted to see me. In the back of my mind I thought waiting until the end of October to meet would have been arduous for both of us.

"Is it possible to fall in love with someone without meeting them?" That answer lies within that INDIVIDUAL's TRUTH.......and MY TRUTH is, I AM IN LOVE WITH THE ESSENCE OF YOU and I hope to be deeply in love with you after this weekend. I can't wait to see you, touch you and to Kiss you. Now that doesn't mean that what we discussed about our sons being our main priority would be changed. Let's strive to become the most compatible future empty-nesters.

Rufus

https://vimeo.com/334193426
Stephanie VLOG

Hi Rufus, how are you doing .... I was also thinking 'cause I was just, umm ... sitting and I was thinking ... I have no idea how we got to this point ... umm, you know umm ... I've fallen in love with you and I don't even know what happened ... and umm, but I want to say I'm really happy that umm, it's you ... and umm, that's it ... (giggles) ...

that's what I really want to say. So have aahh... Great Great Great amazing day for the rest of the day, okay. Bye!

August 31, 2015

Rufus Turnbull

Good morning Stephanie, for the record it is 5:30......last night's conversation made me feel so much joy- and I know you felt similarly. .... we were not lost for words, but we lost time....it felt like we talked for about 2hrs

Stephanie Brock

Good morning. Today is a great, new day! I am so thankful for today. Just the miracle of opening my eyes makes me smile. I have a chance to begin...again. A chance to be the best me that I can be. A chance to love again, laugh again, cry again... I am grateful. A chance to talk to you. I too, enjoyed last night and this morning ;-)) It was wonderful.

Rufus Turnbull

You DID laugh last night.... like no one was listening. ......that was great..."
...burn calories for a living "

Stephanie Brock

Rufus...I checked our phone time from last night. Ok...ready? 6 hours and 53min. That's seven hours!!! Can you believe it? And so pleasurable ;-))

Stephanie Brock

How are you feeling this morning, with very little sleep? I'm at my studio, my next session starts at 10am. I'm energized right now. I know I'll crash later with vanilla ice cream. If only I had a magical wand ;-))

Rufus Turnbull

LAFFING. ....to myself in line at the Post Office. The 3 1/2hrs of sleep wasn't adequate, but I'm good.

Stephanie Brock

Thoughts in my head. I'm still lying in bed. I want my coffee, but I'm not ready to rise from my comfort yet. I reach for my phone to check the time. That is what I tell myself. Really... I'm just checking to see if you are somewhere on my phone. I'm almost giddy when I see your name. It's still raining, I wonder what it would be like to have walked with you this morning. As I hear you catching your breath, I realize it would be a bit of a workout, especially with your strides being so much longer than mine. Of course, I'd like that, a more challenging walk for me, trying to keep up. I really like your smile. I like the joy you exude when talking about your life's experiences. I like the broadness of your shoulders. I caught that while watching you hit a step or two while singing karaoke. I like the fairness of your heart towards humans-natural-nature. Your honesty is beyond compare. I like that deeply, heartfelt love that you had/have for your wife. That's a heart I'd like to touch. Really...just put my hand on your chest, and breathe with its beat

Stephanie Brock
You feel kind of extraordinary.

Rufus Turnbull
I'm talking to Milton on my landline... (340)555-1212...can I call you in a few? I just read your message. ...my heart is also affected by you.

Stephanie Brock
Hi. On the phone with my Mom ;-))

Rufus Turnbull
Yeah yeah ...your phone can Text and Talk.

Stephanie Brock
Call soon. iPhone abilities!!!!
More like text and listen...I never get a word in ;-))

Rufus Turnbull
I'm sorry. .... I AM a great rememberer....and listener. ...BTW, check your email.

Stephanie Brock
Hi. I just watched the cruise videos. Oh my...that's serious business. I'm going to wash my son's uniforms for tomorrow and do some much needed cleaning. Of course, I'd rather be talking to you. What time are you picking Kevin up today? Hopefully we will have a few minutes to talk later? If not, I understand. Big day tomorrow! Is he excited about starting school tomorrow?

Rufus Turnbull
He goes to school next week. I'm arriving in Fort Lauderdale at 9am on Friday I just tried to call you.

Stephanie Brock
Good night.

Rufus Turnbull
You too sweetheart.

September, 1, 2015

Rufus Turnbull
Good morning Stephanie,

This morning I awoke around 3:30- I got my 5hrs okay? - and I decided to do the 3 ½ mile trek around the neighborhood. Moments later there was a torrential rain and I thought it would sidetrack my morning workout, so I laid in bed and read 1/2 of a short book Milton gave me and thoughts of you abound. A half hour later the rain stopped so I dawned the usual walking/running/biking outfit and made a bottle of citrus water and by 4:30 I was out the door. It was dark, cool, peaceful, and for the next hour the streets were mine.

As I explained earlier to you, what makes this walk uniquely effective for me are the drastic change in elevation with the decline and incline of the road. The first 5 minutes starts as a slow rise before descending drastically about 300ft in 5 minutes. The difference today was the road was wet and I had to switch back and forth as I walked or sideways whenever I felt myself losing my footing. Now I won't embarrass myself trying to find the proper muscle group that was burning under my biker short (that's your department) but my front thighs were now awake. And because I had to be cautious, that decent took twice the time as usual.

I am on the lower road now where it leveled for 5 minutes and slowly inclined for another five. I am enjoying the Salsa in my ear and walking at a cadence. Then came the BEAST. I checked my phone to show it was 5:am as I stared at the 40-to-60-degree incline. I remembered the 1st time I walked this beast I stopped several time to catch my breath. This morning it took 10 minutes as the entire length of the back of my legs- to include my calves- were stretched as I smiled saying to myself, "what goes DOWN, must come back up." When I leveled my heart rate increased and my breathing was audible. The worst was over I used to tell myself years ago, today I simply measure whether if I am gasping or breathing normally. I recall when I did damage to my body when I first began this walk because I could walk or run anywhere without any adverse effect. I never hydrated before nor after and I constantly complained about sharp pains in my lower back by my kidneys. My doctor at the Cleveland Clinic recommended a litany of tests and an appointment with a sports medicine doctor on staff, and an emergency MRI because I had to return home to work and they found nothing wrong with me. Six months I am back and still no resolution.

Then I was at the Ritz Carlton working and I met their new Spa manager and we were casually talking about the music system I installed and I brought to his attention my lower back issue. He recommended a deep tissue massage and I had a curious look because I thought one thing had nothing to do with the other. So I said what the heck, made a date with Christine that weekend. The manager was my therapist and to shorten a long story, he said my muscles contracted too quickly *which suggest I ingested minimal amounts of liquid in my diet. I begged to differ while he continued as I described my early morning walks and I immediately realized that I drank no water before, during and after the walks. He then explained further that's when the body needs it most. He even showed me how his body responded to a technique he performed to his thigh and compared how mine reacted.*

A week later I am on a lower impact walk and liquid diet and within 2 weeks the pain was absolutely gone. I realized I was getting older and my body isn't what it used to be. Milton accuses me of Self-Diagnosing now when I tell him I know how my body feels when I FEEL GOOD and when I don't, I compare what I do from time to time and make the necessary adjustment. Anyway, I did my 55-minute walk in 65 minutes because of the rain condition hazard and I was completely drenched before showering. That is my typical morning workout during the week.

YOU HAVE YOUR USUAL AMAZING DAY.

Rufus

Stephanie Brock

I love reading every word that you write. I have a serious affinity toward great writing/writers. Just your power to express emotions on the page, piecing together letters to tell stories. Your writing makes me weak in the knees.

Rufus Turnbull

Blame - or I should say - credit my writing to thousands of hours listening to Audio Books. I am at the Clinic trying to obtain a physical copy of Kevin's Immunization records. I am not used to waiting for stuff like this, but it's a necessary inconvenience.... lol.

Later in the day Stephanie called to tell Rufus that in preparations for his visit, she was considering how best to spend the weekend together and asked about his preferences in foods and particularly spirits. She texted him a pic of her preferred Belgian Ale and asked him what was his favorite beer. Rufus' response was to sing the chorus of a very old jingle of a Puerto Rican beer commercial he'd memorized in Spanish that states:

"Cerveza Schaefer, es la mejor cuando se toma más de una." [Schaefer, is the, one beer to have, when you're hav-ing more than one!] https://www.youtube.com/watch?v=7L6DZfVC7mc Personally, I was very proud of him like a school teacher would be in Spanish class. She on the other hand immediately thought he was batty remarking that she never heard of it. He told her that all she probably drank was "pretty bottle beers." That comment prompted her to send him her most provocative video testimonial.

https://vimeo.com/334193019
Stephanie VLOG

"Good Morning.... (giggles and smile), I see...... that ... you just wanna 'throw down'... right? I cannot believe you're putting down my beer choices like that - like I'm some kinda 'lil Girlie-Girl'... You know, I might look like a lil Girlie Girl, but I'm 'Straight-Up Jock!'... (giggles, smiled, a pause to get into character to 'spit' the following rhyme) ...you know what I'm sayin'.... DON'T MESS WITH THE BEST CAUSE THE BEST DON'T MESS, DON'T FOOL WITH THE COOL CAUSE THE COOL DON'T FOOL.... WHAT? (gangster scowl) ... (she resumed demurely while twirling her hair) Send me a choice, ... or send me three... of your favorite beer choices, okay? .... we gotta do some thangs ...alright? ... alright ....BYE!*

I observed that after he saw that video, he replayed it more often than the 'subtle invitation' video. He was enjoying how effortlessly she changed character in that brief thirty seconds in her car. Consequently, all of her video testimonials - a dozen or thereabout so far - were all recorded in her car. This particular one was like she produced her own infomercial. He was so enthralled that he had to share that video with Milton. He told him the backstory that resulted her response. So seldom missing a beat and with their one-ups-man scorecard keeping both honest, Milton's simple retort was quite timely when he said,

"Rufus, you know you don't know NUTHIN 'bout beers."

They both enjoyed the comment which from time to time he repeats. To that point, Milton had only seen one picture of Stephanie prior to this video and his following comment was emblematic of their friendship and the degreed education he had attained.

"Christine was a quality woman and you deserve nothing less."

September 2, 2015

Stephanie

Hi I just finished up. Just saw your message. If you're still available. Please call. I'm driving.

Rufus

Car is reserved, ...I thought I had dropped the ball when I couldn't find my airline reservations, ...I almost had a conniption. . ....I'm good.

Stephanie

Just saw your video three times. I'm still smiling. I enjoyed watching you talk.

Rufus

I know what you mean. ...I am looking at your smile, (the twinkle in your) eyes, your hands.... it's just so invigorating that you can make me feel so happy....... I forgot, you Burst-A-Rhyme too, with ATTITUDE

After talking on the phone about seeing the Tap video she sent he texted....

Rufus

Be nice or be truthful?

Stephanie

Lol! First time in taps! Shut^....My son said I'm creeping him out!

Rufus

Okay. ...You PAID for the Tap Shoes so far.... NOT for the Lessons. .... I'm just sayin.

Stephanie

Come on! Encourage me......Don't make me cut another step. I'll show you what I've learned on Friday ;-))

Rufus

You will be Great...I mean it.... we will encourage each other.

Stephanie

Yes, we will. Thank you ;-))

Rufus

Good night sweetheart, I am programming the replacement receiver downstairs. Kevin wants to know why there are different types of beer in the refrigerator. He hates fruits so I hid the chocolates in the fruit chiller in the refrigerator. He prefers raw vegetables: celery, carrots...weird kid. ... he got that from Christine.

Stephanie

I'm taking another shower. When I think of you coming I get butterflies. So I'm going to warm my body under the steaming rain of my shower. Sweet dreams Dearest Rufus.

Rufus

I'm smiling at your words

September 3, 2015

Stephanie

Good morning. Thoughts of you in the early morning, floating through my mind. Safe travels today.

Rufus

Thanks sweetie, getting back from my walk. I'm an even keel kinda guy, now I'm really getting excited.

Stephanie

I feel the need to organize our Friday. You have to see your Mom. I pick my son up from school at 4pm. He goes to his Dad's around 7pm until late Sunday. Ok...my thoughts......Breakfast when you arrive. Hang out together until it's time to pick up my son. You then go to Miami to your Mom??? Evening. Let me know your thoughts. So then I can change my work morning to be with you. We have dinner that evening

Rufus

Sounds perfect We're at the airport waiting for our flight. It's a 25-minute flight.

I'm in Puerto Rico

Stephanie

I'm happy you two are safe. Thank you for keeping me in the loop. Enjoy dinner. My tap class starts at 7pm. I'm meeting Heather at her home at 6:20. Then we will ride together from there. I'm so excited.

Rufus

With my Mother-in-law and Kevin at the restaurant ...the waiter was surprised that Kevin and I knew the menu with our accents...... We are chatting and they just reserved a car service to pick me up at 4am

Stephanie

Rufus, I just got home from my first tap class. I was so amazingly goofy! The instructor even started laughing. It was so much fun! I'll be more loose

next Thursday. I'm excited about seeing you. Going to shower, then bed. Sweet
dreams Dear Rufus.

On the evening of my passing seven and a half months ago Rufus
was lying in the same bed in my sister's condo in Puerto Rico unable to fall
asleep which was somewhat poetic. And because of the chocolate covered
strawberries snafu, he purchased an assortment of chocolates that are
made daily and exquisitely package from the local chocolatier The
Chocolate Factory on St. Thomas. He had to forego the flowers because it
would have call into question why he was going to Florida. He simply told
my family that he was going to visit his mother.

September 4, 2015

Rufus
Good morning Free Spirit, I awoke at 2am after about 4hrs of sleep. Today is
going to be one of the most anticipated days in my life. I hid your beer-truce
[chocolates] in my sister-in-law's freezer. No chance of anyone finding it there
because there wasn't much of anything in it. She hardly cooks. Now I see what
Kevin meant when he said that he had nothing to work with when he stays
there when he wants to make an omelet.

Stephanie
My body has awakened me. I'm sure it's just to say "Good morning" to you.
I'll try to sleep more, before its time for me to wake my son for his morning
routine, then breakfast and school.

Rufus
I'm waiting for my ride to the airport and I will chat with you from the cocoon
of the terminal.
BTW, I have already named your video greetings: my favorites are 'Tongue-
tied' and 'Don't Mess with the Best.'

Stephanie
Good morning Rufus.
Today is September 4, and I'll see you soon. I'm smiling.

Rufus
Good morning.... I thought that notification from my phone was you. ...can't
wait to finally see you.

Stephanie

I'm probably fooling myself...thinking I'll sleep more. I wanted to look fresh upon seeing you. But, I didn't even close my eyes until around midnight and now I'm awake already. Darn it!

I do want to make sure that we are on the same page. I'm going to the studio to train an 8am client, then I'll meet you for breakfast. (I have a place in mind), then I'd like to take you to my studio, then introduce you to my home. Now, if I'm correct you are renting a car at the airport? So I can send you the address of the breakfast place. You will let me know when you have the car, so I'll know when to leave the studio to meet you for breakfast. How does that sound? Your thoughts please.

Rufus
I'm at the airport.

I will confirm when I am at the gate. I was preoccupied with TSA, now that I have read your message. .... you are so organized.... plans sound perfect......When I travel I always text each leg of my trip. .... I did not combine your message with my mom's, in-laws and Kevin.

"At the gate"

"On the plane"

Stephanie
Safe travels ;-))

Rufus
See you in 3, or at least I will be in Fort Lauderdale in 3 hrs. Even though there is a personal TV for each passenger, I'm going to watch STEF-TV....your vlog greetings.

"Landed"

Stephanie
Hi there. You ready? ;-))) So happy that you are safely here. Breakfast?

Pelican Grand Beach Resort
2000 North Ocean Blvd
Fort Lauderdale, FL, US 33305

Rufus
Still on the plane.

Stephanie
Hi. Are you still on the plane?

Rufus

Just got my car. ...another Camaro.

Stephanie

Cool................... Red?...................I'm heading over now

Rufus

This time Black.

CHAPTER FOURTEEN

"When you look at me, tell me what do you see?" Then like a skilled
prosecutor in court she added, "And don't tell me I'm beautiful."

I N THE SAME MANNER RUFUS documented the moments leading up to and after his operation sixteen years ago, he also wrote a journal which is the continuation of the Prologue from his perspective about finally meeting Stephanie.

So here I was, in the lobby of the Pelican Beach Hotel waiting with anticipation. I asked two hostesses at the restaurant if someone was waiting for me inside when I provided my name. They suggested that I go inside and see for myself. Upon my return, they told me to go to the lobby where the cell phone service was better and try calling my date from there. I thanked them for their assistance and proceeded back from whence I came.

I'd traversed less than twenty feet when from the corner of my left eye, she seemed to be walking in slow motion exiting the restroom as her facial expression quickly changed from indecision with a quick hesitation, to recognition where smiles met both of our eyes. I was immediately taken aback seeing how impeccably dressed she was for breakfast: Curly flowing black mane gathered without professional restraint via a simple hair clip that allowed her hair to partially flow over a shoulders and down the small of her back. Thin strapped white linen dress accentuating what was visibly pleasing. It draped to mid-thigh, thus equally framing her shapely torso and long shapely legs that were accessorize with designer heels. Her almond shaped eyes seem to immediately light up as their corners twinkled to make my eyes duly smile.

Synonymous to airport arrival greetings, without hesitation or dispensation, we embraced between the hotel's lobby and the restaurant's entry as *our faces grew closer while we beamed continuously and unassumingly kissed totally oblivious to our surroundings. Passersby incorrectly assumed that we had known each other forever. Our mouths organically magnetized as a result of the huge smiles drawing our faces nearer until both our teeth met only to be cushioned by the soft touch of our lips. I hugged her dearly around the waist and felt how taunt her body felt from my embrace as she simultaneously wrapped her arms around my neck.*

At that moment I immediately thought that I had blown it based on how I was attired. Leaving the Luis Munoz Marin Airport in San Juan Puerto Rico at 6am where from time to time I would jokingly state to my friends that no infectious disease could survive in that airport terminal based on the temperature that felt sometimes like a frigid 50 degrees. With that in mind it led me to don black jeans and a heavy sweatshirt with a hoodie reminiscent of Isaac Hayes, aka the Black Moses. When I arrived at Fort Lauderdale International, I swapped the sweatshirt for a personalized New York Yankees jersey in the terminal restroom and thereafter obtaining a car rental where I followed the GPS directives from Stephanie's last text to the Pelican.

As our embrace released, I held her around her waist and whispered in her ear to declare,

"I am so underdressed", emphasizing on the word 'so.'

"No you're not," She immediately retorted.

I disagreed, complimented her on her attire and reverted to the moment as we remained comprised and enthralled staring into each other's eyes.

We remained standing embraced for a minute – which actually seemed like two, but really felt much longer when from the corner of my eye I saw the restaurants hostesses infectiously smiling at us which prompt me to whisper,

"I don't mind being a spectacle standing with you because nobody here knows me, but if we don't get our table we are quickly becoming spectacles."

So after escorting her to the now giddy hostesses, we were led through the restaurant to the outdoor covered patio dining where the Friday mid-morning sun was gloriously reflecting over the Atlantic Ocean. As we sat in adjoining chairs, I held her right hand with my left, as we complemented the sun's rays with the glint in our eyes and continuous smiles.

We hardly ate and we barely spoke, and if you didn't know better one would assume the breakfast date to be a disaster. But we had previously logged significant hours of conversation and hundreds of instant messages. The intensity of her stares were changing as her almond shaped eyes became more mysterious while I tried to discern what – if anything – was developing. Or rather I was over thinking what was going on and dismiss the peering as we were simply catching up with all of the live visual stimulations we were yearning for the past month.

On the way to her apartment, we made a pit stop at her Pilates Studio where I was able to discern a little more about her personality. In addition to being incredibly beautiful, she was equally competitive. She told me an anecdote about training football players when their cocky disposition prompted her to put them in their athletic places. They acted as if they were really in shape belittling the equipment. She then demonstrated a very difficult side-knife maneuver on the reformer still wearing her designer dress that humbled them. Then it was my turn. Oh boy. Without incriminating myself, I would just say that I really appreciated the challenge even though I told her in jest,

"I don't like you anymore."

"Nobody comes into my house and acts as if they run things" She concluded.

Then at her apartment, I was able to observe a little more. A shoe basket at the door, spotlessly clean planked wooden floor, and everything in its place. I also took note of a few things that were peculiar.

On her 5th floor balcony we snacked on crackers, Brie and her favorite imported beer and later she confided that in the first in a very long time she literally let down her hair. After a few hours of talking, she told me of the report she'd given to her girlfriend of this was the first in a very long time anyone had seen her without makeup. I attributed that decision was made after she thoroughly enjoyed the song I played and sang by the reggae artist Tarrus Riley's 'She's Royal'. https://www.youtube.com/watch?v=qGuLqe-NMKg Hell, I even showed her my version of a reggae skant dance.

Tarrus Riley Lyrics
"She's Royal"

No I, never been someone shy,
Until I seen your eyes ....
Still I had to try, yeah ....
Oh yes, let me get my words right and then approach you,
Woman I'll treat you like a man is supposed to,
You'll never have to cry, no ...

I know everyone can relate to when they find that special someone ...
She's royal, yeah so royal

And, I want her in my life.
I never knew anyone so one-of-a-kind, no...
The way she moves to her own beat,
She has the qualities of a queen, She's a queen
Ooo, - Ooo ... such a natural beauty,
No need no make-up to be a cutie
She's a queen, she's a queen ...
And when they ask what a good woman's made of,
She's not afraid and ashamed of, who she is,

She's royal yeah, so royal,
and I need her in my life,
I never knew anyone, so one of a kind,
Until the night that I see the light in your eyes,

I guess the lyric, "...such a natural beauty, no need no makeup to be a cutie." really struck a chord. In the subsequent weeks and months, she would make requests for me to sing acapella. I knew that my singing voice makes paint peel off walls. My voice was the reason why after hearing me sing at my first gig while I simultaneously played the bass in high school, our singers saw it was important to immediately learn the lyrics to ALL of the songs. My singing voice was the reason I never was allowed to be close to a microphone when I played with Priscilla and Company.

Then there was the moment on the small fifth floor balcony after we ate I considered held the most significance of the long date that began with an airline flight from the Caribbean. Face to face without any notice she simply asked of me pointedly,

"When you look at me, tell me what do you see?" Then like a skilled prosecutor in court she added, "And don't tell me I'm beautiful."

If this was a typical first date, I'd have to admit I would have failed miserably in answering her question. Additionally, if this was a first date, it would have definitely thrown me for a loop because everything was going so well up to that point and I didn't see it coming. If she hadn't added the caveat as a follow up, I would have been there like a moron stating the obvious. It was a litmus test of sorts guessing she'd heard those endearing terms several times before. But since the question was asked out of court like in a deposition - to my defense this wasn't a first date; it was the first time we met.

Our first, second, fourth and sixth dates were the long distance marathon phone calls from where both of us poured out our souls. We spoke for hours on end over the previous weekends. And on one occasion, we both fell asleep with the phone still open. We awakened simultaneously hours later the following morning and continued talking like as if we had spent our first night together.

So after all that have been said, it behooved me if I was not in the moment because I was. In my defense, I wasn't perplexed - not in the least. My response came without delay and forethought when I immediately replied,

"You look like a woman who needs to be appreciated."

To reiterate, the response came organically from the myriad of correspondences and text communications with this woman for almost a month on a daily basis. Initially and quite normally even though at times she had been enigmatic and guarded with her thoughts gradually opening up ever so slightly. On the other hand, I was a bleeding heart. In my immediate hindsight, not being able to see her in person was probably to my advantage in really getting to know her. The superficial was not allowed entry into my thoughts or conversation.

She was constantly judged by her looks and appearance and during the past weeks I got to know her cerebrally. So when I answered her question in the succinct manner I did, the expression in her eyes immediately changed to acceptance. Days later she told me that she replayed that moment in her mind over and over when I told her she looks like a woman who needs to be appreciated remarking that it was synonymous to the scene in the Jerry Maguire movie when Tom Cruise said,

"You complete me."

But I thought I had her at "Hello."

◆ ◆ ◆

Time escaped them when she realized that they had spent half of the Friday afternoon together and she had to leave to get her son from the bus stop now praying that the traffic won't cause much of a delay. She hadn't anything to worry because I can work my magic with the traffic lights so she could be there on time. They said their goodbyes and decided to meet again early the following day. Rufus drove away feeling very hopeful and happy.

While enroute to his mother's house, he knew his nosy sister Lena couldn't wait for her Ponche Kuba - I meant - to hear about the details of his day. He noticed that he had received a text message from Stephanie while meandering south on I-95 and purposely did not view it until he was off the highway. After parking he was smiling after reading her endearing message.

Stephanie

The chocolates are delicious! Thank you so much. Please be safe driving to Miami. Please don't drive too fast. :-) Today has been one of the best days of my life. Thank you for being here.

Rufus

You're welcome .... I'm extremely happy that I came.... BTW, I forgot my reading glasses.

Stephanie

I don't see your glasses. I'm sorry I had to run out so fast. But, I was running a little late picking up my son.

Rufus

Ok.... I just got into my room. ....and I took the last portion of your Wrap...loved the apple in it.... BTW, I have a spare pair of reading glasses.

Stephanie

So happy that you are safe. I bought the food for you. I'll make you lunch tomorrow. Do you like pasta?

Today did not feel like the first time we've met............ I miss you already. I'll continue to look for your glasses.

Rufus

Okay, of course if I don't respond to your messages you can assume that I am driving. And to be honest, I am also feeling withdrawal being away from you. I also wish I was kissing you right now.... What are you doing?

Stephanie

I'm waiting for my son's dad to pick him up for the weekend. Then I will shower, and go to bed.

I got no sleep last night and I'm emotionally charged from all the feelings toward you. I'll rest so that I can enjoy our time together tomorrow. What are you doing? How is your mom?

Rufus

I'm at my mom's as I text.... I am going back to the hotel in a few.

Stephanie

I'm really looking forward to seeing you tomorrow. Sweet dreams .... Dearest Rufus.

Rufus

I'm totally smitten by you Stephanie.... I am not trying to make sense out of what happened today, I am just thrilled that it happened to us.

September 5, 2015

Rufus

Good morning Stephanie, I was supposed to call Milton last night but I fell asleep around 10pm and awoke shortly after 12.

To recap, the joy I felt when I first saw you was priceless. The image is indelibly etched in my mind. I wish I had my laptop so I could type faster. Anyway, expectations are high in anticipation of what you are planning for today. I will try to catch a couple hours of sleep to be thoroughly rejuvenated.

In the meantime, I am watching STEF-TV. ...."don't mess with the best ...."

I'm still up.............I shouldn't tell you what I'm doing. ......okay, I will spill the beans. ... I am online researching "pretty bottle beers " for when I return in October

Rufus

I'm at the mall. When Milton was here last week he ordered prescription eyeglasses and he asked if I can pick them up. The Mall opens at 10, I will call afterwards when I am about to leave.

Stephanie
Got it

Rufus

I am talking fashion with Kevin, going to get him a T-shirt. ...I will call you in a few.... On my way

Before he left the mall, he realized that her address was not in his cell phone's GPS directory. He was about to call her when he felt an ominous sense of disconnection. After all their communications, he knew that he had her address. Then he remembered that he had ordered another surprise to be delivered to her apartment and she provided it. He searched his phone for the order confirmation and delivery address and inputted it into his phone's GPS. Before driving off he texted the following message.

Rufus

BTW, aren't you concerned whether I will be able to find your apartment since I only followed you there yesterday?

Stephanie
I knew that in an earlier communication I forwarded my address. If this relationship is important you would have it handy.

The second meeting at Stephanie's apartment began when Rufus found his reading glasses on the ground of the parking lot. They had been run over by the previous cars that may have parked in the space he did because he coincidentally parked in the same spot.

She greeted him with a kiss after allowing his entry in the apartment lobby. Then he informed her of the demise of his eyewear when she commented that she was quite certain he was mistaken after she searched the apartment and did not find them. When the elevator closed, they repeated a shorter reenactment of the oblivious introduction they participated in at the Pelican a little more than 24 hours ago as it slowly rose to the fifth floor. They spent the remainder of the morning and half of the afternoon on the small patio eating and conversing. Yesterday they were mostly reserved but today nothing was taboo for discussion.

As she began clearing the patio table after they had eaten the lunch she had prepared, she lobbed another salvo at him when she caught him looking at her as she walked - similarly like the day before - this time suggesting that she wasn't the typical woman he had dated in the past because of her non-generous flat derriere. She actually said,

"I know my ass is flat, it has always been that way - ain't nothing I can do about it. So if you don't like it you can leave now."

She followed up making general statements that African American men prefer women with big bootys. Again Rufus' spontaneous remarks gave way to another organic response that flabbergast and blew her away.

"I am not your typical Black man. I am attracted to the physically fit female form like Cory Everson and Rachel McLish. But a woman's mind also …"

She interrupted him in mid-sentence after he threw her for another loop,

"What do you know about Rachel McLish?" she asked with her almond eyes following up with a quizzical look and continue to say, "How could you have pulled that name out of the blue?"

Rachel McLish was a throwback in female athletics in the 90's and is no longer viable in fitness media circles so how could he have known that she was her idol. Stephanie continued still perplexed,

"You're kidding me, right?" she queried herself. "Rachel McLish is my fitness idol."

Rufus continued to share what he knew about Rachel McLish and other notable female fitness professionals. She was one of the fitness models I saw in the binder in his office. He concluded that Cory Everson co-starred in and action movie with Jean Claude van Dam which she did not know. And to my credit, those magazines in the binder were very instrumental now in Rufus' socializing process.

She later showed him how bad she was as a tap dancer that amplified the short video demonstration she had forwarded to him. Then she asked him to replay "She's Royal" on his phone like he did yesterday streaming to her Bose speaker. Then she actually told him that she liked his acapella version better. For a brief moment I thought she had hearing issues. https://vimeo.com/334318764

Afterwards he provided a brief historical dissertation of Caribbean music particularly Calypso. He sang Lord Nelson's King Liar verbatim very slowly explaining that the song was forty years old and displays the genius of the art form where comedy was put to a calypso song. https://www.youtube.com/watch?v=cYkqMT6HKD0 Rufus did the same thing in 1998 when we visited my godmother in DC. Her husband submitted it was the most fascinating song he had heard.

It couldn't have played out any better. Everything was working out. And as far as my litmus test was concerned – all of the boxes have been checked including challenging his notions. Did you see what she told him about remembering her address?

At the same time, it was imperative that they got to know each other on a secondary level from a distance. She thought that he really got to know her. And quite frankly, never before had she spent so much of her time with a stranger.

At the end of the weekend, they decided that a long distance relationship was exactly what both of them needed at that moment. But she also had additional requirements that were non-negotiable: First and foremost, their sons came first: hers and Kevin. Their welfare and wellbeing came before theirs. Second, she explained that even though she knew that it was impossible for her to travel to see him now that she worked six days in the week, she needed to see him twice monthly if possible – but monthly would suffice. Third, they had to take at least two prolonged getaways every year together of at least a week. Oh yeah, I almost forgot the caveat. She suggested that when he was in her presence, she will not touch mechanical knobs of any kind - particularly on automobiles and entry doors. Her home door was the exception because she had the key. It was something her son has been doing for her as far back as she can remember.

It all seemed doable to Rufus initially seeing that his only other meaningful relationship began similarly without the first requirement and caveat. The caveat was tested later when they went to dinner for the first time at Trulucks on Sunrise.

Rufus opened the passenger door to the Camaro for her on the way to the restaurant and held the door when they entered. Additionally, they sat next to each other in the booth as they dined. Subsequently, up until that point Stephanie had paid for everything during the weekend: the breakfast at The Pelican and hors d'oeuvre and drinks, including the lunch earlier. When the check for dinner arrived Rufus explained he was not comfortable with her paying. She said,

"I won't expect anything less." That was settled.

Rufus was really feeling good about himself as they left – and to be honest again, he was a little cocky too. She wrapped her left hand around his upper right arm as they strolled slowly towards the door and Rufus held it as she exited it first. As they promenade towards the car, he released her grasp from his right arm in order that he could retrieve the Camaro's keyfob from his pocket. He then pressed the remote to unlock the doors and walked to the driver's door, stepped in and was about to closed the door when he heard Stephanie say,

"Really?"

I'd be lying if I didn't admit that if he was really quiet, he would have heard me laughing.

September 6, 2015

Stephanie
I do miss your presence...your touch.

Rufus
Sweetie, I am on Standby for an earlier flight but lightning in the area has stopped operations.

I'm on the early flight so I should be in Puerto Rico around 7pm.

Taking off now. .... I am REALLY missing your kisses. ...1600 and counting ....and your smile.

Stephanie
:-))
Safe travels.

◆ ◆ ◆

Different songs were becoming his personal soundtrack during the year. Initially he actual found meanings in the melancholiest after my passing. And for the past months, the genre was changing to match his disposition. Friday morning he flew up listening to Corrine Bailey Rae and after the weekend with Stephanie the following song by *Ledisi* encapsulates his present state of mind as it played in his headset on the way back to Puerto Rico. https://www.youtube.com/watch?v=EMSW1Z2UFZQ

Ledisi
"I Blame You"

People keep ASKING, 'bout this glow I seem to have, cause I'm just not, the same.......
They say I'm WALKING different, TALKING different, it's like all of me, has changed ......
Magic that's in my eyes.... I can no longer hide....
Chorus
When they look at me, What they really see,
Is the love you got me feeling, Like I'm dancing on the ceiling.
I can hardly Breathe, Cause you're all I need,
So when they ask me why I'm smiling like a fool.......
I BLAME YOU. ...oh baby.
I BLAME YOU .... oh yeah.

In this moment in their lives, he knew exactly what he wanted, but it was becoming obvious that she wasn't going to make it easy - and she shouldn't. She has her own social norms that she has gotten accustomed and in comparison, the only non-starter I presented to Rufus at the age of twenty-two when we met was when I stated unequivocally I was not going to be his girlfriend for a couple of years. She exhibits the maturity of a life lived and that works for her. It brought to mind an excerpt of a Bob Marley quote that Stephanie literally epitomizes where it states:

> "If she's amazing, she won't be easy,
> If she's easy, she won't be amazing.
> If she's worth it, you won't give up,
> If you give up, you are not worthy."

In the weeks ahead Rufus revealed the following excerpt in his journal.

There are several times in my life, too numerous to enumerate, when my state of mind is truly content and happy. But consequently, there are only few notable moments when I can actually recall being totally ecstatic: The day I realized I was going to marry Christine and the subsequent day we did. The day I learned Christine was pregnant and the day Kevin was born. And the day I met Stephanie Brigham Brock.

When I am happy there is an outward exuberance that can sometimes be infectious: shouting when your teams win a game, singing karaoke knowing that if I had to make a living singing I'd starve, or beaming proud when my son does something noteworthy like writing code to control a radio controlled vehicle at a summer engineering camp.

Inversely, I also show little or no emotions when I am in the state of total euphoria. That's why I was misunderstood when I learned I was going to have a son. I may smile to acknowledge the blessings in the presence of others but mainly I become totally introspective as I contemplate how I may have arrived to that present place and time.

Then during a subsequent weekend visit, my adherence to one of our agreement was tested. Upon landing at the airport she told me that her ex-husband could not pick up their son due to a last minute business trip so our weekend was canceled. I recalled telling her that I was fine when in actuality I wasn't. My first thought was had I known a few hours earlier, I would have spared myself the trip. But a sense of immediate calm overcame me when I was reminded of rule number one. After all, she was notified when I was inflight. And at the same time I realized I was being selfish. That was the agreement we made – our son's came first. And after all, the trips are never a bust because it affords me the opportunity to visit my mother and sisters. And in the end, we were still able to salvage the weekend with a last minute date at the drive-inn before my return.

But in the weeks and subsequent months to come, I did not foresee the state of turmoil that was lurking around the corner and the repercussions I would have to endure due to my euphoric state as a result of my decision to Move On.

CHAPTER FIFTEEN

"What developed later was a misguided sense of loyalty. To use a metaphor to summarized their collective responses, they circled the wagons even though none of us really liked Western movies."

EVERYTHING SEEMED TO BE RIGHT again with the world. The joy he was feeling was palpable and he immediately shared the news with family and selectively with his few closest friends. The responses varied: he correctly assumed what his sisters were going to think about his new relationship and what they would say. He forwarded a pic of a selfie-like photo that Stephanie took of them at dinner. His sister Janet in Port St. Lucie told him she was so happy for him that she no longer needed to call him anymore on Fridays - it was disrupting her weekend TV bilge marathon time. That statement was equivalent to a doctor's clean bill of health coming from her. He knew what his best friend wanted for him. And his clients whom mostly were not local were all thrilled and happy because they could actually see how his disposition had changed in the times leading up to meeting Stephanie.

Some of his local clients and friends collectively made comments about an unwritten mandatory one-year period of waiting before getting involved in another relationship. One of his colleagues - the uncouth, horse-divers friend - actually made a religious reference. I am not kidding nor paraphrasing when I heard him tell Rufus that 'he should not get involved with a divorcée, suggesting that she needed to reconcile with her ex-husband because the Bible says that.' If I was alive they would have heard me laugh. But the response that most disappointed me deeply came from my family. To be totally honest, it was like I had died all over again.

The way everything was misconstrued was another form of awareness that ran deep.

Two weeks after meeting Stephanie he was making plans to return. Kevin was able to spend the weekends at the homes of three of my girlfriends of which two had similar age sons. He had apprised my girlfriend Katherine first of his travel plans and she was ecstatic for him. Against the advice of his best friend Milton who also has a Master's Degree in Psychology, he decided to also apprise my family in the form of an email to my mother, sisters and niece. He surmised what had transpired over the past two months. In his letter, he inferred that he wasn't looking for their approval, but he just wanted to be forthcoming about the relationship and his comings and goings. In essence, he didn't want to continue lying about where he was traveling to like he had twice prior.

My mother's delayed response diplomatically stated the obvious when she mentioned that she knew the day was going to come, but she didn't think it would be this soon. But behind the scene was a different narrative slowly looming within my family. What developed later was a misguided sense of loyalty. To use a metaphor to summarized their collective responses, they circled the wagons even though none of us really liked Western movies.

In most of the pictures I've taken with my sisters, I am in the middle where we look like the symbol for a strong cell phone signal. I also thought we had a strong family unit. With that said, if any of my sisters was close to Rufus, it was the shorter of the twins; the one that he described liked him immediately because of his dark complexion. The one that lovingly refers to him as her "favorite brother-in-law" with him at the moment being her only brother-in-law.

Over the years and during the countless weekends we'd traveled to visit, she warmed up to him immediately. Before we were married, she was with him in front of the television at our home on February 11, 1990 when Nelson Mandela was released from the South African prison and was back later in the evening when both of them watched Buster Douglas knocked out Mike Tyson for the very first time before returning to his hotel.

More recently as an adult, on several occasions they have gone out dancing - with and without me. And on two instances she purchased sought after front row tickets for us to see Rueben Blades, Willie Colon, and

The Gentleman of Salsa – *El Caballero de la Salsa* – Gilberto Santa Rosa perform.

Gilberto took the performance to another level. Instead of a typical orchestra standing static with their instruments behind customized music stands while only the singers repeated choreographed steps during the song, Gilberto Santa Rosas concerts are productions likened to Pop Artists. https://www.youtube.com/watch?v=7kbjKCj-rMQ&list=RDZc13NAc7dvM&index=3

There were professional dancers and themes for the songs. It was as if you were watching a live Salsa Music Video being recorded where one song was sung behind the wheel of a convertible Mercedes Benz. Another began when dancers descended from trapezes in the ceiling. During one of the songs a lady immediately next to us was talking on her cellphone while the performance was going on. Gilberto directed the band to lower the volume so he can ask the lady what she was doing. She said she was talking to her girlfriend. He then instructed her to give him her phone and commenced to sing the song with the microphone and cellphone. Note that I am translating everything to Rufus because only Spanish was sung and spoken at his concerts. Unlike Bobby Valentin, Gilberto's English can only be described best the way Celia Cruz remarked about her limited English, "Thank you for coming, remember that my English is not very good looking..."

After that song was over he returned the phone and told the lady to collect the admission fee from her friend. And another time my sister bought him tickets to see Chris Rock in Puerto Rico for his birthday.

More recently after I passed, on their first trip to Puerto Rico they all drove to Ponce to have lunch and my sister organized a surprise for Rufus at a roadside Sports Bar named Zalza. She had a percussionist there to teach Rufus how to play the congas. But the guy wound up being impressed. Rufus taught himself the various patterns from YouTube video because for Christmas when he bought me the Microsoft Surface – unbeknownst to her – he bought himself a set of congas without the tubular   shells. https://www.facebook.com/rufus.turnbull.9/videos/991663057551003/

The second time they went out with my mother the Easter Saturday which is a big deal in Puerto Rico as a pre-religious outing where Rufus was totally out of it. He didn't dance; he simply just sat and watched. What did happen was my sister ran into the guy she had recently broken up with. He offered Rufus his condolences because the four of us went out on dates in the past. What was uncomfortable for my sister was the fact that he was there with another woman after their recent break up.

Two months later for Father's Day they were out dancing when he got to meet Bobby Valentin. What also made the outing memorable was my sister wore the same outfit. When Rufus met her at the hotel ballroom, he had already begun laughing. She stopped him to explain that the culotte she was wearing was her favorite because it showed off her legs and she hopes that her ex could see how good she looks. Rufus actually said, "You go girl." https://vimeo.com/334333604

With all that said, her response to his email was simply cold; she replied telling him to remove her name from his contact list.

◆ ◆ ◆

My niece at the age of twenty at the time loved her uncle and quite frankly she still does. Back in July after the cruise she posted on her social media page a picture on the ship they took together with a message of her adoration towards him. Two months later it seemed like that message and all those years of experiences together were just pipe dreams.

The Christmas holiday when she was our first house guest when our lower level renovation was completed, she had the run of the entire place when I told her to imagine that it was her own personal apartment for a week equipped with a gym, library, wet bar and home theater. That was when Rufus taught her the rules of football on the 120-inch screen pausing the game several times to explain all of the nuances. She subsequently taught her mother and they have been Tom Brady fans ever since.

A few years earlier we took her with us to Poughkeepsie New York on a business trip around Christmas so she and Kevin could see snow for the very first time when I had to work. At the airport in Puerto Rico, Rufus purposely walked like a pirate sliding his foot because immediately after checking our luggage, the heel of his right shoe was flapping like a loose tongue. There weren't any shoe or sneaker store in the terminal, therefore he had no immediate reprieve. To make matters funnier, he thought if he bought chewing gum it would have the necessary properties to stick leather. The ordeal was over when he changed shoes in JFK baggage claim.

The next day Rufus got into trouble with me after they left the hotel room to get breakfast and I saw that he allowed the kids to have cake and ice cream. Not to mention the several times we've taken her to Orlando with us where I only allowed her to go on the roller coasters if Rufus rode along with her. We even have a picture of one of those memorable moments where they posed outside The Incredible Hulk extreme ride after they went. She would tell me from time to time that she always enjoyed visiting us because she loved the interaction between Rufus and me. With all that said, two months ago she posted the following on Rufus' Facebook page.

Words can't begin to express how much I love and cherish this man! My uncle Rufie has been an amazing uncle to me from day one and I thank God each and every day for him. Thank you so much for all the love and support throughout the years. Thank you for all of the life lessons you have taught me and for the immense love that you have for my aunt Christine (R.I.P. titi I love you and miss you so much) and my family. Thank you for this wonderful trip that I will cherish for the rest of my life. Thank you Rufus Turnbull!!!! THANK YOU UNCLE RUFIIIIEEEEE!!!!!!!

Now her response to his email was a confluence of mixed emotions of which she described as being confused, angry and sad to the point suggesting that how could he have loved me – her aunt – and moved on so quickly.

◆ ◆ ◆

My other sister – the taller twin.... I am pausing to measure my words carefully. I love my entire family dearly. But what she said to Rufus and the subsequent treatment after his email was totally undeserving. I recognize that she was at my side during my treatments and hospitalization and it was obvious how much she loved and cared for me. But Rufus lived up to his end of the bargain even when he wasn't there when I was in Puerto Rico because he was back at home with our son. He was everything that I dreamed for until the end. But the way she besmirched his reputation as a result of her own insecurities was not fair.

At first I attribute her response as her way of coping. My in-laws and aunt were completely confused about her reaction which caused them to suggest whether something else was going on between them. Stephanie even asked Rufus point blank, "What kind of relationship did you have with her?" when he told her about how he was being treated. Again I reiterate, if any of my sisters spent more time with my husband it was undoubtedly the shorter one. His interactions with the taller were mostly of my doing.

Initially he stayed in hotels for the first year. Then after we were married he would isolate himself during the weekends mostly doing 1000 piece puzzles as he warmed up to the family. Then after my taller sister's divorce, she purchased her first condo. I volunteered Rufus to tile my niece's bedroom to save her money before she moved in because of her history of allergic reactions to include carpet fibers that were included in the condo installation. He carried boxes of ceramic tiles up the stairs and completed the project a day before our scheduled Aruba vacation. What no one realize was as a result, he spent half of our week's getaway unable to walk up and down stairs while he recovered from lower back pains. Afterwards whenever she asked him to do anything, he always prefaced his response in the following manner,

"If you didn't divorce, you could have asked him to do yada yada yada."

Like the time she bought her first refrigerator and wanted a water line installed for the ice maker.

"If you didn't divorce, you could have had him install the ice maker."

Or the time she bought her first Plasma television and needed it installed.

"If you didn't divorce, you could have asked him to mount the TV."

But Rufus did more. He purchased a sheet of plywood and stained it to create his signature wall feature for flat panel TV installations. It was beautiful. As I now think of it, it was ten years ago and a precursor to his EB Hotel designs at home. And after I passed away, he overheard her telling my mother that one of her glass panel doors needed a privacy screen because the neighbors can see directly into her new condo at night. In the same manner he surprised me with my last Christmas gift, he took it upon himself and installed a semi-opaque film on the glass and didn't say anything until she realized it was installed.

In all of those things she showed her gratitude. But she expressed extreme outrage upon learning about his new romantic interest. She later told him that she didn't even read his email; it was my mother that told her about it. And as a result she had become totally belligerent and ungrateful towards him.

A lot of things were suggested that Rufus did from the distraught mind of my sister. And they were believed by some of her friends - some whom never even met nor knew him as the narrative she perpetuated was allowed to fester. For those that actually met him but never knew him, it caused them to pause. All of a sudden he was a bad husband - like her ex - and totally unworthy of trust. It all was played out during the weeks leading up to Kevin's birthday at the end of September.

◆ ◆ ◆

As customary, Kevin's birthday celebration at the end of September was scheduled months' prior before meeting Stephanie. But because of the backlash he notified my mother that they were still coming but they were going to stay at the Embassy Suites at the airport to which she insisted that he stay at her house. If he hadn't decided to share his life, they would have undoubtedly stayed at my taller sister's three-bedroom condominium. So on the weekend after Kevin's birthday, after school they flew to Puerto Rico. Rufus' plan was to take him shopping in the mall on Saturday and to have dinner later that evening with the entire family whomever decided to show up.

Now it wasn't unusual that they didn't pick them up at the airport, but not stopping by at my mother's house after work to say hello was very unusual. It was also very rude that when my sisters called in the evening, they only spoke with my mother and Kevin. The next morning, they added insult when my taller sister came to my mother's house, said hello to Rufus cordially by shaking his right hand with hers and presented him with a shopping bag with all of his clothes from her apartment with the other. She then proceeded to greet our mother in the customary manner of cheek kisses. Immediately after she took Kevin in her car and returned him the following day with enough time for them to catch their flight back to St.

190

Thomas. In the meantime, Rufus stewed over how the weekend was hijacked by my sisters. My mother tried to be a mediator but she had her own personal biases.

On the return flight home Kevin asked why they didn't stay at his Aunt's place together. Rufus simply told him the truth.

"Your aunts are angry with me." he began.

He knew that he had to tell him. Stephanie was going through the same delicate situation with her son. And he definitely didn't want him hearing it from my sisters. My niece actually suggested some sort of intervention moment of the right time to apprise Kevin. So when he followed up and asked why they were angry, Rufus curtly replied,

"They are angry because I told them that recently I met someone."

Kevin asked him where did he met the person to which he stated,

"Online on a Dating Site."

What my son said next reaffirm everything about what life is supposed to be about.

"I knew something about you had changed. One night I got up to go to the bathroom and I saw you in bed with your phone smiling .... It was late and I knew it wasn't a client."

He then told him the quick version of the circumstances how they met and how the last time he traveled to the states he lied about why he was traveling. And with the intention of having not to lie in the future about his comings and goings, he told them. Then Rufus asked,

"How do you feel about me dating someone else?"

He thought for a brief moment and said,

"Kinda weird, but I am happy for you Dad."

It was all the validation Rufus needed. Some people have 'a come to Jesus' moment; he was conversely having a 'To hell with them' moment. The only person whose opinion really mattered at the moment was fine. Nonetheless, the subsequent weeks that followed continued to be tumultuous.

◆ ◆ ◆

From my unique perspective it seemed like everybody in Puerto Rico had an opinion – but it wasn't about his relationship anymore – they were primarily concerned about Kevin's wellbeing. Additionally, my family members abroad - primarily my aunt in New Jersey - thought that if the situation wasn't resolved amicably and soon, it would cause the dissolution of the family. My niece at college in Atlanta contacted my aunt and began to mediate over the phone behind the scenes. And upon a scheduled doctor's appointment in Puerto Rico, at their behest Rufus agreed to have lunch with my taller sister and my mother at his favorite restaurant. He flew over on a Thursday for a Friday doctor's consultation while Kevin stayed with one of my girlfriends.

The Saturday morning began with a few documented false starts where my sister initially pushed back the time via text messages, then proceeded to invite and dis-invite our mother from the lunch. Rufus was in a clear state of resolve already coming to the realization that an amicable resolution was possible if everyone was rational. It was finally decided that she would like my mother to be present where he initially requested her presence.

It was immediately apparent that the reason why she requested the time to be changed from noon to 1pm was her salon appointment. Truth be told, my sister is a strikingly beautiful woman and always kept her appearances, until I got sick. In her late teens she was a model and did her share of music videos - most notably as a background dancer in two Jon Lucien R&B music videos. The irony is that Rufus actually knew Jon Lucien personally before he found success mainstream as a great lead singer and guitarist from St. Thomas where during the late 80's they played at the same local hotel nightclubs on Fridays where he too played the bass and their band played mostly calypso. https://www.youtube.com/watch?v=BtqfirOwvwo

I won't be presumptuous to suggest it was part of her strategy, but it was the best I have seen her look in a very long time. On the other hand, his thoughts were all logistical noting that having pushed back the time, at least they were dining at the new Mall of San Juan and a short drive over the bridge that led directly to the airport. There's never traffic on that bridge which is grossly underutilized unless there's a marathon race of some sort. So now with a delay of an hour he made a mental note of when he had to leave to return back to St. Thomas.

It was well into the third month of the new long distance relationship where Rufus was getting advice on nutrition that stuck with him when Stephanie would sincerely ask him on the daily, "Did you eat something green today?" So when they were seated, he ordered the chopped salad for the first time in their presence for his starter. It was the first salvo that was intuitively noted that things had changed.

The lunch began with queries mostly about Kevin's wellbeing. If it wasn't for the fact that his visit was the precursor to his colonoscopy procedure being scheduled for the following month, the diatribe of accusations would have started earlier.

My sister in the middle of Nordstrom Bazille restaurant commenced to accuse my husband of being unfaithful. She conjured up the story of how he met Stephanie on the Tom Joyner Cruise when I was hospitalized 2 years earlier. Continue to tell him he was an awful excuse of a husband for leaving me in Miami and going on the cruise leaving me in the hospital. Although he had apologized to me for leaving me and I had forgiven him, I never admitted to my mistakes and misgivings.

The truth was I was not totally honest with him and mostly hid my condition from everyone. When I was confronted I made trivial excuses. I remember getting very angry at him when he called my mother to apprise her. I actually thought that I would not have been admitted on that Saturday, but if I was, I would be released the following day to catch the cruise. We both had no idea how serious my condition was. Then on Sunday they diagnosed why my legs were retaining fluids and again I now thought I would be discharged before Wednesday in order to catch a flight to Puerto Rico and meet up with the cruise. And it was my idea for Rufus to go on the cruise. At the same time my sister-in-law Lena promised and was there at the hospital every day. He called me every day ship-to-shore and I never told him what the doctors diagnosed. All the while before I made everything seem normal.

We left Miami 10 days later with a full diagnosis of congestive heart failure – that my heart was severely weakened by the aggressive chemo treatments. I was on a care regimen for my continued healing. At year's end I made the difficult decision to have a double mastectomy.

Again, against the advice of my plastic surgeons and Rufus, I decided to reduce my breasts from a D to an A-Cup – where they both suggested C's. I always reminding him that it was my body and I ultimately settled for B's. In the end it didn't compliment the shape of my body and I wound up having expander implanted to stretch my skin in hopes that they could be C's when the time was right for reconstructive breast surgery. In the end I realize they both were right.

The next year I was able to go on the subsequent Tom Joyner Cruise in the best shape and health in a very long time as I partied like a schoolgirl with him til the early mornings almost every day. When we embarked, Rufus was suffering from extreme cramping in the legs. I selfishly left him in the cabin and went out for the evening before reminding him that last year he was here without me. He simply laughed and told me to enjoy myself. When I returned after midnight, I remarked,

"I had so much fun ... and this was only Day One!"

Day Two began with Rufus still suffering with limited mobility until we attended the George Clinton concert on the Pool Deck. Again, I swear the following actually happened.

Rufus and I were against the railing on the pool deck - which was preferred because of my height - and we had a great view of the stage when he began shouting the following lyrics to P-Funk,

W-E-F-U-N-K, y'all
Now this is what I want you all to do:
If you got faults, defects or shortcomings
You know like arthritis rheumatism or migraines...
Whatever part of your body it is,
I want you to lay it on your radio ... let the vibes flow through,
Funk cannot only move, it can re-move, dig?
The desired effect is what you get
When you're in tuned to your interplanetary Funkeningship
Sir Lollipop Man! Chocolate coated freak-in habitat,
Doin' it to you in 3D
So groovy that I dig me.

All of a sudden Rufus screamed,
"My legs are fine!"
"Are you sure? I asked
"I am serious!" he reassured.
"That's great Honey." I replied. Then he said,
"The Funk cured me!" to which caused me to say,
"Really?"
He recapped the lyric that he swears was his antidote,

"Arthritis, rheumatism or migraines, whatever part of your body it is, just lay it on your radio... Funk cannot only move ...it can re-move ...Dig?"

I watched him quizzically and said,

"Okay."

He truly believed it was the music that cured him. In actuality, it was all the adrenaline and the outward exuberance being expressed as he sung loudly along with the large crowd being in the moment. At the same time, I was simultaneously catapulted back in time twenty-years prior when we were at the Lionel Roberts Stadium at a Third World reggae concert on St. Thomas. The music was similarly foreign like all the "Gaga GooGa-Gaga Googa, ... Gaga Goo Gaga" refrain being sung by everyone on the ship. I knew with all certainty, I was the only sane person on the pool deck and amidst the locals back in St. Thomas 20 years' prior who were high on more than adrenalin. And although it was very entertaining, none of the music was familiar. To reiterate, it seemed like I was the only one in the audiences that didn't know any of the songs. Then I heard,

"96 Degrees .... In the shade, ee-ade!" I shouted at Rufus,

"I KNOW THAT SONG!"

"REALLY?" Rufus shouted back while Third World continued,

"Real hot! ... In the shade, ee-ade!" I joined in unison,

"**1963** ... In the shade, ee-ade!"

Rufus started to laugh uncontrollably at me and I playfully punched him and asked what was so funny. After gathering himself he clarified the lyrics were,

"They are saying Ninety-Six Degrees, not Nineteen Sixty-Three."

It was the highlight of that concert for me. Over the years we had countless moments like that. Again I digress.

With Rufus perfectly healthy we participated in the 70's Throw Back party on the cruise where Rufus dressed like a pimp wearing a red velvet suit tiger printed lapel with a matching hat that were two or three sizes too small. He showed me that the elastic waistband on the pants were below his butt and since the length of the jacket was longer than usual, you'd never know. I was dressed like a Go Go Dancer with knee-high pink boots ready for the Soul Train. Rufus kept telling everyone I was his Ho (whore) and I'd better have his money. And most of the evenings we retired to our rooms at 4am.

Even when we disembarked was noteworthy. Rufus saw George Clinton waiting for his ground transportation and I told him that he needs to get a picture with him. He obliged and I snap a pic of both of them having a great laugh together like they were friends. (see his Facebook post) I initially thought Rufus told him about his recent recovery as a result of the song at the concert. Rufus later confirmed that he told him that back in the 70's, The Parliament Funkadelic Mothership Connection was the first cassette he had ever purchased as a kid and after learning the lyrics back then, he continued to tell him,

"No way in the world you were breathing 'Pure Air' when you wrote those songs."

♦ ♦ ♦

Then a few months later, the same symptoms that I first experienced were back and we were scheduled for our summer cruise with Kevin and later a family reunion in Orlando. Rufus wasn't having any part of it this time. He had seen this drama played out before so he vehemently decided that we not go and his family would be understanding. I didn't relent and he came along for appearances. Actually, he unwillingly came along to make sure I was going to be fine.

Then I remember the look on his face when he realized that someone other than him knew more about my situation than he. We were in Cape Canaveral and having just disembarked the ship and were all in the car rental when I called my girlfriend Arlene in St. Petersburg Florida for directions to her condo. As the car idled quietly through stop and go traffic and even though I spoke softly, I knew that he heard when she asked, "...and how are your legs?" I hadn't seen my friend in at least 4 years since she left St. Thomas and in addition to my mother, we spoke almost daily. I had been telling her about my struggles with water retention in my legs and how much I loathe the prescribed diuretic. So when she asked, I knew that he heard and from the corner of my left eye, without moving my head or torso, I felt his stare. And since I am being honest, I actually didn't care.

They actually circled the wagons around me when Rufus said that if I did not go to the hospital, he was not going to drive to the reunion. I compromised agreeing but I did not want to be admitted because I already knew that I would spend a similar amount of time at the St. Petersburg hospital like I had in Miami.

The doctor said all my vitals looked good but my legs were swollen and he wanted to do more tests and admit me and I adamantly refused. It made Rufus very angry because from that point, the vacation was over. He didn't participate any further in the activities with his family. We returned home to find that my cardiologist was not available so the next day I was in Puerto Rico again in ICU. I checked out of the hospital to be the matron of honor for my girlfriend's wedding and upset my mother. Later on we received a bill from the hospital in St. Petersburg for $3,700.00 because our insurance did not pay for the 2 hours I spent there because I checked myself out. Up to that point, we never had a hospital bill because Rufus reassured me that the monthly insurance premium was his most important bill.

I am recalling all of this in more detail because at the moment he was in the restaurant paraphrasing everything – with the exception of the Tom Joyner Cruise - from his point of view to my sister. At one point he even told my mother that he was happy that she was present to substantiate everything he was saying because even though I spoke daily to her, I kept her at bay as far as the really bad news was concerned. Rufus reminded my mother that she even threatened not to come to the reunion if I wouldn't cooperate in St. Petersburg.

But my sister wasn't having any of it. She needed to make her point. Then she began accusing him of telling our son to not answer their phone calls and messages. And after it was all said and done, he summed up the whole sad state of affairs by asking her the following question,

"If I had informed you guys about my relationship two years from now, would you still be accusing me of the same things you have?"

Before he could complete the question she blurted,

"Yes!"

I knew then, I knew there, it was over. A proverbial disconnect switch had been thrown as if to sever the activity in his brain that was now making him very angry. He wasn't going to subject himself any further to anymore accusations. And after it was all said, his favorite entree remained in his plate untouched as he attempted to pay for the lunch and my sister insisted like she always did so he got up and left and waited for my mother to drive him to the airport.

The drive was thankfully short so there wasn't any conversation to be had because his demeanor was stoic and resolute. He knew everyone felt the emotional pain of my loss but now he came to the realization that he had become their outlet to lash out whatever psychological and emotional issue that they kept hidden. It was hidden the several times he and Kevin traveled on weekends. It was kept hidden on the Western Caribbean Cruise. But he also realized that had he not met Stephanie, those resentments in my sister's mind would had remained harbored for an unforeseen amount of time. He even thought that they even had feelings that he may be one of the reason I was not alive. All I could think at the moment was whether all those good memories for the past twenty- five years would sustain them.

With a calming breath he sat in my mother's car as they crossed the seldom used Teodoro Moscoso bridge and concluded that Puerto Rico may no longer be frequented as much. Puerto Rico was his place to getaway for more than twenty-five years: to shop, to dance and to simply chill. And as his flight returned to St. Thomas, a renewed sense of excitement was realized knowing that a new bridge to Florida would now bring him joy.

CHAPTER SIXTEEN

"To reiterate, a sister-in-law, who at the time Rufus was on speaking terms with ten years into our marriage - that still lives on the small 32 square mile island, I never met in our twenty-five-year relationship."

T HE FOLLOWING MONTHS WERE UNCHARTERED territories and self-reflection. But to preface what is about to follow with a case of levity, I remember a conversation Rufus and I had when he commented he didn't know what he would do if I passed away before him. The situation he was referring to was when we were both in our retirement years. I actually said,

"Well, I know what I am going to do …. I am going to marry a young thing." And even though the question was hypothetical, I doubled down in jest saying, "And since you are such a grouch, I am going to put you in a nursing home, then remarry a young thing."

But on the serious side, he was now navigating the reality of that previous hypothetical dilemma. He was learning how to be a single parent. He was figuring out how he fit in a new relationship. And although I am quite certain he did not consider the following, he was now becoming very comfortable being estranged from my family. In actuality, he had a lot of experience with estrangement in his own family.

Although his father is still alive, from very early in his life he chose not to have a relationship with him. It first began out of loyalty to his mother after his parents divorced when he was around the age of three or four. Rufus told me the last pleasant memory he had with his father was at the age of four when his dad took him to the horse races. On the ride back, he remembered sitting on his lap while he steered the car back home.

The next time he had any interaction with his father was in 1985, almost two decades later. It was the first day he was a teller at Banco Popular de Puerto Rico. He saw his father in the queue when he reminded himself of one of the rules where 'Tellers could not service family members.' Rufus walked over to his supervisor and relayed the following as he pointed out his father and reminded his supervisor of the nepotism rule. Then he stated,

"If by chance my father is called when I say next, I want to take care of him because I don't want to give him the satisfaction of hearing me say I cannot service him because he is my father."

The supervisor looked dumbfounded and allowed the irregularity.

With that said, Rufus didn't have any axes to grind, because all emotions were nonexistent. He had detached his identity from his consciousness. In his mind, his father was just another older person that he held a lot of resemblance to. He had arrived at that realization when he was in the seventh grade. While in primary school, the bus took him to school turning to the left of the Estate Nadir intersection and life went on. For the following six years when he attended secondary school until he graduated, the school bus turned to the right of the same intersection. On that route was when Rufus realized how close his father lived. It was less than a three-minute drive - approximately a mile from where he grew up. The house was visible from the highway and he passed it twice every day to and from school. The first times were emotionally difficult especially when from time to time he would see his father as the bus drove by. But as the six years passed, every time he passed the house, he began to detach himself from his father emotionally as if each pass was a proverbial eraser stroke rubbing away the image in his mind.

Then there are his two oldest twin sisters nine years his senior. As a kid, both sisters helped raise the younger siblings while Rufus' mother worked up to three jobs at times. In their high school years, one sister was stoic and militant at times donning an Angela Davis afro and notably wearing military style boots to school while the other sister was more demure, soft spoken and never wore a pair of slacks in her entire life.

During the 25 years I have been with Rufus, I have only met the demure sister. It was during the first two years of our relationship. I moved into Rufus' childhood home shortly after we were engaged and became roommates with his sister Linda and her husband and daughter. We all got along well until the demure sister returned because of her circumstances and moved into the furnished guest room that was kept for whenever their mother returned home to visit. Around that time my clothes were stored in another room in my luggage and it was becoming an untenable situation walking between those rooms when I was getting dressed. So Rufus and Linda simply asked the demure sister to swap bedrooms. The guest room was the largest with a proportionally sized closet and it simply made sense. The demure sister reluctantly agreed and the relationship between us quickly deteriorated.

She began to make me feel unwelcome where in the mornings when we usually showered or addressed our hygiene needs, she would remain in the second bathroom. Linda and her husband bedroom had an ensuite bath and at times Rufus and I had to disturb them when we were readying ourselves for work. The reason why we knew her actions were deliberate was the fact that she was unemployed at the moment. As a result, we began keeping our oral hygiene products in our rooms. As a consequence, on weekends we traveled to various destinations to simply getaway particularly to St. John, St. Croix, St. Maarten and Puerto Rico.

Everything came to ahead when Rufus and I were entertaining my coworker Jacqueline and her husband Cleo - the owner of the flying school - having a couple's night playing board games. We were recently married and reciprocating a recent outing at their home. I made the mistake of offering a beverage that the demure sister had purchased. It was the most embarrassing display of belligerence I had ever witnessed. And quite frankly, it was the last straw. At that moment I knew that I wanted out. I became emotionally detached. And behind the scenes I was looking for an apartment for us to move into. At the same time Jacqueline and Cleo decided to fast track their lower apartment construction. It was completed in one month. 800 square feet and fully furnished. It was the most amazing act of friendship I had ever received. The evening before we moved, I was up packing everything that we owned in Rufus company pickup truck and our car while he slept. He was flabbergasted the following morning when he realized there was nothing left for him to do. We said our goodbyes to Linda and her family and never looked back.

I remember Cleo helping us move in and three years later helping us move out when we bought our home. Cleo later said we were his best tenants. It wasn't because we hadn't signed a lease and still paid our rent before time. It wasn't because after we moved out Rufus returned the week after to repaint the entire apartment with a neutral color. It was just because we were friends. They sincerely congratulated us when we bought our home.

On the other hand, I never met the stoic twin. To reiterate, a sister-in-law, who at the time Rufus was on speaking terms with ten years into our marriage - that still lives on the small 32 square mile island, I never met in our twenty-five-year relationship. Rufus knew it was her religious beliefs that prohibited her from attending our wedding, but he thought that was her problem.

He told me about the time when she taught him how to drive stick in 1985. He said she was the absolutely worst teacher. She took him to one of the steepest roads on the island aptly named Donkey Hill for his first and only lesson. Rufus said the experience was like a cowboy breaking in a wild horse. She made him stop on the hill and continue while cars were honking their horns. He explained he was so nervous to the point that he had no control of his left leg. It was trembling as if it was electrocuted. She sternly yelled at him like Sargent Carter did to an annoying Gomer Pyle when the car bucked like a bronco. But at the end of the hour lesson he was ready to borrow her car on a regular basis. And a year later he purchased his first new car.

While we were married Rufus never spoke much about his stoic sister. He only told me from time to time he had ran into her during the nineties. Then in early 2001, Rufus and Kevin were at Kmart in the checkout line when he saw Sargent Carter in another checkout line. He called her name and she answered remarking that it had been a long time since they'd seen each other. This conversation was going on while she was being checked out. Rufus told her to come over and meet Kevin who was in a baby carriage on his shopping cart. To his extreme disappointment, she left without acknowledging the presence of her nephew. Since that day they have not ran into each other and have been estranged ever since.

At my memorial service the demure sister was in attendance and gave Rufus her condolences. She also took the opportunity to actually apologize for how she treated us - particularly me. Rufus thanked her for the sympathetic remarks but he also told her in no uncertain terms that her apology was twenty years too late. She tried to justify that she was in a dark place and apologized again. The weeks that followed, she really tried to make amends with her kid brother by calling him regularly to see how he was doing and whether she could genuinely be of assistance. His remarks to her were like Kevin's, terse F.O.G. variety. After about three months she stopped calling him all together.

So I knew firsthand how comfortable Rufus has been being estranged – especially when he knew that he wasn't at fault. I know he gets very comfortable with disengagement to the point he will pass you on the street and wouldn't recognize you. Like immediately after he resigned his job at his cousin's electrical contracting firm. The circumstances that led to it again wasn't of Rufus' doing, but his cousin disrespected him personally usurping his authority for the last time. In hindsight again, he was ready to go. In Afterlife UHD it is crystal seeing those circumstances coming into play.

Rufus always had the notion of getting into the custom electronic installation sphere and by the mid-nineties ran the idea by his cousin. His cousin had no designs to venture out from the core business while at the same time hiring guys to do what Rufus was proposing and never really satisfied. At the same time, Rufus was too scared to venture out on his own. So the summer of 2002 while his cousin was on vacation and Rufus was in charge, one of the guys was late and wasn't allowed to get the necessary materials to work on Saturday. This was the same guy who Rufus kept telling his cousin would report that he had worked on St. John while being seen on St. Thomas.

But this Saturday everything came to a head primarily because the evening before we were both up all night because Kevin was sick and had a fever. Rufus went to work early and immediately returned home to give me a break. Later in the morning his cousin called because he was told than Rufus failed to report to work by the other guy. Rufus told him that not only did he go into work while his son was sick, the guy was the only person that did not show up. His cousin told him to return because the guy was there now and Rufus told his cousin he wasn't going to and furthermore the guy could sign for whatever materials he needed at another electrical supply store on the company's credit. His cousin told Rufus to,

"Get your fucking ass back to work..." when Rufus hung up before he could complete his thought. He then came to me in bed with Kevin and said,

"I think I just quit my job."

His cousin was scheduled to return to work on Tuesday and Rufus had prepared a letter of resignation over the weekend. On Monday, Rufus reported to work as if everything was normal and only told his coworker who coincidentally is the same person that told him not to date divorcees. The following day his cousin asked him whether he had something for him. He was actually hoping for an apology to subsequently reprimand him but Rufus handed him the letter. It stipulated that it was effective in two weeks. His cousin told him to leave immediately because he did not want his notice.

Again like puzzle pieces falling into place, Rufus left and before he could hop into his truck, he saw the proprietor of a Fire Alarm and security company that had offices in the same industrial park four doors down. He told him that he just resigned and the guy told Rufus, "I need you .... let's talk." The conversation was brief because they knew each other very well and Rufus told him that he needed to take the rest of the week off and he will see him on Monday.

After that day, we have never been back to his cousin's home and they haven't been over to ours. And at the same time working at the new job put him in the field and gave him the confidence to work on several subsystems like gates, cameras, and alarms. He knew that he was not going to work there for long primarily because the only holidays they had were the three major: Thanksgiving, Christmas, and New Years and in all actuality, it conflicted with our travel schedules. Additionally, there was a sense of impropriety Rufus felt from his new employer that only results when race is factored - Rufus being Black, his new employer being White.

Months before I bought Rufus a brand new Chevy S-10 pickup truck for his birthday in August. It was fly if I say so myself. It was black with mag wheels and even a front spoiler. He really loved it but his torso was too long. He really tried to make it work but he was conflicted.

The decision to finally change the truck occurred when Kevin in his car seat kicked the shift out of gear when Rufus was getting gasoline. He traded it in for a Ford Sports Trac - the four door mini pick up and Kevin was now in the back seat where he belonged. That truck was new and nicer than his boss's older and slightly damaged. Then his boss bought a new truck.

Then during Rufus' lunch hour, he cleared a shipment for a new High Definition television when that was the new craze and left it in his pickup bed. The secretary – who was Italian and the wife of the boss – told Rufus to take the TV home before her husband sees it.

But the last shot across the proverbial bow was when his boss mentioned how nice our house was in one breath when we bought accordion shutters from the company and had them delivered and later told him that he's paying him too much. That comment did not sit well and at that point Rufus knew his days were numbered. He lasted a little more than a year and while working there Rufus had that meeting with the Philadelphia Mogul.

In the end, there's a simple nod of acknowledgment when they see each other in the field, but Rufus goes out of his way to say hello to his wife whenever he sees her. And after he quit working for his cousin, his wife only spoke to me and Rufus was happy to oblige to her narrow minded behavior. Subsequently, both his cousin and his wife were absent from my funeral.

♦ ♦ ♦

I didn't want this for my family so I know that the longer it takes for a resolution the harder it is going to be for reconciliation. And any quick resolution was immediately dismissed when my niece enthusiastically called the late afternoon when Rufus returned home from having lunch with her mother and grandmother – after all – the lunch was her idea. She was wholeheartedly expecting that a truce was going to be forged. But instead of providing a little background to limit her expectations by prefacing that fact that my sister suggested that Rufus met Stephanie on the first Tom Joyner Cruise when I was unable to go, when my niece asked,

"Uncle, how did lunch with my mother go? Without thinking he said,

"Your mother is delusional."

He immediately knew what he said was wrong and those words could not be retrieved. He quickly apologized but he knew that he'd gone too far. The conversation was a lot shorter than both anticipated as he apologized again for what he said to her – but at the same time – he really meant it.

That wrathful relationship was now another quest I had to remedy. And in order for me to attempt to mediate this tenuous situation I think it's only right for me to admit to my own alienated relationship of consequence. Now that all the seasons had passed I was hoping things would be more amenable for a reconciliation. But I knew exactly what they were doing because I was also guilty of similar comportment.

You see we all learn that awful lesson of tribalism when my parents divorced. My mother packed up her three young daughters after saving portions of the allowances given for household expenses until she had enough for airline tickets to Puerto Rico. I was seven and was a little excited and confused flying at that time. But when my mother told me that we were going to live with my grandmother, I happily replied "Okay Mommy." After that we only saw our father during the summer school breaks in New York as young children traveling on airplanes. At first I traveled alone with the flight attendant assistance being under age and because I was five years older than my siblings. Later the three of us flew together.

Coincidently around the time my mother remarried, the child support payments from our father seized. My father wasn't cooperative in resolving the situation because from his point of view, his wife left with the children leaving him in New York. His pay stubs showed that his wages were being garnished regularly and his support payments were up to date. Over ten years past and that animosity grew throughout the family with no resolution. At the age of adolescence and adulthood, we collectively stopped communicating with our dad. Then in early 1990 – a few months after meeting Rufus – another confluence of circumstances slowly materialized that profoundly changed the outlook on all of our lives.

While working on St. Thomas after the hurricane, I monitored the progress of home repairs and one of my jobs entailed me delivering claim checks to the insured based on the progress of their repairs. One of those clients was an older gentleman by the name of Mr. Carty. After I delivered to him another check he asked me,

"What is your title?"

At first I didn't understand what he was referring, so I told him my position at the insurance company. Then in the local vernacular he reiterated,

"Who's your people?"

I thought it was personal and became guarded with my response. He saw the apprehension on my face and in the same manner the two inebriated men who identified Rufus at Carnival in the evening and the British Virgin Islands agents did similarly on the cruise ship dock on Tortola, Mr. Carty explained that I had the resemblance of his friend living in Puerto Rico. I thought it was now harmless to offer a little more personal information so I told him my full name. He then asked what is my father's name. I told him Eric Bell. He told me that the name of his friend is Wilfred Bell and quite possibly he could be my uncle. I told him that my father was an only child and what he was suggesting was literally impossible. Additionally, I told him that my uncles were from my mother's side of the family. Nonetheless, he then asked whether I can give him my telephone number so he could have his friend call me. I noncommittally provided him my office number in Puerto Rico and thought nothing else of it. In my later communication with my mother that evening, I told her about my encounter when she interrupted to explain that she vaguely recalled a conversation when my father told her about a brother that he never met.

The following week while working back in Puerto Rico, I received a phone call from Wilfred Bell who spoke Spanish very well suggesting that he was quite possibly my uncle. He asked me what was my father's name. He continued to explain that he has a younger brother that he never met of whom he was 18 years older. He explained that he spent all of his formative years in the military. He was actually blowing my mind when finally, he suggested that we meet someplace mutual over lunch. I immediately called my mother and told her about the phone call.

So after my mother and I were able to clear our schedules, we decided to meet Mr. Bell a few days later in a park nearby my office. The moment was serendipitous. When we saw each other there wasn't any doubts. We both began to cry. He instantly became my Uncle Wilfred. We actually had each other's eyes.

A couple of weeks later I received a phone call to learned that my father was vacationing in St. Thomas. Uncle Wilfred sought out to find his only brother in New York and told him where I was working and he wanted to take Rufus and I out for dinner after learning that I was engaged. The uncanny fact we learned that evening was my father was actually born on St. Thomas. He was visiting his ailing uncle whose sons were both musicians and grew up in the same neighborhood as Rufus. Rufus made the association that my father resembled Sherman Helmsley the actor from the 70's comedy show The Jeffersons. They were similarly short, animated, walked the same, and were equally loquacious.

I learned a lot about my father that evening and we hung out with him a few more times before he returned to the mainland. Even though the moments were cordial, our relationship remained strained. In the end we decided to be friends and to stay in touch. I also invited him to our wedding a few months away. I was very disappointed when he didn't show up. But even though I was fashionably late on November 3rd 1990, Rufus told me that Uncle Wilfred and his wife Julie were the first guests at the church after he arrived.

Eleven years later I received another call at work from my father when he was vacationing with friends on the island of St. Maarten and was hoping that we could drop everything and meet him there. The audacity of him I initially thought. After calling Rufus and apprising him, Rufus suggested that he probably wanted to see his grandson. He hadn't met any of his grandchildren to that point because of the estrangement and my taller sister wasn't particularly amenable to anything to do with our father. It was like deja vu how she was now treating Rufus.

So after requesting leaves from both of our employers, on a Thursday morning in May 2001, the three of us were on a plane for the extended weekend in St. Maarten.

Rufus and I met my dad's wife for the first time there. Kevin was eight months old. We were picked up at the airport and swept away on a watercraft for an excursion around the entire island. Additionally, we met many of his friends from the island and the mainland. The beachfront hotel room where we stayed literally steps from the sand in downtown St. Maarten was owned by one of his friend that lived in New Jersey. The car rental we drove for the four days was owned by another friend that lived on St. Maarten. The restaurant where I later taunted to all my girlfriends on St. Thomas and Puerto Rico as having the best mussels in the world...you got it.

That weekend ended as fortuitous as it began. Every now and again Rufus shows glimpse of wisdom. While we waited at the airport for our return flights to our two destinations, we sat with my father and his wife. Then my father excused himself momentarily to the restroom. At that moment Rufus indicated that my father was in the bathroom crying. I asked him how did he know. Rufus simply replied,

"After the weekend we had, that's what I would be doing right now if I were him."

We said our goodbyes again like a decade earlier and again he decided to keep in touch. This time many of those bricks that built that proverbial wall of estrangement were compromised and brittle. This time he did call. He called to tell us that he arrived home safely and he confirmed what Rufus suspected about him crying in the restroom.

Afterwards, he continued calling every Sunday. With every phone call, a proverbial brick fell. The frequency of the calls tapered off to once a month when Rufus would announce his calls by saying,

"Mookie, the phone's for you."

And at the year's end I was pleasantly surprised to receive a phone call on my birthday from my dad. It was the first of its kind in a very, very long time. But because I can review everything in Afterlife UHD, I now realize that it was Rufus who moments before, called my father and reminded him that it was my birthday and he should call. He never told me he did that gesture.

Unexpectedly, shortly after our reconciliation, my mother received a lump sum check for child support from the social services department in New York for all the years we thought my father was purposely being delinquent with the department's apologies. She never told me how much - even though I can always see it in her warehouse now and I know the amount. She need not worry; I will keep her secret.

The years to follow my father visited us in St. Thomas for a two-week stint. At the time my shorter sister decided to reconcile with him when she flew over to see him during the weekend.

Years later we visited him in New York where for the first time Rufus was able to see where I grew up. Then in 2004, my uncle and father decided to both relocate to Oviedo, a suburban neighborhood in Orlando Florida. They both bought homes in new developments in close proximity and in the months it took for the construction completion, I traveled a couple of times to provide input in choosing the plot, cabinets and bedrooms furniture for what my dad suggested would be my room. Even though he didn't swim, my dad added a heated swimming pool and screened-in lanai for his grandkids.

And as the saying goes, 'if you build it, they will come.' Shortly after my father met my niece for the very first time. She was with us on a Disney vacation. Thereafter my taller sister reconciled with him.

Another poignant moment was a party held in 2005 at my dad's house for Rufus' birthday where the entire family was present: three daughters with his three grandkids, two sons-in-law, my Aunt and her daughter, my grandmother and my mother. My mother later told me that my father congratulated her for raising remarkable young women and poignantly admitted that he was an asshole and understood why she left.

Sadly, in June 2008 my father passed away as a result of complications from kidney failure. He was on dialysis for several years awaiting a compatible donor. He was sixty-four years old. At the same time my Uncle Wilfred was suffering from dementia and was never notified about his brother's death but inevitably found out on his own metaphysically when he passed away two weeks later.

I was always my Daddy's Girl. I was reminded subconsciously of that in the end. The Law of Attraction brought Mr. Carty into my life to set forward the series of events that I described. The truth is I yearned for my father and the cosmos answered. So in order for any reconciliation between my family and Rufus to begin, they would both need to be amenable. He could not rationalize how a relationship that was seemingly healthy at all fronts quickly disintegrated so fast. But he actually admits that a simple apology from my sisters would suffice and he would inevitably forgive and hopes to quickly forget. But it takes two to tango.

◆ ◆ ◆

The passing of my father and uncle also fostered conversations between Rufus and I about what kind of internment we would prefer when that unfortunate time for us was realized. Rufus unequivocally stated that he wanted to be cremated and proceeded to tell me about a funeral he attended at a local private school on St. Thomas celebrating the life of their headmaster. There was only a picture of him. Friends, family, and well-wishers gathered under a canopied tent where his favorite music was played. The following day his family sprinkled the ashes in the ocean. Rufus concluded saying that he wanted something similar but with Salsa music.

At the moment I was unsure. What I was certain about was I didn't want the preparation of my funeral to be like my father's. I was disgusted how the funeral director tried to aggressively upsell us with the releasing of doves. He also suggested that the higher tombs were sought after and cost more to house the casket as if they were selling real estate.

Although I did not make a decision, Rufus made the right decisions for me. He told my mother about our discussion and she too was conflicted. Rufus made the decision based on one criterion. My mother wanted a traditional funeral with a casket and burial. Rufus remarked that would involve transporting the body via air freight to St. Thomas and he could not come to terms of having to prepare shipping documents that would leave lingering psychological effects when he cleared my body through Customs and Border Protection.

"I was his wife, not cargo," he thought. In the end he knew himself because every time he had to present my death certificate to update legal documents, he actually goes into depression.

The decision to have me cremated was the best. My mother wasn't amenable at first. The crematorium made an exception for my mother where they allowed them to see me in my physical form for the last time. Rufus kissed my forehead with tears in his eyes and afterward my mother did similarly while running her fingers through my hair. As they drove away my mother asked Rufus to pull off the highway to the side of the road and stop. She thanked him for requesting the exception of being allowed to see me for the last time and not only expressed that cremation was the best decision for me, she was now considering it for herself.

◆ ◆ ◆

I remember how the family treated my sister's ex-husbands. We remained cordial towards them because they were the fathers of my niece and nephew. Rufus only disliked the husband of my taller sister, and for plausible reasons. Initially Rufus expressed his disdain when he learned that he was bilingual and refused to converse in English with him. It was a weekend when we met my sister's brother-in-law who told Rufus that his brother was an asshole. Then there was another weekend Rufus and I spent at my taller sister's apartment when she was married. Rufus and her husband went for a drive and my sister and I thought it was going to be a great bonding experience. They returned less than a half hour later and Rufus said nothing until I pressed him to tell me what happened when we returned to St. Thomas. He explained that he was a bet. My sister's husband drove him to a friend's house, the friend took a look at Rufus and said something like, 'Diablo!', reached into his pocket, paid him, spoke for another 5 minutes, and then they returned. Rufus hated him more ever since if that's possible.

Our family also estranged ourselves from my shorter sister's first ex-husband after they divorced. Rufus always insisted that she was not ready to get marry then. He suggested that my sisters saw my happiness and wanted it for themselves. He continued his point saying that the taller was ready for marriage but she just happened to marry an asshole. He thought that my other brother-in-law was a great guy and my sister proved Rufus correct when she dissolved the relationship.

I remember when Rufus told us a few years after the divorce that he saw him in the mall with his new family and they spoke for a while. I remember my sisters actually reprimanded him for speaking to her ex. Rufus wasn't having any of it. He told them in no uncertain terms can they tell him who he can speak to. As I recall those series of events it seemed to be a precursor to what he was now going to experience.

◆ ◆ ◆

The week before Thanksgiving Rufus wrote the following email that expressed the way he was feeling after being alienated by my sisters. He aptly described it as Deafening Silence. Additionally, he forwarded a copy to my aunt and Stephanie.

It is obvious that the silence in Puerto Rico has been deafening. It is also obvious that the recent decision I made has caused a sense of disdain where I am concerned. What is incredible about all of this is I chose to seek happiness and all of a sudden I have become the pariah to people who have been very close to me.

Many people seek lifetime soul mates and I was fortunate to find one in your sister/aunt/daughter for half of my life. No one can nor will ever replace the memories and the joy that Christine brought into my life. No one knew how I have endured over the past seven months, but it was a burden I was forced to accept and to put the pieces back in my life: like expecting to see her walk into the kitchen from time to time, like only able to sleep on the edge of our bed and expecting to hear her voice from time to time. I truly wish this sense of emptiness and loneliness to no one. Consequently, the changes I have made to the Living, Kevin's, and my rooms was more therapeutic than cosmetic. It was a sign that I needed to change.

Someone very recently asked me 'What do I want out of life' and I replied that the answer would be different based on the circumstances that were occurring. I continued to explain that if I was asked that 5 years ago my answer would have been to have a long life with my family; two years ago I would had replied that Christine be healthy and since I was asked the question last week, I simply stated that I wanted to be happy. What makes me happy now is seeing Kevin doing very well in school as I try to keep him engage since I have taken away most of his distractions and have developed some semblance of a weekly routine.

If pursuing someone to share my happiness with bothers anyone, I will not apologize. Everyone knows what kind of person I am; I can be engaging to those that I allow into my inner circle and I exude whatever energies I receive from the people that are around me who have my wellbeing in their hearts. As a result, my sisters on the mainland are totally overjoyed - at least the three that I have told. Conversely, the inverse is also true for my sisters-in-law.

In Closing, I simply chose to be honest with my feelings instead of lying about my intentions; I chose to pursue happiness opposed to the status quo.

This weekend will be the FIRST in over 100 times - over a period of 26 years - I am going to feel unwelcomed by some when I go to Puerto Rico. I hold no grudges- and if it's time they need to cope with my decision, granted - but the decision to move on with my life is mine.

It is no secret that the person who asked him 'What he wanted out of his life' was Stephanie because they discussed everything. Having received a copy of the email the he sent my mother before her classes, she forwarded a very subdued poignant response. The few words she carefully articulated below took a minute and a half to express by evidence of the video time stamp. The several pauses are why.

Stephanie VLOG

Good morning Rufus, ... how are you ... umm, ... (a sighed breath) ... I just read your email ...and .... umm, ... Wow. Pretty heavy stuff ... Everyone's afraid that things are gonna change for them ... I get it .... I mean, ... things have changed ... they've lost a sister, they've lost a daughter ... you've lost, your wife. (another sighed breath.) I guess that everybody wished that things would stay the same, umm .... wow.........I don't know what to say ... umm... Somehow I feel as if it's my fault – like I've done something – I mean I know better but, ... yea ... umm ... that's heavy stuff. Hmmm, ... Alright, I'm going to get started and have a good day.

Thanksgiving was another celebration he had preplanned and already had the airline tickets months in advance. Quite frankly if he hadn't, the chance of him traveling was very low to have dinner with my family – and in hindsight – he which he hadn't. It was the saddest state of affairs I have ever bear witness to.

My Guys traveled after school on Wednesday and overnighted at my mother's house. Early Thursday morning my taller sister was present and cordial but the shorter sister was an intentional no show. The tension was palpable with the lingering residual taste from the last time they had sat together to eat. The tension should have also been on the menu because it was so thick that it could be sliced. In the end, there was nothing to be thankful for.

Having anticipated the situation and knowing that Stephanie hadn't planned anything for the holiday weekend, earlier in the month Rufus made roundtrip reservations from San Juan to Fort Lauderdale on JetBlue for Friday and return early Sunday to return home with Kevin. After a few hours with my family, it was apparently clear that the day was going to be uncomfortable. As a result, it was the first Thanksgiving where dinner was served before noon because of the tension in my mother's house. And after everyone ate, Rufus decided to notify my mother of his intention to leave immediately and travel standby. He also anticipated that Stephanie's son was going to be present so he called her to notify her of his change in travel plans where he was going to take the opportunity and drive an hour and a half north to visit his sister Janet in Port St. Lucie. Janet hadn't seen him since my funeral and they were up all night talking.

The following day Stephanie drove her son to his dad's early so they could spend the rest of the weekend together. And on Sunday, my mother drove Kevin to the airport where Rufus intentionally layover so they could both return home together.

CHAPTER SEVENTEEN

*"Everyone that knew me are all going to be very surprised
that I was registered Republican in the mid-nineties."*

T HE SUBSEQUENT WEEKS THAT FOLLOWED were perennial three and four day whirlwind weekends that at times included a few false starts like delayed flights and other un-eventualities. Spirit Airlines for the foreseeable future had become Rufus' mainstay. He procured tickets at least a month in advance to take advantage of the best prices. While everyone complained about how their pricing structure charges you even if you changed your mind, the funniest joke by far about Spirit was that they charged a woman an additional fare for delivering a baby in flight. But jokes withstanding, Rufus really knew how to play their game. On average he only paid $200.00 roundtrip and a lot less with miles.

One time when I was alive Rufus actually flew roundtrip for nine cents each way. It ended up being thirty-seven dollars with airport fees because the local port authorities did not care whether the airline had lost their mind, they still wanted to get paid. The key back then was you had to fly on the exact date they provided. And since he was self-employed at that time, he took a lot of those opportunities to visit his mother.

Another airline coup we both took advantage of happened in 1990. We were engaged to be married at that time - because I wasn't going to wait 5 or 6 years - was he 'crazy in his ass?' That doesn't even sound right as I wrote it. Only local people can say that phrase correctly. Anyway, our travel agent called me to report American Airlines made a huge mistake in their reservation systems. And since we flew to Puerto Rico frequently, she said until it was corrected, roundtrip tickets were forty bucks. I called Rufus at the bank and we both sat by our desk calendars and we chose every other weekend for the next six months to weekend including the extended weeks leading up to the wedding and honeymoon cruise. I remember when we flew with those tickets for the first time, the ticket agent at the airport actually said,

"I see you guys have one of these."

Rufus corrected her saying,

"We have a lot of these."

Subsequently we were awarded upgrades and free hotel accommodations for being working class frequent flyers.

So flying has been transfused in Rufus from all those times spending twenty minutes in the sky initially flying to visit me. And now an additional two hours in the air was the price to pay to see Stephanie. The irony is the average price he pays now to go to Fort Lauderdale is what we use to paid to go to Puerto Rico back then. Go figure.

When the late Friday afternoon flight from St. Thomas arrived in Fort Lauderdale between 7:30pm and 8, it was made for a very short window of time to enjoy the evenings happy hours. At first it was necessary to rent a car which at times made him wait an additional hour waiting for the shuttle and going to the car rental center. Then after becoming an Elite member at Enterprise and Budget when agents became familiar with him - in addition to the upgrades and expedited service - it reduced the waiting time in half. He kept looking for ways to shorten his ground transportation options.

Shortly after Stephanie introduced him to Uber when one evening they went out dancing. The driver that picked them up was a recently retired school teacher and an aspiring comedian. It was one of the best social experiences he had to that point. The driver explained that his back seat was his club and practiced his routine on them for the ten-minute ride. He was actually good.

Stephanie also suggested that he should keep some of his clothes at her apartment so he would not have to add to Spirit Airlines' bottom line by traveling with a carryon - but more importantly - for him not to appear like a foreigner with a backpack in the nightclub waiting for her arrival when their weekend commenced.

So now immediately after deplaning, he could be observed on his phone thumbing an Uber when upon arriving to the designated Ride Sharing pickup location, his car was either there or moments away. And most of the time he was the only passenger on the plane without luggage and dressed to go dancing.

On Saturday mornings when she worked three hours until noon, he would take the opportunity to drive to Miami to visit his mother and sister in her car having taken it to the carwash before returning to pick her up. Afterwards the variety of activities they attended or participate in were similar to when Rufus and I dated in the late eighties and nineties.

Back then I did the Puerto Rico Department of Tourism proud when we visited the rain forest at El Yunque, the Arecibo Radio Telescope, and the underwater river system at the Cavern at Camuy. His dates with Stephanie were more sophisticated as she began to culture his behind taking him to the Theater in Palm Beach, a Latino Variety Show in Hollywood, and the International Art Basel show. She perused the weekend's calendar of events before his departure to decide their weekend itinerary.

But clubbing at Blue Martini quickly became his favorite night spot because it reminded him of the life he had on the stage 30 years in the past as a musician. The entertainment was always top notch with a rotation of bands that made it seem at first like there were different concerts. It seemed like everything was going to work out.

◆ ◆ ◆

Those weekends began typically after he arrived at the Cyril E King airport on St. Thomas. I met Rufus back when the airport terminal was a quaint airplane hangar that appeared out of a Banana Republic and was named after the 33rd president of the United States Harry S Truman. After its renovation, it is now the Cyril E. King International Airport to commemorate the 2nd elected Governor of the United States Virgin Islands.

Rufus told me Governor King left an indelible impression on him when he was a kid. He explained when he played biddy basketball around the age of twelve, he was almost 6ft and the basket was 8ft. The governor could be seen in the audience in the neighborhoods watching intra-neighborhood basketball games. They weren't photo-ops - he genuinely loved attending the games in the evenings. Rufus even has a newspaper clipping of the governor tossing the ceremonial jump ball with him in the picture winning the tip off at the beginning of the playoffs. What stuck out in the black and white news clipping was the they had no uniforms and the governor was there in his suit. He said he was thirteen then.

And at the age of 18 he registered to vote under the same political party affiliation Governor King founded, the Independent Citizens Movement or the local ICM Party. Coincidentally, Rufus in some way or manner: met, spoke to, worked for, or is a personal friend of, or is related to every elected governor of the United States Virgin Islands. Although he was seven when the first governor was elected, he met Dr. Melvin H. Evans when he later became their non-voting representative to congress when he attended the Presidential Classroom in 1980.

I was even a celebrity of sorts when people associated my last name with the sixth elected governor Charles W. Turnbull. He is Rufus' second cousin. But Rufus told me a funny story about Governor Turnbull being thrown in jail with a desk when he was the Commissioner of Education in order that he not be distracted from doing his job.

As for myself, everyone that knew me are all going to be very surprised that I was registered Republican in the mid-nineties. Back then Rufus told me to get involved in the community shortly after we were married. With my affinity for travel, I learned that if you were a local party official you could travel with the delegation to the National Conventions. Since the local Democratic Party was very active and their officers were established, Rufus told me that the Republican Party - in his words - was a joke locally. And since it wouldn't hurt proving him wrong, I attended a meeting. When I returned home, I was nominated to be the party's secretary and I accepted.

That kinda stuff seems to happen to me a lot when I was alive. Like when I attended my first PTA meeting at Kevin's private school. As Rufus loves to tell the story, "You made the mistake and asked an important question at the PTA meeting and came home as the Chairperson."

I was very proud of my time there where I began initiatives to fundraise to get the teachers what they needed and at the end of the fiscal years we used the surplus to buy the teachers Christmas gifts. I even got Rufus to volunteer his time in after school programs where he started a Chess and Sudoku club and my employer allowed me to be a substitute Spanish Instructor.

All of that was a result of Rufus' backhanded encouragement when I got into local politics on the sly. But instead of ridiculing me, he told me to buy the book Robert's Rules of Order in order that I can become familiar with parliamentary rules and procedures. And although my experience with the local Republican Party ultimately proved Rufus correct, it was a necessary stepping stone in my managerial skills.

The party meetings were a social club and a colossal waste of my time. In the end, it has been almost two decades since I attended a meeting. The funny part is after my passing, Rufus really got a kick reading letters from people on the mainland that corresponded to me seeking my approval to become part of the Virgin Islands delegation at the 2016 Republican Convention – I AM NOT KIDDING. He even shared some of the letters with Milton.

◆ ◆ ◆

Anyway, although the new airport terminal has been in operation for over a quarter century, they might as well have kept the old hangar. The old hangar was not air conditioned and you knew what to expect upon arrival. If the A/C worked in the new terminal you were pleasantly surprised. And the claustrophobic classroom of a gate for Spirit Airlines has been so uninviting, there's a permanent industrial fan as a fixture as you wait. It feels like a place where you wanted to spend the least amount of time when you travel.

Right before I passed, Milton was the Human Resources Director for the Virgin Islands Port Authority and Rufus blamed him for everything wrong at the airport. Every time Rufus got wet boarding and deplaning the planes, he would call his best friend and ask him when the jet bridge was going to be completed. At one point he even suggested that Milton could look into getting some of the cold air from JetBlue's terminal in Puerto Rico. But I digress again.

The following is a potpourri of different occurrences that actually transpired over various weekends to describe how he was now celebrating his life.

The weekend began with a fellow passenger coughing and sneezing in Rufus' close proximity in the Spirit Airline terminal. It continued on the plane because the person sat in the row behind him and Rufus unfortunately began experiencing flu-like symptoms. He was certain that his weekend was going to be ruined.

Upon landing in Fort Lauderdale, he quickly queued an Uber and caught it shortly after exiting to the Ground Transportation area and was on his way to Blue Martini on Sunrise Boulevard in Fort Lauderdale. Instead of driving Stephanie texted him to notify that she would also catch an Uber immediately after her son's father picked him up. She also shared the ride with the App so he could see her coming to his location in real time on his phone.

Upon his arrival he decided to remedy his flu like symptoms with a prescription of alcohol. He was cerebrally reaching trying to remember whether he had seen a movie where a character drank their way back to health so he began ordering his cocktail of choice...Mojitos. And since one of the ingredients is mint, his rationale was that it must have some kind of medicinal properties. And if it worked, he would duly tell Milton who undoubtedly would have quipped,

"Is that what they taught you in medical school Dred?"

At the same time when the first drink arrived, an older Caucasian man stopped by his booth to compliment him on the jacket he was wearing. The guy actually said,

"I love that jacket man."

Rufus graciously acknowledged with a nod saying, "Thanks."

Then the guy added, "I just had to tell you that...and I'm not gay."

Rufus looked at him quizzically and replied, "Okay?"

Blue Martini is a social hotspot with many franchises in South Florida and even one in Puerto Rico. It's like Hooters, but with class. Oh yeah, and the food actually tastes good. It's the kinda scene where people go to be seen and have a great time in between. The seating arrangements mostly catered to people who spend money on drinks by the bottle. The others could be observed standing with drinks in their hand trying to strike up conversations. (Cue the creepy older Caucasian guy) Then the guy returned again to compliment Rufus' jacket – not forgetting to remark again that he was not gay.

Rufus was seated and told his waitress that his date would be there shortly and to keep the Mojitos coming. Then Rufus texted Stephanie stating that if she didn't hurry, he was going to be picked up. When the Uber App indicated that she was two minutes away, Rufus went outside and paid for her cover and returned to his table. I kid you not, the creepy guy was again back. Rufus narrowed his eyes in the guy's direction to suggest that he wasn't interested in his attention. Then he also realized that he was the only person in the club sitting at a table alone and the guy probably wanted to have a seat at his table.

When Stephanie arrived she looked amazingly stunning as I remembered when I saw her those few times on St. Croix and the first time they met at the Pelican. Her dresses always seemed to fit her body right. She was partial to one-shoulder form-fitting garbs that hug short of mid-thigh thus showing off her shapely legs. At 5ft 7, she wore 3 ½ inch heels to complete her statuesque appearance. At times they would act as if they were meeting for the very first time even when Rufus had already prepaid for her cover at the door. And since the manager had become familiar with them over time, he would signal to the security at the velvet rope to let her through - essentially allowing her to walk in past everyone else in the queue on or about when the band began to play.

The bandstand at the Blue Martinis are uniquely positioned behind the bar where the stages are the same height as the bar counter and the bartenders work the wells in between. It's a subliminal spectacle that keeps your attention dually on the entertainment and at the same time enticing you to buy another cocktail. The bevy of beautiful buxom bartenders and servers are also intentional.

Their evening continued when after mulling over the wine list, Stephanie then ordered their usual: lamb chops and flatbread chicken pizza with a bottle of Camus. This particular evening Rufus spilled some wine on the jacket that the lurker admired and his pants. Like Superwoman, Stephanie flew into action running to the bar to get club soda and cloth napkins and immediately cleaned it up before it was able to stain. After diffusing that small fire, she told him that she was going to the lady's room.

It was a far cry from the time I witnessed when they went out on an evening soiree on the ocean's edge across from the Hilton in Fort Lauderdale on the beach. It was the 10th anniversary party for Venice Magazine. Huge temporary canopies were erected where various arrangements of seating were situated for the guests to network and mingle.

Rufus got Stephanie a glass of wine upon their arrival and he didn't realize that the plastic wine glass was leaking. After she felt the liquid around the stem, Stephanie asked him to have it exchanged. When he finally got to the bar again, the bartender poured another glass of wine, took the glass from Rufus, and blindly tossed it towards the trash receptacle setup behind the bar. Likened to Shaquille O'Neal shooting free throws, the glass flipped on the trash bin's edge and splattered red wine all over a guest similarly attired like Stephanie was at the Pelican. For all intents and purposes, her evening was through. Rufus actually felt responsible after reenacting the episode to Stephanie wishing he had disposed of the wine himself.

I described those series of events to set the stage for what happened next. When she returned from the Ladies Room, she pulled him on the dance floor because the band was playing a familiar tune and they were at it for a few songs. Their exuberance while dancing gave license to others to do similarly. At one point she stopped to hug him on the dance floor. He stopped and felt her body shudder within his grasp, loosening his grip to realize that she was crying. He asked her what was the matter to which she replied,

"I am so happy right now." Then she continued, "When I was in the bathroom, I realized that Christine had to die for me to have the happiness I'm experiencing now."

Rufus held her to reassure as they slowly swayed back and forth. When they danced, I guess she subscribed to the mantra "Dance like nobody's watching" because all her inhibitions seem to have disappeared. She danced so freely as if everything was right in the world while Rufus simply kept up. She also seemed to give license and permission to others not to be so reserved as they found the confidence to also dance freely. She yearned to be led, held, and spun; every now and again returning to their table in step for a sip of wine then return on the floor for more fun. And at times when the music was up-paced, they would do what was contrary and slow dance, if only to take in the moment or simply to give him a chance to catch his breath.

During that moment she once told him she loved the fact that he really knew how to dance and he ungraciously retorted, "You're not bad yourself." Which led to a quick playful jab in the gut as her reminder to check himself.

Then as if she was leading, she quarter-turned him so they were perpendicular to another couple a short distance away also on the floor dancing. The man was an older Caucasian and the lady was significantly younger and Black. Then she said,

"Do you see that couple over there?"

After Rufus acknowledged she continued,

"That used to be me." then proceeded to lay her head on his chest.

Rufus had already known. He was allowing her to reveal as much of her past as she deemed necessary.

When they returned to their booth, there was an unfamiliar glass on their table and a handbag draped over the corner of their chair. The couple was periodically taking sips as they danced. Rufus and Stephanie looked at each other like they were being punked. They decided to let it pass and until the steroid looking, t-shirt bulging Black guy ordered another drink and now there were two glasses on their table. They looked at each other again. This time Rufus said,

"Dude, what are you doing?" loud enough that he would hear.

The guy acted obtuse so Rufus pointed to the glasses.

"My bad." he began and continued to remove the cocktails, "I thought you wouldn't mind." Rufus retorted

"We didn't, but you didn't ask."

Later the guy ordered a flatbread pizza and stood as he ate. Stephanie quipped,

"If you hadn't said anything, that would be on our table too."

After all of the drinking, dancing and near altercation, Uber was the responsible means of transportation to get them home safely. Ironically as they pulled away less than 10ft, in the presence of a Fort Lauderdale police officer, their Uber got side swiped by another patron who had too much to drink.

On Sundays she'd prepared breakfast that was salmon, scrambled eggs, with spinach greens salad. On the balcony they toasted the weekend with Veuve Clicquot champagne. Then she would take him to the airport and say their goodbyes like they did that first time they met.

♦ ♦ ♦

Before the end of the calendar year, after their initial meeting at the Pelican Hotel for breakfast, Rufus subsequently traveled to Fort Lauderdale eight additional times: with Kevin for the NFL game, when he cut short the CEDIA Trade Show weekend in Dallas and left on standby and changed his returned tickets to leave from Miami, the Thanksgiving weekend and they even attended the Art Basel weekend extravaganza in early December and for the Christmas Holiday.

A month earlier I got a little concerned when I felt a little emotional distress emanating from him on November 3rd but immediately realized he was commemorating our anniversary alone in solitude. It was actually Stephanie's idea. She suggested that he should have that day for himself by her not contacting him. The following day's call, she lamented about how hard it was for her not to speak with him saying it was like self-inflicted purgatory she put herself through. They were becoming totally inseparable during his consistent bimonthly weekend visits.

They also attended the Kravitz Center in Palm Beach and the Hollywood Performing Arts Center to see Mozart's Sister – a one woman play – and a traveling Latin Music review at the respective venues. It was so funny watching him trying to stay awake in the front row during the actress's performance staving off whiplash but was totally lucid when it was all over. A stark contrast to the toe tapping, finger snapping, infectious time he had at the Latin review where she simply enjoyed watching him. Or the weekend she picked him up from the airport so that they could see the last sets of a jazz quartet and wound up at Cafe Iguana in Pembroke.

Back in the nineties our favorite nightclub in Florida was Facade located on the Beaches off 163rd. Rufus' keen sense of perception suggested after our first time going there that the club was a money laundering operation. Most evenings were Ladies Night which not only meant that women gained entry for free, their drinks were also.

But hands down Blue Martini in Fort Lauderdale and Miami were Rufus and Stephanie's favorites.

And there were many times Stephanie noticed how tired he was whenever he visited even when he said differently. He would nod off at times in conversations and swore he hadn't. He would lie like a big kid and when he got busted, he would 'fess up' saying that he had traveled so far and didn't want to miss anything during the weekend. She later told him that she would purposely take hold of his hand while they chatted until his grasp loosened to confirm exactly when he dozed off. Thereafter she would treat him like the big child he was acting like and send him into her room where it was purposely darkened void of most light and made sure that the

A/C was frigid. Then she would actually tuck him in under the covers...I am not kidding. Always one to protest, he once suggested,

"I wouldn't need to be covered if you turn up the A/C."

She knew that she should ignore him, but she was the oldest child in her family and didn't take crap from her siblings and instinctively retorted,

"Shut up and sleep."

A girl after my own heart.

♦ ♦ ♦

During the Holiday break, her son stayed at his father's while Rufus and Kevin were spending their first Christmas without me. I knew if I was alive I would have protested against Rufus purchasing the hoverboard for Kevin for safety reasons. But I loved the way Rufus helped Kevin find his center of balance inside of my mother-in-law's home when he stepped on it for the very first time and similarly cringed the following day when he rode the hoverboard around the neighborhood among the slow driving cars when he became confident. My argument would have been, "*What if he fell?*" while Rufus reply would have been his usual default saying, "*He has a lot more falls to get.*"

Stephanie on the other hand made it extremely clear after the Mike Tyson hoverboard fall went viral. She told Rufus that if he rode the hoverboard and falls, she would break any of his remaining good hip or limbs. She further explained that in her experience rehabilitating her clients, their serious injuries were sustained for longer periods the older they were. She never missed an opportunity to remind him that he was old. Again, a girl after my heart.

Finally, Rufus took three days after Christmas to makeover his mother's living accommodations. The gesture made him more endearing to Stephanie and she actually told her mother how special she thought he was. And after he completed he took the time to reflect about the entire year when he posted the following entry on his Facebook page.

At the end of the most emotionally trying year of my life, I would like to thank the people who provided me with the kind of support that made possible to carry on:

My sisters on the mainland that consistently called me on the weekends to check on my wellbeing. What I've learned later was after they each spoke to me, they would conference each other from time to time to compare notes of my metal disposition.

My best friend Milton for always being available to talk. He should send a bill for the invaluable advice I received. One week after the funeral on St. Thomas, he stopped by un-announced to see how Kevin and I were coping. Upon his arrival he called his wife to tell her that 'they need not worry about me because I was in the process of preparing and storing foods for the week like rice and potato salad and had already ironed Kevin's school uniforms for the week.' He continued to tell her that they could learn to organize from me.

My Mother-in-law and I have become a lot closer despite the drama that was brewing in Puerto Rico where over the past year she'd remind me about issues concerning my health.

Debbie in New Jersey who kept reminding me that I was her special nephew and to never let anyone steal my joy.

The parents of Kevin's friends – they know who they are – that allowed an immediate sense of normalcy when Kevin slept over and allowed him to stay longer whenever I had to travel.

My clients, who constantly inquired about my wellbeing and were very understanding whenever I had to adjust my schedule when it conflicted with the new realities of my personal life.

My son Kevin, who from time to time expressed himself with the kind of honesty that makes me pause, reflect, or simply makes me smile. He actually said, "Our life was perfect before 2012."(The year Christine was diagnosed.) On the evening she passed, I told him that my priority in life now is to take care of him for the rest of my life.... his response was, "Dad, you can't guarantee that." That comment hit me to my core and as a result I have been embarking and maintaining a healthy lifestyle of exercise and diet. Last week while driving home from school he actually turned down my NPR on the radio - I reminded him what Chris Tucker explained to Jackie Chan "You Don't Touch a Black Man's Car Radio." Kevin should know ... he has seen that movie too many times...but he did anyway to tell me, "Dad, I tease you all the time about the stuff you chose not to eat to stay healthy, all the exercising that you do, and the upcoming colonoscopy test next...." He summarized by saying, "I really appreciate all that you are doing to stay healthy." My son is a Tightwad as far as spending money on someone else, but that statement suffices as my Personal Christmas Present.

For the 25 years that I spent with Christine, I truly know what love feels like and that is what I have grown accustomed to.

At the year's end Rufus and Kevin flew back to St. Thomas on my birthday December 30th. Then on New Year's Eve, he dropped Kevin off at the airport so he could visit my family for a week before he was to return to school. After Kevin's departure he hung around the airport and waited for Stephanie's arrival when they celebrated the New Year. Prior to leaving Fort Lauderdale, after her last class she forwarded the following serenade via email in anticipation of her first trip. Boy did I get it right when I checked off the 'She Can Sing' box. https://vimeo.com/334199125

When he brought her to the home, he took a cue from his friend that invented the home control system that had been the core service of his business.

In a training seminar the moderator explained that programming home electronics not only could be practical, it can be fun. Rufus explained that the instructor suggests that everyone knows when the mood is right to make love. But what if you had seven kids like the instructor kept repeating he has. How would you know when the time is right? He proceeded to describe the parameters in which he programmed his house: when at a certain time in the evening, if all of the doors at the kid's rooms were closed, Marvin Gaye's Let's Get It On will play in the Master Bedroom beginning with the guitar pick-up lick, ... Wah-wah-wah-wah... And if any of the kid's doors open, the music will immediately stop. And upon their return and the door was closed, Wah-wah-wah-wah ... *"I've been really trying baby, to hold back the feelings, for so long ..."*

Rufus did a similar programming trigger to the home control system for Stephanie initial arrival. The song that she has grown fond of, She's Royal began to play when he opened the front door. That was a short lived coup because the following day Stephanie was in Home Depot buying cleaning products .... again, I AM NOT KIDDING. Rufus really thought he was doing a good job as far as keeping the house clean. But he wasn't affronted – he was incredulous that she was cleaning his house.

A few days later they celebrated her birthday on St. Thomas on the 5th. And as careful as the schedules were made, after Rufus and Stephanie said their goodbyes again on St. Thomas – likening to the first time they met at the Pelican – he remained to watch her plane taxiing for takeoff as Kevin's plane was landing.

♦ ♦ ♦

It's not without forethought that I now choose not to refer to Rufus and Kevin as My Guys anymore. I am so proud of how thoughtful Rufus and Stephanie have navigated their relationship around their sons. At this point both boys knew about the relationship of their parents even though they hadn't met each other. The circumstance when Stephanie initially apprised her son was when he told her that it had been a very long time since he saw her happy. After that comment, she openly spoke to Rufus in the presence of her son on the phone without seclusion. She even had his framed picture next to her bed for a while and thought better of it after realizing that it could be seen from the common space potentially by her ex.

After an accumulation of those calls had transpired, Rufus noticed an intriguing pattern of interaction between mother and son. Every time her son left the room she was in, he would say "I love you." He would politely interrupt her while she was on the phone – or he would abruptly barge in wanting her opinion about something he recently learned – or to tell a joke – or just to be a nag. After she gave her advice, laughed at the punchline, or dismissed him after being annoying, he would say, "I love you." Every time without fail.

After overhearing that scenario played out several times Rufus asked her how and why did she start doing that. She first corrected him stating it was her son who started from very young. He came home from preschool crying because he had forgotten to tell her that he loved her and imagined that something terrible had happened to her. He vowed thereafter to never forget again. As a result, Rufus immediately implemented the same terms of endearment with Kevin and everyone that he loves.

And as far as her mother is concerned, I literally held mind proverbial breath when Stephanie told her mother about Rufus. The homely offspring comments came immediately to mind. Stephanie was also concerned about what her mother was going to say after she forwarded the pictures she took at Trulucks. I did not want to hear the paraphrase – I wanted to hear the unfettered response after the fact that she now has pictures of Rufus in her warehouse – so I wanted a firsthand account of her disposition and not only to hear what she was going to say, but to also see for myself.

"I like this one," her mother began. Then she called her husband to see the pictures. "Pumkin, come and see Stef's boyfriend."

As her father neared he said,

"I told her don't bring anymore White guys up here."

"Then you gotta see this one" Her mother continued.

Still on the phone with Stephanie, her mother couldn't help herself when she remarked,

"Is his head really that big?" as she compared the sizes in the picture.

"Momma?" Stephanie pleaded while her father chimed in after seeing the picture,

"Leave that man alone."

After her father left the room her mother asked,

"Stef, you say he's a fine young man?"

"Yes Momma." She replied.

"But do you have to lay with him?"

CHAPTER EIGHTEEN

"One long time crisis averted - one truce implemented - one groin pain subsided. I think I should go to Geneva to celebrate and have a treaty established. I heard it was beautiful this time of year."

T HE PREVIOUS ACCOUNTS IN A NUTSHELL were their lives for the concurrent biweekly weekends until the early new year. But as turmoil likes to lurk, the both of them never could have foresaw what was next.

The new year of 2016 began where the majority of my omnipresence was spent navigating the warehouses of my family in Puerto Rico. While I observed their slow healing processes as they continued to mourn my passing, I watched and waited for opportunities to intervene whenever possible to ease their emotional pain and to ascertain whether the time was appropriate to foster amends between my household on St. Thomas.

Regardless of what they thought about Rufus, they all had their personal biases with relationship separations in some period of their lives that inevitably led to mistrust issues. And in the middle of all the turmoil was Kevin. His loyalty was cemented with the person who he had observed pulling himself out of the deep quagmire of depression during the past months. Nonetheless, they all felt justified in their behaviors.

When I got sick, Rufus continuously said that our lives were on 'pause' until I got well - not stopped. He insisted that we go out after my final chemotherapy treatment at a fundraiser and he couldn't wait to get me on the next year's Fantastic Voyage where we dance to ole school music until 4am.

On the other hand, they were still indifferent and seemingly obtuse about the fracture they created after Rufus' decision to date again. And as I patiently waited on the sidelines, I observed the uncivil war being waged as both sides seemingly entrenched themselves in their own foxholes.

The lessons learned from their estrangement suggested that although my shorter sister totally severed all ties with Rufus for the moment, she would be more amenable for reconciliation. Stephanie in her wisdom actually mentioned that observation to him. That sister never said anything that got back to him that was derisive.

At the same time, Rufus continued to submit he was cognizant of what was happening and totally understood that time eventually heals all wounds - psychological and emotional. He made the association that what my shorter sister said to him could be considered as a kick in the groin - painful, but it inevitably subsides. And even though what my taller sister accused him of was equivalent to superficial fresh cuts, a sincere apology would be a Band-Aid and those lacerations would heal eventually in time. But those scars remained open, and as time passed, they became infected.

The fact that communication was nonexistent was a blessing in disguise where the moment at the restaurant was allowed to die a slow death of sorts. It was a symbolic truce and a cooling off period. But the Facebook post that Rufus uploaded from Blue Martini during the Christmas holidays didn't help the situation either because it briefly showed him having a great time with Stephanie. Quite frankly, he didn't care because my sisters had already unfriended him.

It is impossible to determine how long people should mourn because it is a path each individual has to follow. The sorrow of my passing still lingers and it has been a hard process trying to reconcile their anguish. Their requests of the universe weren't anything positive and uplifting that fostered reconciliation. They emanated prayers for me reliving my past while at the same time dreamed about the time they would see me again in their afterlives almost a year after my passing. As a result, the Laws of Attractions began the very slow process of granting their wishes as I began to observed the declining health of my mother and my taller sister where medication prescribed and a short hospitalization period was recognized for them respectively. I was happy when they contacted Rufus to apprise him of that matter. He provided the usual emotional support he was accustomed wishing them well and I continued to work behind the scenes looking for opportunities to repair the damages.

In order to turn the corner, I could only intervene if the situation was amenable on both sides. That's why there are truces. My niece in her very short life subliminally recalled some ancient world history from her previous studies and recommended the truce over lunch. It should have been an easy resolution she thought knowing the easygoing kind of person he has been after spending so much time with us. Like on her first Disney trip when she was seven, Rufus kept telling her,

"I hope you're comfortable, because I'm not ...." because she had her own bed while Rufus and I had to share a full-sized while Kevin had a Disney crib. During the week he continue,

"I hope you're comfortable, because I'm not ......" because the only channels on the television were Disney programming. My niece simply giggled.

Fast forward to the pirate walk on the way to New York, the football talk where she has become an avid football fan and has celebrated more recent Superbowl wins than him because she's in love with Tom Brady. Not to mention when she felt she needed to be present at my second memorial service while at college, Rufus was and still is the uncle she described on Facebook. With that farsightedness she also knew that all he required was a sincere apology – nothing more, nothing less. That's how he has always been wired. If he is wrong, he would be first to apologize after showing him the errors of his ways. But he wasn't going to allow himself to be subjugated.

The notion that there's a particular way one is supposed to act after the passing of a loved one is a fallacy. Everyone goes through their own cycle of despair individually. So as far as the state of mind of my family, they were stuck in their personal limbos. From time to time my mother still refers to me in the present tense. The tenant that resides on the upper level of her home has a slight resemblance to me and there's a picture of her where my picture used to be in her guest room downstairs. On the other hand, my shorter sister continues life where she goes dancing from time to time resuming what has brought her joy while my taller sister continues working hard on her job and in private slowly sinks into the rabbit whole she unknowingly created.

Their communications between the family became fewer as the weeks past when Kevin purposely ignored the calls from his aunts and seemed to only answer the calls from my mother arbitrarily. My taller sister became the most affronted because Kevin's cellphone was a long time gift from her and he was on her corporate account. It came to the point where Kevin asked Rufus to get him a new phone so he could be off his aunt's plan and not have to read her text messages where some were reprimands. And because my sister was being ignored, Rufus now began receiving assaults via text messages that he was now telling Kevin not to respond to their texts and calls.

At one point while he was on the job programming, he received one of her accusations and was so angry that his state of mind needed relief because he could not concentrate on what he was doing. He realized that the input of an incorrect code in the system would really compromise the installation, so he went home to clear his mind and returned the following day to complete the task. During the ride home he called her with the intention of letting her know what she was saying was lunacy, but her phone immediately went to voicemail. She then text saying 'she was busy and that they would discuss it later.'

It was that moment Rufus realized it was all a power play in her attempt to manipulate. She could call and launch a salvo interrupting his work, but she was too busy to be interrupted. After that, he decided not to subject himself to her overt maneuverings where he now began ignoring her calls and texts.

In effect she was slowly gerrymandering the family by trying to maintain its division. It also became obvious that her strong will was now adversely influencing my mother's disposition towards Rufus when she no longer spoke to him over the phone, but would only ask about his wellbeing when Kevin chose to speak with her. My other sister seemed to already have her vote and her daughter communicated less with her uncle. So now the party lines were now being spread for our son's loyalty.

Rufus maintained the service to my cell phone for a very long time for two reasons: in case anyone called who hadn't heard the news and most particularly to hear my voice in my voicemail message from time to time. I remember how painful it was for him when on the day after I passed my phone rang. It was my childhood friend Annie. We went to the same elementary school in Puerto Rico and she now lives on St. Croix. She called to find out why I hadn't called her the day before for her birthday like I've done for my entire life. The way she framed her question made it harder for him to disclose. Rufus eventually closed my AT&T account and gave my iPhone to Kevin with one specific directive at the AT&T store in Crown Bay Marina while sitting on the stools,

"Text me your number." Kevin obliged.

"And you must give your grandmother the new number and always answer her calls." Rufus continued. And since he was a little perturbed about the whole situation he concluded to say,

"And frankly I don't care who else you give your number to."

◆ ◆ ◆

It was now five months since Rufus had last spoken amicably to my twin sisters on their birthday in early September – two days after meeting Stephanie. Additionally, it was the week before the anniversary of my passing when my shorter sister finally reached out and called Kevin to see how he was doing. He wasn't enthused; he was far from it. He maintained distant but was cordial with his terse 'FOG" responses: "Fine", "Okay", "Good."

When she asked him about how Rufus was doing, Kevin added more words to form a simple indelible sentence when he replied,

"Ask him yourself."

The difference in how she treated Rufus after he informed my family about his relationship isn't any different than she would have behaved towards him if I was still alive. She hardly ever called him directly – definitely on his birthdays and if there was a Salsa concert looming weekends ahead. And if for some reason we hadn't traveled to Puerto Rico in that same period of time, we still would have spoken regularly on the phone when from time to time she would only ask about Rufus in passing comments – similarly like she just did with Kevin.

So shortly after she hung up with Kevin, she called Rufus. At the same moment he was talking to Stephanie when the caller ID read her name because he hadn't deleted her from his contacts. In his excitement, he told Stephanie that he was going to call her back because of who was on the other line.

The call was pleasant where my sister indicated that she just needed time to come to terms with the whole situation and apologized for not speaking to him sooner when she explained what Kevin said prompted her to call. She even texted him a long apology because although she is bilingual, her English at times includes many Spanish words like "como se dice..." (how do you say) And before they hung up, she promised to keep in touch regularly.

One long time crisis averted – one truce implemented – one groin pain finally subsided. I think I should go to Geneva to celebrate and have a treaty established. I heard it was beautiful this time of year. But before I was able to celebrate, another small battle was looming.

When Rufus called back Stephanie, she was now the terse individual on the other line. She told him that her first intention was not to answer the call, but that would only perpetuate what she wanted to immediately get off her chest. She reminded him that my sisters were totally awful to him while she was the constant emotional support and comfort in his ears for all those months. And now that one decided to come around, she was being summarily dismissed. He knew that it wasn't the case even though everything from her point of view was absolutely true. He apologized and she accepted with another caveat, only their sons call, business or an emergency could interrupt their calls – that's what voicemail is for.

After they hung up, the situation lingered where she was feeling uneasy. After what my sisters put him through - making him feel alienated for all those months - Stephanie felt she was being shunned aside. She wouldn't have taken it so personally if the relationship remained amicable like it was when they were a secret and only talking and texting, but they had taken it to another level. The mere suggestion that she met Rufus more than two years before they actually met in September 2015 was – for lack of another word - insane. Stephanie also predicted that my mother was going to later uninvite herself from the Alaskan Cruise. And even though she had her reservations about the kind of relationship Rufus had with my sister even when he categorized it as a 'brotherly rapport' after being temporarily shunned, she was having second thoughts again.

She suggested very early after hearing Rufus' account of the whole sad state of affairs that my shorter sister was "smartest" when she emotionally removed herself from the equation. She continued to predict after sufficient time had passed, she may be the first to apologize. Her insight led me to realize she was really emotionally invested in their relationship. And conversely, my family also acted like they had a vested interest even though they weren't telling him how to move on with his life; they felt that Kevin should be shielded from Rufus' affair.

CHAPTER NINETEEN

*"I immediately knew what was causing his distress fearing whether
the circumstances that brought them together may have begun
to broke down and wondering whether it could be salvaged."*

EVERYTHING WAS GOING SWIMMINGLY with Rufus and Stephanie, or so I thought. Their stitches in time spent together on weekends appeared blissful on the surface while an underlying problem over the past several months was being camouflaged beneath. The relationship was now in its eighth month and it still felt new as if every weekend visit was a renewal to the first time they met at the Pelican. With the same diligence she took every morning in preparing an amazing workout for her clients at the studio, she planned different things for them to do to make every weekend they spent together special.

They spoke to each other regularly every day – even when they hadn't anything to say. And from my visual perspective, their future together was hopeful and bright. And as far as I was concerned, half of my Afterlife quest was complete. Now I can focus all my energies towards the individual healing of the other members of my family who are still bereaved and try to foster a reconciliation towards how it used to be.

My kindred spirit remains with everyone whose lives and interests were intrinsically entwined in mine. And if their dreams for the immediate future were hopeful, I was now in the position to kickstart a new beginning.

But late in the evening on Friday April 15th, my state of being intuitively recognized signs that I on purposely allowed to go unnoticed. I ignored those funny feelings you get when you know something is wrong even though everything on the surface appeared to be alright. Those feelings were not being addressed and were allowed to fester for too long where one was not being entirely honest with the other until it could no longer be dismissed. They both actually discussed it a couple of times, but among friends it was debated where an unsubstantiated narrative was being subscribed. Now at this present moment, it all came to a head.

It was confirmed when I became aware that they did not tell each other goodnight, yet they both were lying in bed and not asleep. Now lying awake is normal for Rufus, but not for Stephanie. Even her father still referred to her as his Sleeping Beauty.

They did not have an argument because I definitely would have been aware. So what did I miss? She was in Fort Lauderdale; he was at home on St. Thomas and still up after 1am in bed and both visibly distraught. From my unique perspective in Afterlife, the full spectrum of light revealed everything that is otherwise unseen. His light spectrum imminence was like an amber siren alarm similar to the evening when I passed away but not with the same intensity. The difference was fifteen months ago he was writing on his iPad, now he had a blank stare.

I immediately knew what was causing his distress fearing whether the circumstances that brought them together may have begun to broke down and wondering whether it could be salvaged. After all, everybody has arguments – even they had their few when they were together and even when they were apart.

Like the time while on the phone having a typical conversation, she asked him right out of the blue why he wasn't circumcised. I immediately knew that discussion would have implications because Rufus and I had a similar conversation – but it was during my pregnancy and it was in reference to having the procedure performed on Kevin immediately after he was born. It was an option that the pediatrician recommended while Rufus stated it was the doctor's way of paying for his new car.

After giving birth, the nurse was in the process of preparing Kevin to be circumcised when Rufus adamantly protested. He went as far as telling them that the procedure had no medical health benefits other than an archaic religious practice and inquired whether we were going to have to pay for the procedure even when he did not approve nor gave his consent. I was totally out of it being incapacitated from the pain medication after the cesarean. And to be truthful, I wanted the procedure performed merely for cosmetic reasons. Rufus summation brought our conversation to an impasse when he stated,

"I wouldn't tell you what to do if we were having a girl."

So it was settled weeks ahead of the delivery date. Although I knew that the doctors probably didn't fully understand what he was saying knowing how he gets when he's upset, I also knew that Rufus was going to get his point across.

So when Rufus argued his position about the subject with Stephanie, he was coming from a deep seething position he had already resolved and felt he was more qualified being the male in the discussion. In other words, Milton would have been a better advocate to debate her points to this subject. Additionally, his position was reinforced and solidified in the nineties when he listened to the likes of Dr. Dean Adel on afternoon syndicated talk radio while he ran his cousin's electrical contracting firm. Discussions of how the sensitivity of the penis 'glans' is severely affected after circumcision when a growth of dry skin replaces the foreskin rang through that in effect diminishes the pleasure similarly like having sex with a condom. He even bolstered his position reading the recommended testimonials on www.nocirc.org website. So he totally tuned Stephanie out when she said "she did the research" jokingly suggesting to himself that he may have taken her more seriously if she had a sex change. He countered her argument when he suggested why she didn't have her genitalia mutilated similarly like it's performed in many African countries and the Middle East. After that comment, she duly tuned him out. That discussion resolved to a slow death of silence where they both hung up frustrated.

The second time their discussion became heated was over the mundane classification of the piano. Again, I am not kidding. When I say they spoke about everything, that's exactly what I mean. Rufus' position was that the piano is a percussion instrument because of the mere fact that in order to play the piano it had to be struck by the fingers, similarly like playing the drums and the congas. Stephanie said it was a string instrument because the sounds were produced by the strings.

"But you don't play the strings" he argued.

"That is what you hear ", she countered.

They went back and forth as they sat outside on the patio lounge of the Fort Lauderdale Ritz Carlton Burlock Coast Restaurant. It was a chilly evening where they were previously snuggled across from the outdoor torched fireplace after dining on what they considered was the best hamburger where their conversation was now providing the warmth. She even checked Wikipedia on her iPhone which solidified her position stating

"*The piano is an acoustic stringed instrument.*"

He said anyone can edit Wikipedia and probably a non-musician wrote the article she read. He continued recalling what he learned in high school from memory and later referenced Google on his Android cellphone where he read the following from a published encyclopedia,

"*Although an acoustic piano has strings, it is usually classified as a percussion instrument rather than as a stringed instrument, because the strings are struck rather than plucked.*" Then he added,

"So what type of instrument is a synthesizer?"

They were relentless as they continued and eventually tuned each other out after no one gave ground.

Then to further stoke the conversation when that fire seemed to be losing it steam, she brought up another musical reference when she told him that in his earlier discussion, he probably didn't know the meaning of the word 'luthier' and how he probably used it for the very first time. The truth was she admitted not being familiar with the term. But that comment really stuck in his craw.

As a lover of Salsa music, from time to time Rufus tried to explain to me that the acoustic-electric bass that most of the Latin bands used has the best resonance and the fattest bottom. We would be driving or mostly at home listening to music and the quarter panel on the car would resonate or the stud walls would vibrate. Then he would do a thing with his eyes squinting as if he could see the notes. Not to mention, those basses are only manufactured by the Puerto Rican luthier Ray Ramirez out of wood or fiberglass. They are actual works of art. He said he was going to eventually get one if he ever learns to play the acoustic upright contrabass. But on a personal level, the suggestion that a bass player not knowing the classical name for '*a person who makes and repairs string instruments*' is blasphemous and really struck a chord. He was so affronted he told her he was ready to leave knowing that to argue that point with someone who admitted to hearing the word for the first time an hour ago would definitely be futile. She told him that she wasn't ready to leave – not until she finished her wine. It was a quiet ride home. The following day they forged ahead where they began recording exercise videos for their website. I surely got what I bargained for when I requested from the universe someone to challenge him.

So with all that said, they had no further flare-ups to my knowledge and definitely nothing since they last spoke to each other. And although I made sure all of the signs of compatibility were checked off before and after I proverbially relieved myself from my duties, in any healthy relationship there would be hiccups. As far as I am concerned, my quest of finding a soulmate for my husband was over and I wasn't about to now second guess myself. She was absolutely genuine and contrite with her requests of the universe. But was there now a possibility that the kind of lifestyle she had become familiar with and grown accustomed to, she was now beginning to miss even though she expressed otherwise? She had only visited him once so far while in eight months he had visited her sixteen times.

Her one trip to visit Rufus was unlike the weekly first class variety on American Airlines to St. Croix when she dated the doctor. JetBlue with the Big Front Seat sufficed. Nor was it on a private plane to New York for dinner or Broadway Show or to Colorado for weekends in Aspen. Or possibly like the other relationships, this one had simply run its course where she was simply having a change of heart. I didn't have any answers at the moment so I simply had to wait. In the morning I would see exactly what was going on. Two hours later I observed as he finally fell asleep.

I remember how much I loved to see him rest. There is a calm comfort in his breathing similar to when I watched Kevin as a baby that made him appear to be more endearing. His tireless work ethic made sleep a currency he unknowingly deprived himself. Now lately as he got older he was unintentionally getting a late reprieve - after all - he simply needed it.

It actually began when he went into business for himself and was striving to be a success. He worked unconventional hours if the project allowed. Like the time he did the different music systems at the Ritz Carlton on St. Thomas. At times he intentionally worked evening from 8pm because the attic space was too hot during the day and still work regular hours on his other projects. Or another time he got involved in a completed project after the contractor failed to install structured low voltage wiring for Ethernet systems. He couldn't mar the new interior wall finishes of faux paint and leather wallpaper. So he recommended running exterior conduit parallel to the roof guttering and told the owner he was going to commence work at 4am when it was cool and would stop eight hours later or as soon as the sun became unbearable. Today he cringes whenever he sees the local roofers working in the island's summer afternoons. So anytime he had a moment to relax, I let him. And Stephanie did the same for him similarly.

Like on our first cruise with Kevin when he was four, while he spent the day at the kid's camp, Rufus slept. When we embarked on St. Thomas, Rufus did a gate system repair then returned to the ship to sleep. His client later lauded the service that was rendered while we were on St. Thomas on vacation. And the following all day at sea while I explored the ship, he slept.

I remember when our families spent another summer vacation at the Melia Coco Beach in Puerto Rico. Rufus got a call to begin a new project immediately after we checked in. He had to leave the next day so I made sure he was undisturbed by Kevin. He took the opportunity to sleep and I took him to the airport the following day while we stayed. And when I became ill and my breathing was labored, he told me that he hardly slept then. So whenever he appeared so peaceful with his mouth opened, I watched and simply smiled.

◆ ◆ ◆

They seemed to have awoken simultaneously very early at dawn where it could be suggested that they both had each other on their minds and were both obviously sleep deprived. Having developed habits and rituals in their mornings, they appeared to be out of sync. I immediately knew it was very serious. It also appeared that he was now reluctantly reading an email from her on his phone. Based on his expression, it was obvious that he had already read it before.

After he was finished, he deleted it, but not before I was able to read its contents and implications. I immediately knew it was bad because this was the first email from her that he had ever deleted. It confirmed my worst fear; it was more serious than I anticipated. What I just read came totally out of the blue, but it now made perfect sense why he was in emotional despair. The evening before on Friday April 15th - the metaphor of being emotionally taxed with the email received on the exact day he had filed two years' worth of income taxes seemed like a very cruel joke. In essence, the email he just deleted precipitously ended their relationship. Just like that.

In her form of literary prose, Stephanie accused Rufus of "not keeping her safe." The email was an indictment of sorts charging him with the crime of "failure to inform her about bed bugs." I too was taken aback when I questioned whether I had missed something. She suggested her apartment became infested as a result of Rufus' frequent visits. And in its end, concluded he was more concerned about his pride rather than telling her the truth that would have prevented all the pain, discomfort and emotional distress she had to endure over the last four months.

Again it was like another case of deja vu similar to when my sister accused him of knowing Stephanie before he actually did. So he again rationalized that there was no point defending what was untrue. That's how many people wind up imprisoned when they fail to defend themselves from the ridiculous and incredulous. They believe that eventually the truth will be realized. So even though he was deeply in love with her, I again immediately knew what he was going to do.

Stephanie was very proud of her body having over the years worked very hard to maintain its fitness and appearance. Scores of people would either admire from afar or compliment her on her physical appearance. In a previous casual conversation, she told Rufus that her body was her business; her body was her billboard.

In South Florida, plastic surgeries are such a common place where women frequent doctors to maintain their physical appearances. One of Stephanie's many unclaimed fame was the fact that she had never been under the knife. On the job she always wore crop tops with short sleeves as her unofficial uniform at her studio to show off her abdomen and arms.

So in early December when blemishes were now appearing on her body, to say she was freaking out would be a major understatement. All of a sudden she began to purchase longer sleeved garments to wear. Every other day or there about, she seemed to contract another. The thing was early on she visited two different dermatologists where they took cultures of her skin and both determined that they were bug bites. She insisted otherwise because she didn't see any evidence of them. While going through her ordeal she told Rufus about an earlier time in her life when she had experienced similar lesions on her body that were later deemed psychological. That was another reason she was adamant with the dermatologists. She explained to Rufus that during those previous occurrences, she was in the presence of her doctor and she was able to produce them by mere thought. At that point she realized that she needed to cleanse her mind and body of all maladies. He thought that the story was eccentric but, it was her personal experience and he accepted what she said and made no further comments.

So for the following three months her body was constantly irritated where the discoloration appeared and the only thing that made the discomfort go away were repeat scalding hot showers. After each occurrence it left small discolorations on her body.

At the end of the year, it took a lot of intestinal fortitude for her to visit Rufus in St. Thomas even though she wasn't feeling her best. If the circumstances were different where she had visited him prior during the early months of their relationship, she would have definitely passed on the holiday trip. But she also knew how much it meant to Rufus for her to finally meet Milton. During their brief meeting at home she showed Milton her visible marks on her arms. Coincidentally, she also told her ex-husband who learned from her son when he mercilessly remarked that no one would want to be with her now that it appeared that she was growing spots. Rufus' only corroboration to the accusation was that the malady began before she came to St. Thomas.

Since I am making a correlation that the email was a literary indictment, I am now going to testify to defend my husband. Approximately a year before I passed we did have a bed bug issue in Kevin's room and it was remediated immediately after. It was a result of a recent sleepover he had where he suffered from the bites. I even remembered calling the exterminator where in addition our termite issue was also treated. Rufus told that much of the story to Stephanie in one of their casual discussion and nothing more was said or suggested. But even before they met, Rufus went further for different reasons. He bought a new bunk bed system for Kevin in July and built an integrated desk/chest of drawers wall system so Kevin would have the feel of a new bedroom. And as I have already described, he redecorated his room for his birthday in August to remind him of the EB Hotel where his final evidence of innocence was the purchase of the Sleep Number mattress that arrived a few days before his birthday. Subsequently, all the clothes he wore and left at her apartment –

including his underwear - were all new. Finally, and because all of the additional expenses she incurred as a result of the skin condition were non budgetary, he offsetted those concerns for her.

As the problem persist, she returned to her primary dermatologist where he recommended the use of steroid pills to keep her skin from discoloring. She made the conscious decision where she weighed the adverse effect of the steroid prescription against her life expectancy. Afterwards, the subsequent legions she endured didn't leave discoloration and weren't as painful.

At the same time, her business partner and clients at her Pilates studio were concerned about her skin malady and were in her ear suggesting that her new boyfriend must be the culprit. Additionally, they became certain after she told them that he has clothes at her apartment even though she did his laundry and took care of his dry cleaning. When she finally found bed bugs, she actually stored them in a Ziploc bag and began mulling over her thoughts as if they were her jury pool. And after that point, she began sleeping uncomfortably on her living room chaise.

Suspiciously around the same time, the wooden floors in her bedroom were slowly becoming warped to the point where the doors to her room and closet failed to close properly. Rufus told her to notify her landlord because that kind of repair was more than he was prepared to do over a weekend visit. The fact was that the situation with the floor had begun months before shortly after Rufus began visiting her. He immediately noticed the slight change under his feet when he removed his shoes and made an association that he kept to himself.

He remembered the first time he saw a Pilates reformer. It was on St. Thomas in a client's personal dance studio. The job involved mounting flat panel TVs on the mirrored wall. He remembered the room's wooden floors cupping similarly and later buckling after being subjected to moisture from the condensation of the cistern below. There was no cistern below Stephanie's fifth floor apartment, but he knew for certain there was a water problem. Her landlord immediately found there was a plumbing issue where a pipe in her bathroom wall had been leaking over a period of months to the point the unoccupied apartment below also showed signs of major water damage on its ceiling.

For the next three weeks her landlord moved her into a hotel while the repairs were made. At the same time, an exterminator was hired to rid the apartment of the pest. During that time Rufus visited her during one of those weekends in February and he saw the extent of the damages and repairs. And after the problem was remediated, as a result of her medical esthetician's experience, over time she was able to remove the discoloration with chemical peel and her microdermabrasion machine. Then when she moved back in Rufus told her to replace her mattress by telling her to get a bigger size than the full. She apprised him that the apartment was rented furnished and the bed wasn't hers. He made arrangements with his Rooms to Go account over the phone and even bought a chest of drawers big enough to include some of his clothes.

◆ ◆ ◆

His thoughts were spinning a mile a minute as he replayed the past several months' events in his head. His thoughts had become a huge quagmire muddied now by the equally absurd accusations he had previously rejected and was the reason for his overnight lack of sleep. He actually thought that everything between them was okay, but now he began to feel that pit in his stomach similar to 15 months before. It felt like another death in the family, but different.

When he was younger, it would be convenient to say that when Ms. Credit Card broke up with him, he suffered from a broken heart. But after a lifetime lived with someone that he truly loved, a broken heart is no longer misconstrued from his perspective. When I passed away it was apparent to everyone that knew him that his heart was broken. What he was also experiencing at the moment was broken expectations. Those expectations were renewed after meeting Stephanie. The expectation that if he kept up his part of the bargain she would reciprocate. He wholeheartedly thought that his immediate future was again going to be bright.

But nothing she claimed made sense. Everything he was accused of was the furthest thing from the truth. He even considered that it must have been a cruel joke and for a very brief moment wanted to call her for an explanation. But the simple act of picking up the phone and calling her was a non-starter. His rationalization was simply the fact that he was innocent and she was the one who broke up with him where he wasn't allowed an opportunity to defend himself. So he immediately came to the realization that he would be sentenced to being single again.

His pride suggested he was okay with that, while his ego wondered whether pouring his soul out to her like a bleeding heart was really worth it. He second guessed whether if he had done things differently he would not feel as empty as he presently was feeling and surmised he would not have done anything differently because he would then be inauthentic. In the end, so much time was invested and at what cost. Chalk it up to another one of life's lessons he thought and wondered whether he had the temerity to start over again. Instead he actually thought that a hiatus would be warranted. And to add insult to injury, her verdict wasn't presented in person like it's done in court, it was rendered via email.

Compare now the circumstances with the last break up with Ms. Credit Card. She waited for him to travel by plane to do it face to face when at that time in his life, a phone call was preferred. Now older and wiser, the opposite was true based on their geographic realities. Face to face is always preferable and a phone call would have sufficed as a preferred alternative method of notification instead of the email. He actually thought to himself, "Is that how it's done nowadays?"

Although he was psychologically fragile at the moment, he was self-assured to the point where under no circumstance was he going to call her. It would be synonymous to being allowed to render remarks right before sentencing in court darn well knowing that you were absolutely innocent. The line in the movie Law Abiding Citizen comes to mind, "*It's not what you know, it's what you can prove.*" He didn't feel he needed to explain nor prove anything. He may have been prompted to defend himself and may have even provided a timeline if she had called. He thought that was the least she could have done to sever their relationship. That was how adults communicate.

Still being true to himself, he actually found a little humor in his situation. He remembered stories where people actually broke off relationships on Facebook and was happy she did not maintain any active social media accounts. And at the same time, he actually quoted Sergeant Murtaugh in *Lethal Weapon* stating to himself,

"I am getting too old for this shit."

♦ ♦ ♦

By mid-morning Stephanie realized he must have received and read her email. If he hadn't, he would have called last night and they possibly would have had an awkward conversation or quite frankly she wouldn't have answered the phone to suggest she was asleep and further delaying the inevitable. Otherwise, by this time he definitely would have called simply to say "Good Morning Babe" if he hadn't read the email.

Regardless of the circumstances, she assumed that Rufus was going to call – they always did she mused. After all the Doctor from St. Croix called her after they broke up and continued after she began dating again. The most recent time she asked him not to call her anymore because she was in a relationship and that new information really upset him. She then followed up by telling Rufus about a year before, the Doctor took her out for lunch with thoughts of rekindling the relationship when he was in Miami but she didn't commiserate. Afterwards she always feared the possibility of running into him since he has a medical practice downtown. It was becoming understandable why from time to time she repeated the term "she needed to feel safe."

So with that premise, she cancelled her Saturday classes and waited for her phone to ring. She had discussions with Rufus where she expressed all of her previous relationships ended on her terms. Whether the circumstances were precipitous or gradual, invariably her fiancé's all called to find out why her sudden change of heart. Rufus, on the other hand decided to reciprocate in the same manner he was notified making it known that he had received her email. He carefully worded the following without any ambiguities so there weren't any doubts when he forwarded the following message without the usual endearing salutation.

There were many signs I failed to see, even though a few times initially you tried to warn me. But I am looking back with regret....and yet I am not. Metaphors like 'I am a beautiful tune' and 'you are broken' initially seemed frivolous then, but I should have dug deeper although with that citation so early in our relationship, there was no context to refer or compare.

You are an incredibly amazing woman and for the limited time I have known you were very memorable- to be discreet. What I now know is you are broken because you choose to be and if you feel that ultimately you will be alone with what you have going on for yourself, I won't pity you with platitudes, I will simply say, ... "wow".

As for the bedbug issue – before we met, Kevin and I traveled frequently last year and our families have yet to comment about any such infestation. The problem we experienced was caused by a sleepover he had with his friend in 2014. Christine had extermination services address the issues including termites. The replacement of our beds were additional mitigation process I did just for a change of scenery to make a new start. The clothing that I left at your apartment were all new including the underwear. You found yourself many times cutting tags from my clothes when we went out. My explanation for your infestation was the leaking water issue that slowly caused the floorboards in your apartment to warp over a period of months which may have stir up what was hibernating. And although I know that what happened to your skin was devastating, suggesting that I did not keep you safe is a far reach. What I did do was made you whole as far as restoring you back to pre-infestation....and would gladly do again to 'keep you safe'.

There were signs later in the relationship where my intuition made me pause, but I still failed to question. Every time I told you "I'm going to leave that alone" were suggestions I neglected. I spent the day reliving the feelings of doubt I have been feeling lately and in hindsight, I am questioning what caused those recently heightened uneasy feelings.

Take care of yourself,

Rufus

His email wasn't a gauntlet being dropped; it was more like a door softly being closed. I remember Rufus telling me about how painful his last break up with Miss Credit Card was and the manner in which he coped. He described how he went into preservation mode. He became consumed with playing chess for hours on end not having to go to work because he was on a month's vacation.

He unceremoniously described how he got his ass kicked continuously over and over and over again when he played. As a result, it made him angrier and angrier and angrier every time he lost. Day after day after day, loss after loss after loss. It was another form of self-imposed insanity – doing the same thing over and over with similar results.

Then like most brilliant artists and musicians, the brief periods of delusion create extraordinary works of art and music. When one practices over and over and over fosters the kind of mastery that creates masterpieces. Rufus told me how he devised a plan to beat the computer. I didn't understand how to play chess at that time, but he explained his strategy to sacrifice the queens in the beginning stages of the game. The algorithm in the software design didn't account for that possibility. As a result, the magnetized self-moving computerized game no longer was able to win. He had gotten rid of that game right before we were married because of the bad memories. He now wished he still had the game, but immediately dismissed it because he hadn't played chess in decades.

He then thought about practicing on his bass guitars and somehow becoming a virtuoso of sorts. That notion was dispelled immediately because he needed more than a weekends time knowing that he had pending projects and had to return to work on Monday. He even contemplated about the eventuality of dating again realizing that finding true love truly is complicating. His zealous thoughts that he had lucked out two times in the relationship department was now being questioned why should he be twice as lucky. The twenty-five years he spent with me was a great run and began to reconcile. His thoughts were fleeting and irrationally rational. It was bad…. it was really bad. When he was able to finally calmed down his thoughts, he decided to stay in the bedroom and remain in bed.

Moments later the phone rang and he momentarily became excited until he saw it was Kevin. Unexcited to receive a call from our son was again - another bad sign. He was in Puerto Rico for the weekend to be with my family, but particularly to buy him something. Kevin was calling from Plaza Las Americas Sports Memorabilia store where Rufus bought our personalized Yankee Jerseys. He was asking what name and number to put on the jersey for Stephanie. The jersey was for the upcoming Tom Joyner Fantastic Voyage Sail Away pool deck concert where everyone would wear something representative of themselves or from where they hailed. Rufus and I wore our personalized Yankees jerseys on the only cruise I attended and we were a hit. He figured when he and Stephanie went they would have a similar effect. That's when he realized that they were supposed to be going on the cruise the following weekend. He immediately came to terms that he would be alone again on the ship for the second time in four years since it was too late to invite someone else because he already had the travel documents. He even forgot he hadn't answered the phone when Kevin shouted,

"Dad, what do you want me to put on the jersey?"

The question brought him back to the moment as he solemnly replied,

"Forget about it."

"What happened?" Kevin asked

"Stephanie and I broke up." he responded being forthcoming.

"What did you do? Kevin questioned.

"What did I - Really?" then he added, "What makes you think..." he thought better of it and concluded, "I will tell you about it when you come back."

So for the next forty-hours, knowing he was not responsible for what he was being blamed, he began the process of clearing his head, metaphorically detaching the synapses in his consciousness of the last eight months of his life.

He made mental associations in his mind where he equated the past weekend memories as linear network patch cables. The patch cables represented the sequence of events from the air travel, nightclubs, dinners, picnics, and copulations. The patch cables were plugged into a 16-port network switch from which he illogically figured he had traveled at least twice a month for eight months so the 16-port network switch would suffice.

One by one he was metaphorically unplugging each cable from the switch to symbolize the erasing of a weekend spent. Like the Art Basel weekend where she sought out and found two original Basquiat paintings and apprised Rufus why he was one of her favorite artists. Or the amazing time they had when she took him to Fort Lauderdale's Blue Martini compared to the time at Miami's Blue Martini where she was visibly annoyed when they were unable to get a table. Or even the weekend with flu like symptoms where Mojitos were his prescription remedy and his jacket was almost solicited by a guy who reminded him repeatedly he wasn't gay.

He continued to search his brain for more occurrences that he wouldn't have otherwise immediately forgot. But to his chagrin he couldn't. More often than not, the weekends were simply memorable. So instead of trying to parse specific situations, he decided to remove the emotions from the process and simply unplugged them all including the first time they met at the Pelican Hotel.

Then he realized that the memories weren't only of the weekends, but they also included their marathon telephone calls. As a result, he now needed a network switch with more connection ports so he imagined it to now have 48. Which also meant 48 patch cables of different lengths and colors - all of which he had prepared in the field of his mind: fabricated, tested, and ironically terminated.

Then there were the video testimonials which now required a 96 ports switch...and then all of the letters and poems they shared ... he was an emotional mess.

◆ ◆ ◆

The silence was deafening at her apartment that Saturday morning. The kind of silence one hears immediately after a standoff and before the subsequent gunfights that are infamous in western movies. The kind of silence that is ever present in deep space. The kind of quietness she welcomes when she's about to read or write something. The kind of silence she had grown too familiar with on weekends until eight months ago when Rufus came into her life and began occupying her thoughts and her time. But this was different because it was prolonged....and for hours at that. The silence was amplified because of the twisted hands of fate that somehow failed to give Rufus the script. It was obvious that she was becoming uneasy in each passing 1/2 hour and it was becoming apparent that she was having second thoughts.

Then after reading his email for a few times, she felt the resolution in his words. It was calm and terse. And unlike a closing argument when the defendant's attorney tries to make a case, his email was a weak summation to say the least. He simply quantified the facts from his perspective of all he knew that was true. But that didn't matter at the moment because her prosecutorial tendency still believed what she wrote and what was stoked by her colleagues and friends. But in the end, the sentence that rang through to her in his closing argument was *"I won't pity you with platitudes, I will simply say "wow"*.

Exactly what she did not expect. I knew he wasn't going to apologize because as far as he was concerned there wasn't anything to warrant it. But on the other hand, he did express regret. He felt awful that she had gone through the entire episode and now that it was over, he simply wished her well. In essence, she was also suffering from broken expectations.

She had actually confided with her business partner days before and even forwarded a proof of the email she had written to review. And as the day progressed she called her Jamaican girlfriend Natalee who later came over to her apartment to be her sympathetic ear. She explained to her that she expected Rufus to call but he emailed instead and was now considering whether she was too hasty.

Rufus actually met Natalee briefly on his 2nd visit. He was on the way back to the airport a Monday morning and stopped by the studio to say goodbye during one of the classes. As he walked in all the women in the studio said in unison, "Good Morning Rufus." It made him feel enamored immediately realizing that she had told her clients about him. Natalee took the opportunity to whispered the following in his ear with her Jamaican accent as she walked by,

"If you messed with my girl, I will fuck you up."

Rufus replied in his manufactured Jamaican accent,

"Why yo wan to-GWAN so?" (Why do you want to go on so or why you want to act that way.)

Stephanie wasn't amenable to listening to any advice from her friend because her relationships were not of the healthy variety. But her company was welcomed because she needed to know that she did the right thing.

Natalee began by suggesting good Caribbean men are wired differently than their typical American counterparts. They are surrounded by something intrinsic that mainland Black men seldom see ... role models ... for better or for worse. In the islands they are the Governors, the Prime Ministers, the doctors, lawyers, business owners and different kinds of teachers. They don't have to look far to see their future.

Natalee reminded her of the journal entry she wrote down a year ago describing the type of guy she would eventually like to meet. Natalee actually had a copy of what was written and expressed the following to her: generous, an artist, fun to be with, etc.

Natalee continued to remind her how strikingly beautiful she is being very cognizant of all the attention she garners whenever she walks into a room - welcomed and unwelcomed. She continued to lecture her about how she had gotten accustomed to men literally falling heads over heels, practically sustaining whiplash whenever she walks by or when she is in a captive room. But after it was all said and done, her beauty seems to be a curse. She said although the other men she dated treated her very well, you broke those relationships off for various reasons. You complained about always having to be made-up in their presence and how that made you feel like their accessory and arm candy. Natalee reminded her how surprised she was when she told her that Rufus genuinely cared less whether she wore makeup or not. And continued to recap how she unstintingly tried to chase him away like when she asked, 'what did he see when he looked at her.' Even though Rufus was an open book telling her everything about himself even before they actually met, she was enigmatic about her past - and understandably so.

Natalee reminded her that she thought it was a very bad idea to apprised Rufus on their first meeting that she had been engaged to be married three times and the kind of lifestyle she forego. For most men that can suggest a red flag. Rufus actually stated that he had an idea about her previous relationships even though she wasn't as forthcoming about her past. It was confirmed when he saw how she was dressed at the Pelican. He also referred to one of the pictures that she forwarded in late August where she was seated in an Aston Martin. She clarified that Natalee took that picture while they attended a Car Show and that particular car cost was in excess of $300,000.00. But she further elaborated that one of her fiancé actually ordered a green one for her.

Something weird actually happened after that brief dialogue. Rufus expressed how much he was enthralled knowing that she has a true affinity towards cars. In one of their marathon weekend phone calls she suggested that in the future she would love to put a roadster kit car together and drive it around. She on the other hand commented about the confidence Rufus exuded having the forethought that she owned a six figure automobile and would still have the "balls" to step to her and felt no differently when he first followed her back to her apartment when she drove a Jeep.

She explained that her former fiancés were all significantly wealthy and she was unapologetic about the breakups admitting she was genuinely happier for it. Rufus didn't apologize for having considerably less net worth and most definitely couldn't provide the kind of lifestyle the other guys she's dated were able to. Recognizing that the cycle of relationships was untenable, that she was unequally yoked, she came to the realization that she was the problem and sought therapy. After more than a year of celibacy during when her mother made the comment about her being eaten by her dogs when she dies, in 2014 she wrote the following edict to herself:

"Never accept less than what you deserve in life and love.
Be patient enough to wait for what you truly deserve.
Be strong enough to let go of old comforts where you are no longer served,
You are worthy of a great life and great love."

But she admitted that for the past eight months, Rufus made her feel free in the end. Natalee concluded that it now appeared that he was now willing to walk away stating that based on everything she had told her about him, Rufus is the guy you wrote about.

For all intents and purposes, during those moments of reflection, Natalee was her mirror retelling the life she once knew. In addition, she was providing a prospective about another culture of men where Stephanie hadn't a clue.

After being reminded of it all by her friend, I actually thought contrition was going to be the order of the remainder of the day. Instead Stephanie was still affronted by the fact that Rufus still hadn't called. Additionally, she was also offended by the audacity of her friend being totally candid. After all, she was her father's princess and a modern day Helen of Troy with a face that launched a thousand ships or turned a hundred heads. With her temerity waning ever so slightly she thought to herself, "Natalee had the nerves to talk to her that way.... how dare she." If Natalee was the Mirror in the fairytale Cinderella, Stephanie would've broken it and forego all those years of bad luck to follow because of simply being told the truth.

She later called her mother and apprised her she would drive north and visit for a week since she had the time off.

CHAPTER TWENTY

*"The fact that Rufus took the extra day over the weekend to reestablish
his personal constitution made everything less superficial and
more fundamental about what he really wanted for his future."*

M ONDAY CAME AROUND AND RUFUS still wasn't emotionally ready to return to work. He needed an additional day alone to get over the past nine months to include August when they met online. If he didn't have to pick Kevin up from the airport on Sunday and take him to school on Monday, he would have spent every minute of time in the master bedroom during that fateful weekend. Early in the morning after he awaken, he evaluated his mental state and figured another twenty-four hours alone would be sufficient to again move on with his life.

Over the weekend he took some of that time to resolve upcoming issues. He figured that he was going to go on the Tom Joyner Fantastic Voyage alone; not to mention his class reunion Alaskan cruise. He had invited my mother earlier and she later decided not to go after she assumed that Rufus had invited Stephanie. He never told her directly and actually booked separate cabins with the intention to have Kevin room with her. With the new reality, he had earlier consolidated the payments for both cabins into one. As a result, now, he wasn't looking forward to having the conversation with his classmate Amazia to now remove Stephanie's name from the roster. The travel agent had already charge him fifty dollars when he consolidated the room and another fifty bucks when Rufus saw that Stephanie's passport had her maiden name and requested another change. He now knew he was going to be charged similarly for another itinerary change. Rufus decision was to now shorten Kevin basketball camp duration by a week and to take him on the reunion cruise in July.

He remembered how his classmate Amazia was so happy when he told her to add Stephanie briefly telling her about how they met. At that moment she promised to communicate with him separately about travel details away from the regular group chat. In the end he thought, it would just be him and Kevin. Kevin would continue the STEM camp in Puerto Rico for the summer and then go with him to Alaska in July. He actually thought that Kevin was going to love flying first class for eight hours. He had it all figured out.

Tuesday afternoon after returning from work Rufus concluded that he had one more issue to settle. His sister Linda and her daughter were at the house. They had been there during the entire weekend, but you wouldn't have known it the way Rufus isolated himself in his bedroom. He apprised her about Stephanie's email immediately that Saturday morning and was a recluse thereafter.

Linda was visiting because of the funeral proceedings of her ex-husband. Ironically, she was present to witnessed the reprieve and theatrical break up with Ms. Credit Card and now she was back twenty-six years later to see him through it again. Coincidentally, she was also the first person in Rufus' family to meet me one month after I met him. It was at a surprise baby shower in December for her daughter Cherise. At that party I also realized for the first time how generous Rufus was with those he truly cared for when he flew down his sister Lena to surprise Linda. Subsequently twenty-six years later, Linda was again the first to meet Stephanie. For her birthday in November 2015 – two months after The Pelican meeting – Rufus bought Linda an annual membership to workout at Stephanie's Pilates studio.

As far as he can remember, he had never bought his sisters anything before. But from time to time he would help her out financially whenever there were crises. He figured they were repayment for the times she sent him cash in the mail when he was in college. He never asked, but whenever he felt financially destitute back then, an envelope with fifty dollars unexpectedly showed up in the mailbox every now and again. Ultimately this last gesture of the membership was his superstitious way of gaining Linda's approval. He actually said Linda's opinion was good luck. She intervened with Ms. Credit Card. She was first in his family to be introduced to me and we spent twenty-five years together. And he was hoping for similar results with Stephanie.

As a result of notifying Linda, his other sisters automatically knew about the break up and were again concerned about his wellbeing. Over the weekend they all called but this time he did not answer. When they finally spoke to him on Tuesday, the other sisters expressed their deep contempt for Stephanie. Rufus interrupted them stating that they were making derogatory statements about someone that neither of them had even met.

That was different I immediately thought; it was actually an extraordinary sign of growth. It was a far cry from the ventriloquist scowl and the airplane headset show off days of his past when we saw Ms. Credit Card at the commuter airport in Puerto Rico. They actually dated for the same amount of time he has known Stephanie and that sighting in Puerto Rico was fifteen years removed. He was still holding a lot of animosity towards her back then, but now there wasn't any. Then I immediately concluded he was again ready to move on.

But there was still one small issue that he wanted to address. So after talking with his sisters on conference, he returned to his bedroom and texted the following message to Stephanie.

Rufus
I am just writing to let you know that I will be coming up at the end of the week to go on the cruise and I am wondering whether I can come by to get my clothes.

Rufus allowed a few minutes to pass after he didn't receive a reply and followed up writing.

Rufus
If you have a problem with me coming over, I will appreciate if you brought my clothes to the studio on Saturday so my sister can get them for me.

After he sent that last entry, he waited but again there was still no response. He figured that was it; she probably disposed of his clothes anyway having thought that they were infested. He visualized that chapter in his life had ended. It was over and he actually felt resolute.

On the other hand, I felt the need to intervene, although my intuition suggested that I should let everything play out. After all, the circumstances that brought on this impasse was emblematic of another series of puzzle pieces similarly to the figurative one I construed to get them together. The difference now was there were a few pieces which did not perfectly fit into this particular puzzle and were forced to complete.

We have all completed puzzles with the last two pieces out of place. After stepping back and looking at the entire picture, you see the error and swap the pieces to make the correction that was seemingly out of place. In other words, if there was any chance of salvaging their relationship, there were circumstances yet to be addressed and resolved.

You see, there are reasons in everything that we do. If she hadn't suggested that he should leave clothing at her apartment, Rufus would have had no other reason to communicate with her after his email on Saturday. Consequently, that would also suggest that the break up email would never have been written because there were no clothes to be the blame for the break up. Which now also suggests that there was something else being unsaid.

She did have concerns about his mental state initially when Rufus unknowingly kept comparing me to her. Early in the relationship he stated that he read an article about how the growing population of widowed individuals cope. It suggested that 'a relationship with a widower is an alliance of three.' He told Stephanie about the article and she didn't comment.

Then he kept telling her what 'he was accustomed to' whenever they did things that were familiar. Additionally, in his many of his writings to her, he corresponded in the second person instead of the first or third. She called him out on those instances where he honestly didn't realize his errors. She had become so concerned to the point she sought the advice of Linda after a Saturday exercise class. Stephanie asked her whether I was anything like her to which Linda stated absolutely not personality wise. But Linda also told her that she needed to talk to Rufus about how uneasy she was feeling.

So in her calculations – in her proverbial puzzle - she knew Linda was going to be visiting Rufus and under what circumstances. And although she had written the email a few days prior, she decided to forward it on the weekend when his sister was going to be with him so she could be an advocate to express her concerns. What she miscalculated was the length of isolation Rufus subjected himself to and had grown accustomed after my passing. So while Rufus spent the weekend reconciling his immediate past to the point he was ready again to move on with his life, conversely Stephanie's weekend was unresolved.

His clothes were already compiled in a garbage bag and now sat in the closet. After reading his text messages, she took the opportunity to look at the closet where behind it's bifold doors the bag now sat on the floor. She was again affronted because instead of calling, he texted – twice – and he was only concerned about his clothes.

The song *Back Together* by Jill Scott would have been very timely at the moment, but unfortunately she wasn't listening to any music. She spent her weekend in a state of limbo and went about her Monday and Tuesday in the stoic manner her clients had grown familiar before she had met Rufus. She even told him that her clients actually called her out when her disposition changed commented that there was a certain joy in her voice. But the music she streamed over the past months was from her heart and although certain things were unsaid, she still loved how it felt.

◆ ◆ ◆

Rufus was back in the living room finally being the kind of host to his sister and niece that they were accustomed where Linda talked about meeting her ex-husband's son for the first time at the funeral as she solemnly introduced herself to his widowed wife when the phone rang. It was her. He excused himself and went into his bedroom for privacy and after the third ring he answered,

"Hello?" There were a few seconds of silence before he repeated when she answered.

"I can't believe that you didn't call me." she began.

Incredulously Rufus pondered at what he heard and replied,

"Call?" He paused to sensor his immediate thought of blurting out something like 'seriously' or 'are you kidding me?' and appropriately replied,

"You broke up with me. I figured that you had made up your mind and I just text because I wanted to get my clothes back."

Still affronted she retorted,

"I am here suffering and all you care about are your damn clothes?"

Rufus reminded her of what she had accused him of and she repeated what she thought was her truth. It was actually a civil discourse as they went back and forth at times talking simultaneously. But the conversation was quickly going nowhere when after a minute Rufus finally stated,

"Stef, I don't want to continue going back and forth. Frankly if we can't get past this, it's best that we go our separate ways."

There was a longer than usual silence. It seemed like a brief period of reflection and evaluation when she finally said,

".... I need to see you."

Her response was reminiscent to the video testimonial when she told him "I really want to **see** you." He seemed to have metaphorically replugged that specific patch cable into the network switch to relive all of the emotions he had initially felt when he saw the testimonial.

"I am already scheduled to fly on Friday but I will see if I can come up on Thursday so we can talk."

"I would like that very much." she contritely replied.

◆ ◆ ◆

This perspective of hindsight 20/20 or my Afterlife UHD is quite enlightening. In reflection, even though that discussion over the phone took less than 2 minutes in actual time, they both needed that entire weekend off and then some to step back and take a sighed breath. Rufus did.

Truth be told, before that email, he was madly in love with her. And although Stephanie was equally enamored, she remained emotionally guarded. The fact that Rufus took the extra day over the weekend to reestablish his personal constitution made everything less superficial about her and more fundamental about what he really wanted for his future. He actually did not think he would ever see her again and was now willing to see what the weekend would bring in two days. Life would have gone on and their paths would have or would not have crossed, but in the end, they would have still wished each other well.

Like the time before Stephanie knew Rufus, she ran into her Jewish fiancé at an elevator at a hotel. The brief moment was poignant and they simply hugged each other and said their goodbyes again.

♦ ♦ ♦

Blue Martini was bustling even though it was a Thursday evening. He sat alone in one of the 'U'-shaped dining booths with a Mojito. She told him that she would be arriving a little later so he should have something to eat because she had a meeting that was school related and would be there immediately after. Around 9:30pm he saw her approaching and he stood to greet her with an embrace like they were separated for a lot longer than a weekend. She was more relieved that she appeared and after that truncated time at the club was over, they later vowed to always be totally honest with each other regardless and nothing was sacred.

The first salvo of truthfulness came the following day when she explained that she didn't want to go with him on the Tom Joyner Cruise. He accepted her wish but at the moment he didn't understand. The dichotomy of it was almost a year ago someone he hadn't known was eager to go on a cruise with him and now someone he was intimately involved with didn't want to.

He went ahead alone and thoroughly enjoyed all of the entertainment that the cruise provided. But in the solitude of his cabin he was able to reflect. They communicated via various mobile messaging platforms until he was able to call her when the ship embarked at St. Thomas where normal cellular service was available. Both expressed the desire to be with each other where she emailed him the following poem:

From The Horizon

Many years ago, men went to sea, and women waited for them. Standing at the edge of the water, scanning the vast horizon for their ship.

Now I wait for Rufus. He vanished, six days ago. I think I may have made him up. But still, I wait for him. Each moment that I wait feels like a year, an eternity. Why has he gone where I cannot follow?

I love Rufus so much...But I can never love him as much as I miss him right now......

He was actually touched after receiving the above poem and his devious mind remark at the second paragraph's query of "...why has he gone where I can't follow?" He thought, "you chose not to follow." - he really couldn't help himself. But during the separation her untold apprehension about not going on the cruise was slowly being revealed but his mind was still too clouded for him to see.

Upon his Sunday return from the cruise there was a very short window to meet before her son was back from visiting his father. The morning traffic from the Port of Miami to Fort Lauderdale was kind and the Uber driver instinctively drove with urgency to make up their lost time. They made the best of the limited schedule and later had breakfast at Shooters restaurant on the intercostal nearby her Pilates studio. Afterwards she took him to the airport before noon as she had several times before to say their goodbyes.

This time on the plane during the two-and-a-half-hour return flight Rufus was equally inspired when he wrote the following on his phone:

SPRING

It's Spring, the season when all thing new are abloom
Like flowers and lovers and the wonders of life resume
When one tends to wonder what the future may bring....
It's love, Stephanie...whenever I'm with you, it's Spring

It's passion, when the sunlight reflects between our eyes
Two flowers facing each other, swaying in the breeze,
Cross pollinating smiles, It's the love everyone sees,
That seemed to come so easily
From the seeds of renewed trust planted by you and me.

It's a dream- or so it seemed - lives starting over we thought had end
From finding each other - not just another lover, but more importantly a friend
But with Spring comes renewal, and another chance to proceed
'Cause with you and me and spring, for right now is exactly what we need

It's Spring, with quivers in hand, Cupid's aim was true,

Granting our wishes for a special someone, who can make our hearts two
Would completely fulfill your life, and keep you safe as I again promised to
always do
Together conquering life's challenges as they are experienced with you

It's magic, how the short days turn into long nights, nocturnal lovers we've
become
Everything would be alright, should we never again see another sun
And whether or due to weather, if it fails to shine, with each other there will
always be light
Time seems to stand still whenever we are together, which tells me we will be
alright

And if all else fails, ...should we go our separate ways....
It would have been a shame if we did not fight for us.
By clearing the air, remembering why we are here– particularly how much we
still care.
Because only in Spring can couples fall in love all over again.

CHAPTER TWENTY-ONE

"Stephanie was extremely gracious with my son hugging him and expressing how well-mannered and handsome he was. I was just so happy that he visited the barbershop the day before to tame his hair."

A GAIN, IT WOULD BE UNTRUTHFUL for me to suggest that everything was back to normal as their relationship resumed. On the surface, appearances were deceiving because there were still underlying reservations. From Stephanie's point of view, dating someone of the same persuasion for the first time really didn't matter in the lease. On the other hand, she did take note of the kinder eyes observers had when they were together. In addition to being closer to his age as a couple there was another visual form of acceptability. After her divorce in her mid-thirties, she found that she had nothing in common with the men around her age intellectually. So the older suitors fulfilled that need at the same time being introduced to their lifestyle, but also on their terms. Then Rufus came along at 52 and made her feel things she had never felt with the sincerity of his written and spoken words.

From Rufus' perspective, she filled his emotional void immediately and at the same time hadn't dated anyone so strong willed. He attributed it to her practically raising her siblings and from time to time not taking any of their crap. To further substantiate his assessment, Rufus was present when she received a call that her oldest brother was arrested after he physically abused his girlfriend when he was inebriated. The way she sternly relayed her consternation over the phone provided insight that she is respected by all of her siblings.

But specifically, he now desperately wanted to find out why she was against going on the first cruise.

Then there were the underlying fears that remained with both; she wasn't comfortable sleeping in her room anymore because of her recent issue with the bed bugs. Although an exterminator warranted his treatment of the apartment, it still wasn't enough to reassure her. Rufus apprehension occurred whenever he received emails from her fearing a repeat of the April 15th episode. She was very open with him about her entomophobia telling him of the many times she slept in the living room. She even kept a few dead bugs in a Ziploc bag which he kept reminding her that it wasn't healthy nor helpful for her healing.

On the other hand, he wasn't forthcoming about his issues. He continued to text her on the daily with well wishes, but he paused at times when he saw emails from her. The good thing was emails from her were very few and far between. As the weeks transpired, both of their mental health issues were slowly normalizing.

Stephanie decided not to renew her lease and was really looking forward to moving at the end of June and her gracious landlord understood. The fifth floor apartment held some significance to Rufus because of how he was greeted every time he traveled to see her there. It was a secured complex with a guillotine style barrier arm for the residence and small parking area for guests. Outside the lobby was a tele-entry system that could be used to buzz guests in, but Stephanie preferred the dramatics. Like a fairytale, Stephanie never allowed him to get that far. To announce his arrival, he would either text or call simply saying, "I'm here" when he parked or was dropped off by Uber. Moments later she would exit the apartment door visible to him below and she would periscope back and forth over the railing in attempt to identify him from five stories above in the guest parking area. He once told her that her smile was infectious as he looked upward reminiscent of the Grimm's tale of when the Prince told Rapunzel to let down her hair. Instead she'd descend in the elevator and meet him in the lobby.

In anticipation of the move, she hired a realtor friend and even involved Rufus with her decision process forwarding him emails of prospective apartment choices. As a result, both of their fears were now being addressed proactively where he became less leery every time he received her electronic files of a potential apartment and she looked forward to moving away from a place that caused her so much physical and psychological harm. After all he couldn't tell her not to forward anymore emails because of the outside chance he might receive one with bad news. So in essence, their trust was again being rebuilt.

♦ ♦ ♦

The next time he traveled to Fort Lauderdale was for the Memorial Day four-day weekend and this time Kevin was with him. The last time they flew together to Florida was during the Christmas holidays. Back then upon their arrival, they caught an Uber to Stephanie's apartment where she left the keys to her car under the mat and she left a modest gift for Kevin inside the car. He and Kevin then drove to the Aventura Mall and stop by Five Guys for burgers and later to his mother's house where Kevin would stay and hang out with his cousins and Rufus returned to Fort Lauderdale. This particular weekend - although five months later - the arrangements were the same, but it also included an additional trip to Tampa so they could see the facilities where Kevin would be attending the basketball camp in the summer.

Everything was going according to plan when they arrived that Friday evening. Then out of the blue while they rode in the Uber to pick up Stephanie's car, Kevin asked if he could meet her. From Rufus' point of view it was totally unexpected.

Full disclosure alert. Kevin is my son. And although this memoir is about Rufus, the time may come when he allows me to write his story. In my inimitable way of influencing, I compelled Kevin to request the meeting similarly like when I awoke him to see Rufus smiling the first in a very long time chatting in his room.

Rufus called Stephanie enroute to apprise her of Kevin's request. Her only concern was whether it was solely Kevin's idea. When they arrived the meeting was everything I thought it would be. And seriously, quite frankly it was way overdue. From Kevin's point of view, they were no longer a secret. He would answer and relay her calls with the least of conversation at home. Kevin also knew about the several times when she would get on Rufus' case when he didn't want to go to his school meetings because he complained about how long they kept the parents having them stand and sing the three anthems: United States, Virgin Islands, and the

Negro – in addition to hoarding them like cattle in the auditorium treating them like they were in detention. One time Rufus fell asleep next to Kevin when he had to elbow him when he snored; another time he watched ESPN Around the Horn on his phone to starve off being bored. So there was absolutely no possibility of Rufus being nominated to chair or be part of any the school activities. So quite frankly, Stephanie was Kevin's advocate 100%. Invariably, she was my voice in absentia.

Their meeting was poignant. Stephanie was extremely gracious with my son hugging him and expressing how well-mannered and handsome he was. I was just so happy that he visited the barbershop the day before to tame his hair. That moment was a huge step forward in their relationship. She even commented that she wished her son was there so he could finally meet Rufus and Kevin both. She asked him how he was coping and about school and his responses were a little more than the FOG variety. Before they left for Miami, Stephanie told Rufus where to find a closer Five Guys in the event there was traffic on the interstate and possibly arrived after it closed. She hugged them both goodbye whispering in Rufus' ear, "This is good." As they drove off Rufus asked Kevin how he was feeling. He replied saying,

"I was actually scared at first, but I am happy we met." He concluded by saying, "I like her a lot."

Less than twenty-four hours later they were in Tampa and the following Sunday morning they were touring the IMG Sports Camp facility in Bradenton. It was amazing. I was very happy that Kevin was going to attend; it was something Rufus and I always wanted for him.

IMG is known for the development and training of just about every notable professional tennis player from Pete Sampras, Andre Agassi, Maria Sharapova, Monica Seles and Serena and Venus Williams. At the same time, professional athletes from all major sports also go there in the off season to hone their skills.

IMG is also a high school academy year 'round that mostly caters to affluent student athletes from abroad. There are several homes and apartments on the campus away from the school as temporary housing for parents, students and guardians in addition to the dormitories for on campus attendees.

Kevin was attending because Rufus grew impatient teaching him how to play basketball at home. He even got frustrated with an opposing local coach at a game when he said,

"The kids shouldn't be competing because they are having fun." My husband shouted back,

"Then there shouldn't be any scores!"

I researched some of the camps that were sponsored by retired professional athletes where the reviews were lackluster. IMG tuition was considerable but at the same time they had a track record for being hands on and rudimentary. One of the counselors came in on Sunday and gave them a tour in a golf cart showing them the courts – both tennis and basketball – the dorms, cafeteria, infirmary, game room and all the levels of security. Kevin decided to attend the Three Week Program instead of the Five. He was going to return in five weeks.

On the way back to the hotel I compelled Rufus to contact my girlfriend Arlene in St. Petersburg. They had lunch at an Applebee's and later caught up with her husband Ricky at their apartment. Arlene volunteered to be Kevin's 'in case of emergency' while at the camp. She even offered to pick him up and return him to the airport even though that was one of the services the camp provided. Later on, her offer of being his "in case of emergency' came into play when the camp was under lockdown due to a security concern off campus in a nearby neighborhood. Arlene went to investigate and really provided Rufus with a peace of mind.

◆ ◆ ◆

A lot of apprehension was resolved over that weekend. There was a general feeling of inclusion after the introduction of Kevin. During Rufus' subsequent visit Kevin came along because school was out. They flew up early in the morning and they had lunch with Stephanie after her last class on the Friday. She now felt a little pressure to cross that bridge of when she would introduce her son to Rufus. The opportunity wasn't conducive because it was now summer and her son was spending weeks at a time at his father's – not only the weekends.

But there still was one issue left to be resolved in Rufus' mind and he kept it very close to his chest. Everything else was put to bed so to speak with the exception of one issue that remain unsaid. He actually wondered whether she was going to be a no show for his reunion cruise.

Two weeks before he was there to help her pack and prepare for her pending move. They even drove by the new apartment so he could see where it was. And the weekend included choosing furniture together to be later delivered after they returned from the Alaskan cruise.

But the reunion cruise to Alaska almost wasn't for Rufus as far as his participation was concerned. It was one of those sick jokes life plays as a precursor to a lesson to be learned.

You see he now wasn't being totally truthful and honest and he had a litmus test to see whether his relationship was sustainable with Stephanie. It was the secret he kept to himself for the months following their 'breakdown' – the term she coined to solemnly remind herself of their brief break up. And although they decided to be entirely honest and truthful regardless in the future, his edict was that if she failed to accompany him on the cruise, he was going to sever the relationship. It was that simple. He rationalized his position where she backed out of the Tom Joyner Cruise with no real explanation and if it happened again, at least he was going to let her know face to face.

As ridiculous as that sound, I hoped that maturity would prevail where he would reverse the notion by talking about it face to face and simply ask her directly. But life has its way of reminding you that things could happen beyond one's control and the possibility of regret is the product that remains before one's truth can be told.

I preface that statement to suggest that there was an imbalance in their relationship again, but this time Rufus wasn't being truthful. So with his energies out of whack, bad things can result. Stephanie was quite attentive and if she had the opportunity to see him regularly, she would have brought it up.

This situation reminds me of a gnostic text said to be transcribed from Jesus and considered heresy and rejected from scriptures in The New Testament that simply states:

"If you bring forth what is in you, what you bring forth will save you.
If you don't bring forth what is in you, what you don't bring forth will destroy you."

Those words to live by simply carries your burden. People that struggle with addiction, infidelity, gender identity can all use those words of wisdom towards their own path of redemption. And as far as Rufus was concerned, those truths almost came to pass.

Two weeks before the Alaskan cruise, Rufus fell off the roof from a ladder and landed head over heels in front of our home on the back of his head. The imbalance was he failed to make a prudent decision that could have potentially caused him grave harm. It was raining very hard. And although he knew the tendency for the roof gutter to be clogged by the leaves from the nearby trees, against better judgement he went out anyway to clean the gutter while it was raining. The fall was serious. It was so bad that I compelled Kevin to immediately go outside and attend to his father. With the sound of the rain pelting the galvanized roofing and with the double hung glass window always closed for A/C circulation, the house is generally soundproof from outside noises.

Rufus suffered a severe concussion where he actually said inside his head sounded like a coconut falling on a rock. He was extremely lucky he didn't lose consciousness but for the foreseeable future he began to suffer from chronic headaches and backaches from the precarious way he wound up trying to break the fall. If that mishap had occurred a year earlier, Rufus would have immediately called my mother first to notify her. But the circumstances being as they were, he instead called Stephanie. He told her about the incident when she told him to go to the hospital after she chided him about going out in the rain on a ladder.

"What were you thinking!" she exclaimed.

She even told him what he did was extremely selfish reminding him about his promise of taking care of Kevin. She told him that she didn't mind taking care of him - but not for stupid shit. She concluded with her own salvo stating unequivocally,

"If you do anything like that again I will kill you myself."

Now as I am writing this story about my before and afterlife with my husband, from my vantage I immediately recognize the potential life changing circumstances that fall could have brought forth. Additionally, I know that my head would need examination where I can actually say that I found a dichotomy of humor in Stephanie's edict and what that other girl promised to do to him similarly 30 years ago after one date if he ever looked at another woman. Both vowed to 'kill him' - the local girl said 'kill him dead'. That's another local saying that used to crack me up - but I digress. The first threat was based on insecurity and this most recent threat was based on love. It was honestly the most endearing moment of their relationship from my point of view.

Then one week later, after Kevin attended a religious summer camp summit for teens in Orlando sponsored by my local church, my girlfriend Arlene picked him up as promised and took him to the IMG Academy for orientation. After the first day he called Rufus to complain about ailments. He described that his entire body hurt – especially his chest. From my point of view again, Rufus' response warranted another fall from a ladder – but not on his head because he was still experiencing headaches and stiffness in his neck. But as his mother I felt empathetic and my nurturing nature wanted to console him. Instead Rufus laughed and the story became about him.

He told Kevin that was expected because he wasn't physically in shape and he had been through a similar experience while in high school when he tried out for the team. The counselors at IMG were also prepared for that eventuality where for the next two days in addition to lower impact calisthenics, he would have a trainer massage his tight muscles.

It was a far cry from the local basketball summer camp he attended where Rufus got upset whenever he picked him up. Every time he saw the kids watching movies he was reminded what a colossal waste of money we had spent. He said the camp was nothing more than a huge glorified babysitting operation in the high school gym. That following year Rufus decided to teach Kevin how to play the piano at home during the summer and was adamant. He integrated lesson with his work schedule returning home to check on his progress and disabling the Internet. He had Kevin doing finger exercises where he complained that his hands were hurting. Rufus reassured him that after the pain subside he would eventually learn. Again I was concerned and he was correct. He later had him playing scales with both hands and in the end taught him how to read music. At one point Rufus did something that I thought was ingenious quite frankly.

To dispel the notion that Kevin was simply memorizing the musical exercises and songs, Rufus photocopied a piece of music without the title from his library and told Kevin to play it. After a few false starts, he read and played Corrine Bailey Rae "Like a Star." Upon completion Kevin said,

"Dad, that's one of the songs you always play."

That statement from Kevin confirmed that he had achieved a level of confidence and acumen on the instrument during that summer. I was so proud I had Kevin playing for my mother over the phone. We visited Milton's family where both of his son's took private lessons on the piano. Before Milton could say, 'Rufus you know you didn't teach Kevin how to play Dred', his older son complimented Kevin on his form. Then his older son proceeded to play a very difficult classical piece by memory.

It didn't make Rufus a great music teacher because he absolutely wasn't. He simply lacked the temperament and patience. In the end he seemingly only had enough of both to teach our son.

◆ ◆ ◆

The last week leading up to the cruise Stephanie had her own logistical details to navigate as far as her son was concerned. She made arrangements to have him picked up after summer school by her girlfriend Natalee during the days she was going to be away where he was accumulating extra credits and to drop him off at his dads. And for the very first time, she came to the realization that she finally had to tell her ex-husband about Rufus after being in the relationship for eleven months. She had put it off long enough even though for the past decade her private life was absolutely *none of his business.* Her rationale was simply the fact that while she was at sea, she will be incommunicado and it was the responsible thing to do in case of any unfortunate emergencies. She anticipated that whenever the conversation was had, it would take a tenuous twist like many discussions she had with him of late.

Like when she moved from the 5th floor apartment with all its security to her current 1st floor apartment 'on the other side of the tracks'. It didn't matter that the apartment complex was in a well-kept development in Oakland Park where a considerable amount of her neighbors were owners and adhered to their strict Homeowner Association Bylaws. She always remarked that she loved well-kept environments and seemingly salivates when she uses the word "maintenance."

The fact that her ex-husband observed considerably more African American in the neighborhoods than she normally had compelled him to buy her 'Soul Food' takeout as a housewarming gift. Quite frankly it was a racist gesture and insensitive knowing her stringent nutritional habits even though he would often leave her with a bottle of wine from time to time when he was in a good mood.

She was also very careful not to put herself in the precarious position where her ex-husband could accuse her of any improprieties. To that end. she made the point that she and Rufus should not spend the night together under the same roof as their sons. And for the sake of her son in the past she has traveled as a family unit with her ex-husband and son annually during the spring breaks where the same rule was implemented only requesting that she have her own sleeping accommodations.

Prior to this confrontation their most recent trip was to Quebec a few months ago two weeks before the break up. She apprised Rufus of the arrangement she had participated in years past and added that she had already told her son it was going to be the last time because she had met Rufus. Her son totally understood because even though he commented that it was cool visiting both of his parents in different hotel rooms, when they had dinner together, there was a different dynamic. He stated that it was also obvious that his parents got along better when they were apart.

Her ex-husband on the other hand seemed to have never gotten over their separation and the dissolution of their marriage. She admitted that after her daughter died, emotionally everything changed. The bond they once had was gone. No amount of couple's therapy was going to change what had become her new reality. Her truth was their relationship had simply ran its course. After she left him, he wholeheartedly expected her return similarly like when she told stories about running away from home as a child. But she was resolute and the struggles that endured afterwards affirmed her personal constitution when at times she wondered whether she could do it on her own.

He undoubtedly hadn't gotten over their break up even when both were involved in new relationships. From time to time she would amicably offer advice and counseling when he had impasses with whomever he was currently dating. The most recent came to a precipitous end after weeks of asking her son how he felt about his father's latest girlfriend. The weekends passed where her son either pivoted the conversation or simply bit his tongue. When he was ready to respond, it was confirmation of the deep seethed loathing that still remained after all the years of separation.

Her son told her that his father's girlfriend talks badly about her when he is there. Having met his girlfriend briefly a few times Stephanie immediately knew from where her consternation derived. She also knew that her ex-husband had to make a choice of loyalty after her son refused to visit him in the future if his girlfriend was there.

So having just notified her ex-husband about dating Rufus for almost a year - making sure to mention his full name and where he was from, she knew the following series of events would follow. Immediately she recognized the quizzical look of familiarity on her ex's face because - and I AM NOT KIDDING - one of his email addresses is actually 'rufusyadayada@yada.com' even though his name is NOT Rufus. I too was immediately taken aback about that coincidence. He was trying to catch his bearings because although he was not notified directly from his son, he knew that she visited St. Thomas for the new year. Her son never revealed her personal information to anyone only telling his father that she went to the islands for the holidays. He called her briefly to notify her that he was hospitalized. He then even went as far as calling his mother-in-law to see whether Stephanie had told her mother about her trip contemplating briefly if she had gotten back with the doctor on St. Croix.

His mind was reeling from this new information that he simply didn't foresee and absolutely did not compute in his logical state of mind. How could he not see the signs? Why didn't his son tell him as he briefly pondered where his loyalty lies.

Coincidentally, Operation *'None of His Damn Business'* was almost foiled on Rufus' second visit to Fort Lauderdale. It was the Saturday morning when Stephanie left Rufus in the apartment alone to teach the studio morning classes to return in the afternoon and when he rented cars for the weekend. Rufus told her that he was going to sleep in until she returned.

Even though his body needed its rest, I compelled him to get up and to visit his mother briefly in Miami and return before noon. So as he was reversing out of the guest parking, her son with his father were pulling into the lot and their cars actually passed the other. Her son was returning home briefly because he had forgotten to take disposable contact lenses for the weekend. Stephanie learned later about the near mishap from her son and told Rufus.

Her ex-husband quickly shrugged off his lapse of attention and proceeded with the following remarks that were intended to be hurtful and condescending. He has a way of weaponizing his languaging to leave psychological lacerations. After all, the premise of his carefully chosen remark was predicated from his personal knowledge that in her recent past, she needed his legal assistance after breaking up with her previous suitor that lived in St. Croix. He opened a practice in Miami to be closer to her and in the end, he had to threaten the doctor with a restraining order being filed against him. But instead his contemptuous comment actually backfired. He strategically began by simply saying,

"Typical."

To which Stephanie's response was,

"Typical of what?",

"You know exactly what." He retorted.

She paused knowing exactly what he was referring and considered since he wasn't going to be forthcoming with his speculation, she decided to fill in the blanks for him.

"Well, first of all, he's not rich..." she began, pausing for effect the way she learned in her acting classes. Then she followed up stating,

"... and he is not White." She purposely left out Rufus' age for the time being because she knew that he would ponder whether there was the usual age disparity as his term 'typical' also suggest. She also knew that he would now perform a background investigation on Rufus similarly like my mother did.

Up until I passed, Rufus' social media presence was limited to Facebook posts to interact with classmates around 2011 for their 30th reunion. But after I passed, he was a bleeding heart. He wrote extensively about his thoughts and posted several photos of his life. There he would find that they were the same age among other things. As it sunk in she ended,

"And he's your age."

He was actually taken aback momentarily being in the unfamiliar position of being unprepared for this discussion that was unexpectedly sprung upon him. He was totally off his game seeing that lawyers typically only ask questions that they already knew the answer to in court. That's why they do research and hold depositions, and carefully script their questions to find inconsistencies. And as far as he was concerned, she was consistent and predictable. She did break off engagements. And for his own selfish reasoning he still helped her out. But at the same time, at her behest their son has completed his freshman year at the most prestigious school in South Florida and he initially barked at its tuition cost. And he also knew if she filed a suit for more child support, the state would definitely find her case compelling. So in essence, him taking care of the issue with the doctor made them even.

If he was in court during this current exchange the jury would have seen that he had been rattled. But his cross examining skills from his profession caused him to quickly regroup to say the following shruggingly,

"It can't be that serious anyway because P hasn't met him." referring to their son knowing her predisposition of never having her suitors meet their son. Again without foresight his comment backfired tremendously. She simply replied,

"Ask him yourself."

In actuality, Rufus and Kevin met her son weeks earlier. They were at the new apartment and her son was in his room when Rufus and Kevin came in an Uber to get her car to take Kevin to Miami for the weekend. Stephanie texted him that her son was there and to come inside because her ex had to work late and was going to pick up her son early on Saturday. The meeting was simply a formality - a 'finally get it outta the way' kinda meeting. The boys were both low key and spoke briefly. They sized each other up when they shook hands where both admired the others hair: Kevin's natural unkempt Afro faded and detailed around the ears and Stephanie's son curly long pass-the-shoulder length braids. Kevin remembered Rufus told him that her son was two days older but Kevin was considerably taller.

When it was time for them to leave, the boys instinctively left their parents alone to say their goodbyes where Kevin went back to the car and her son retreated in his bedroom. On the drive to Miami, Stephanie called to tell Rufus that her son remarked saying he thought Kevin was cool and their goodbye kisses were grossly too loud.

After that additional unexpected information, her ex-husband rested his case and simply left obviously now having a very bad Sunday afternoon in her court. Moments later she heard her son's cell phone ringing. Then as if she was witnessing the next series of events from my unique point of view, she knew exactly who the call was from. On cue, her son left his bedroom and went outside. After a few minutes he returned and reported,

"Mom, you should have never told dad about Rufus."

CHAPTER TWENTY-TWO

"I consoled him with my usual default response to everything that embarrassed him."

NEEDLESS TO SAY ON THE DAY of the cruise Stephanie showed up. There weren't any doubts that she was going on vacation with him from my perspective seeing that she was addressing all of the minor details and the possible eventualities that may occur in her absence. Also, she was living up to their two extended trips annually requirement. Her contractual circumstances made for the fact that up until the day before the trip she had Pilates classes to teach in the morning and they both traveled to the airport separately in Ubers on Friday saying goodbye to her son before going to summer school earlier and Rufus did similarly to his mother and sister.

His classmates were already group chatting and posted pictures of their whereabouts enroute from the various airports on their way to Seattle. Some had flights laying over in Miami, New York, and Chicago. Rufus' flight was direct from Miami to Seattle. He only posted two pictures in the group chat: one of his name on the Uber driver's phone with the GPS map destination to the airport and the other standing outside of Miami International where he was waiting for Stephanie.

We had never been to Seattle. The only time we've been to the west coast was the time Kevin and I met up with Rufus in Anaheim California. He was in Denver at a trade show the week before and instead of flying back home, he spent an extra day and flew to California on Monday. Insurance companies were having a conference for recertification courses and we decided to take Kevin out of school for a week. The hotel was in walking distance to Disneyland and on two of the four occasions they went, Kevin told me that they were the first into the theme park.

On the last day Kevin told his father that it wasn't fair that they were having fun every day while I had to work. So Rufus gave him his credit card and Kevin went into one of the Disney gift shops and bought me a bracelet. He presented it to me that evening over dinner with all of the employees. It was another one of many moments I cherished.

In the meantime, the traffic from Fort Lauderdale to Miami was horrendous and Rufus was emotionally suffering inside. She texted him with traffic updates - even informing him that her Uber driver had to detour for gasoline - and he was relieved upon her arrival. They had a two hour wait and he immediately came to the realization that the following ten days were going to be the longest period of time they were going to be spending together.

Their eight-hour trip was enjoyable as they unwound mentally and went into vacation mode. The Admiral's Club staff served them cocktails in privacy and the service continued into first class on the flight where they mostly talked about how well both of their sons were doing. Kevin was having a great time and her son was accumulating community service credits. With all the time Kevin spent at church, he had already satisfied that requirement his sophomore year.

Upon arriving in Seattle at midnight pacific standard time they both were deprived of sleep as they waited for their luggage in baggage claim. They were both surprised about the inactivity around the airport and later it was confirmed when they realized that no Uber were available. So they caught a traditional cab and overnighted at the Hyatt Downtown and she began to immediately see the effects of his recent concussion which now made her very concerned.

He was not spatially aware of his close proximity surroundings. In the hotel he kept bumping his head on the corner of the window treatment and his right shoulder would bump into the edges of walls and door frames when he walked too closely. He had been taking OTC Advil to manage the pain, but Stephanie brought 800 mgs ibuprofen and gave him one that put him down like a horse.

The following Saturday morning before checking out of the hotel they took the opportunity to explore the city on foot and had breakfast at a diner and snapped pictures. They walked for hours in the morning taking the city in. Stephanie immediately saw a sign that read the Amazon Rufus 2.0 Project was being constructed creating several blocks of urban sprawl to be developed into green space, dog park, walking trails with the landmark of the Amazon Spheres. He realized that Milton wasn't going to be on the cruise and he knew it was going to be a futile argument if he told him that Jeff Bezos was developing a project with his name. That didn't stop him from telling him anyway. Afterwards they sought out and found a liquor store to purchase their quota of two bottles of Veuve Clicquot to bring on the cruise.

There were no signs of any of the classmates even in the large embarking station. With the process streamlined over the years where you can check in online, most of the passengers didn't and they were really slowing down the process where the queues appeared like a maze. This was Rufus' sixteenth cruise and he knew better always saying that the time spent waiting in lines unnecessarily you can never get back so he sought and found the expedited express line. He immediately noticed how Stephanie's persona changed from anxiety to relief when she realized that the waiting would be considerably shorter. It was at that moment when quite frankly he had an epiphany. He realized that she was deeply terrified by crowds. While they stood in the express check in queue, he thought back about anytime they were together when they had to negotiate a large group of people in the hundreds. Art Basel in December immediately came to mind. It was a few months into their relationship and he wasn't sure about her reaction with the large crowds because he had nothing to compare, but it was similar to a moment ago.

Now as they waited in the short line, he began recalling what he told her about the Tom Joyner Cruise. At first she was very excited talking about being able to see Ralph Tresvant of New Edition up close and personal - not to mention the opportunity to have her picture taken with Shirley Caesar as a present for her Momma - when he forwarded the lineup to her. He even sent her an electronic copy of the Cruise Chronicles - which was the electronic magazine of past cruises - and asked her whether anything caught her eye. There was a picture of Rufus walking around the ship's track from a previous cruise and she thought that was cool.

But when he showed her a picture of the Sail Away concerts that we had attended where at least 3,000 people gathered around the main pool that is magically transformed into a sound stage, all she said was "That's serious business" and proceeded to do her laundry. He thought nothing about it back then because doing laundry can never be associated with the Tom Joyner Cruise. It was now becoming clear. The pictures of the crowd densely packed on the pool deck spooked her.

Then Rufus realized that he was actually fortunate that she didn't attend that particular cruise despite all of the amazing entertainment like Diana Ross, Patti LaBelle, and Johnny Gill. The disembarking was the absolute worst experience. In the past Rufus was able to get a photo op with the legendary likes of Bootsy Collins and George Clinton when he left the ship.

To Tom Joyner's defense, he warns all of the potential passengers and all of the artists that if you go on the cruise and you have court warrants pending, the authorities will be waiting for you when the cruise returns. This kind of entrapment is not specific to the Tom Joyner Cruise – it happens with all international travel when your passport is logged. It happens a lot with the airlines too. Of all the time Rufus has traveled, it happened at least ten times and during the past year of visiting Stephanie, it happened twice.

After the captain turns off the "Fasten Seat Belt Light", automatically the passengers get up at their leisure to retrieve their belongings. Then the announcement over the intercom requests that everyone return to their seat with the exception of one perpetrator that they call by name to identify themselves and deplane the aircraft first.

That exact incident happened in 2016. Over the ship's intercom they called one specific passenger to the gangway and no one could leave before he identified himself to the authorities. One guy in Rufus' proximity jokingly stated that it was a rapper's Government's Name. Everyone waited as the elevators, stairs and hallways became densely populated with more passengers with luggage while the announcement continued. It became so untenable that a passenger hyperventilated and fainted in Rufus' close proximity. The doctor was unable to get to the person until the captain decided to countermand the authority's directives and allowed the passengers to disembark in order that the doctor could administer to the passenger. Then and there he realized that her instincts served her well. It could have actually been Stephanie's first and last cruise.

◆ ◆ ◆

After finding their cabin, she wanted to locate the gym so that they could establish their daily routine for the week: exercise at 6:00, breakfast at 7, after breakfast cocktail, shower thereafter and explore the ship or go on their excursions. Her philosophy was to 'get it in early so you won't have to worry about it the rest of the day.' And Rufus' philosophy was to acquiesce to the physical fitness professional that happened to be his girlfriend.

He still hadn't seen any of his classmates in the perpetual game of hide and seek. They were no sightings even during the safety briefing and the following all day at sea towards the first port of call. But the class secretary Amazia had other plans. She remembered from the little information Rufus provided about Stephanie and her Pilates Studio, the gym was the only place she would most likely have a Rufus sighting. So while the other 3000 passengers were hoping to see whales, she planned to stakeout the gym bright and early on Monday.

Like a scene out of a romance comedy, Amazia and her other half Leon actually beat Stephanie and Rufus to the gym. They had to be there when the doors opened at 6am. And like a gumshoe, Amazia was willing to spend the entire morning waiting. What was comical about Amazia's stake out was the fact that she had no workout attire. She had no workout clothes because she had no intention of working out. But she was in the gym wearing a cotton pajamas pant and matching button top with her hair in rollers with slippers. And to fit in she sat on an exercise bicycle peddling and tried to blend in while Leon simply leaned on the apparatus next to her.

Blend in she didn't because as soon as Rufus and Stephanie arrived, he immediately saw his classmate at the corner of his eye and smiled knowing he was busted as they made a beeline towards two available adjoining treadmills and proceeded to do their morning miles. Stephanie ran while Rufus walked inclined at a brisk pace. What I really appreciated was she was also his personal trainer. She loved to preface statements in jest like, 'at your age' or 'old man', but would continue to advise him how to properly workout. Rufus complained once that in the early morning when he ran and jogged, he twisted his knee and it was never the same. Her response was, "It won't be the same because you are old, man." Then she explained that the hills around his neighborhood were challenging enough to just walk around after she witnessed it when she visited him on

St. Thomas for the new year and her birthday. She continued to explain that the constant absorption of the knee with less cartilage is a recipe for sustained injuries.

Rufus told her while he was on the Tom Joyner Cruise alone this year, he always saw Tom's son on the track jogging. He explained that four years ago he saw him where he ran. The second year he saw him again running, but he had one knee brace on. This year he was wearing two knee braces. Rufus told Stephanie that he took the time and had a brief discussion with Tom's son to simply relay what she had taught him when he then admitted that his doctor told him similarly. The next day he took heed and stopped running and walked around the track.

After they were finished on the treadmills they proceeded to the hand weights where he followed Stephanie's lead and walked by Amazia's stakeout. Before Rufus could say anything, Amazia raised her hand and said,

"Don't talk to me." as he walked by.

Stephanie was about to engage with the weights when Rufus said,

"Amazia is here."

Stephanie in her excitement replied,

"Really? Where?" Rufus pointed in the direction and continued,

"Over there on the exercise bike."

"It's great that she's getting in a workout." she commented. Rufus corrected,

"She's here snooping. As far as I know she just wants to see what you look like."

"That's silly." she remarked.

"Trust me, after today we won't see her in here again. Anyway, let me introduce you."

Rufus graciously introduced Stephanie to Amazia and Leon where Amazia continued to playfully ignore him. Moments later, the stakeout was over.

Another thing she did to help with his concussed skull was prohibited him from lifting weights and taught him how to stretch. Additionally, she incorporated an exercise noodle for him where she instructed him to lie down with it on the base of his neck while she did her thing.

◆ ◆ ◆

The highlight of the cruise was the Mendenhall Glacier Helicopter Tour and Guided Walk. Truth be told, in the same manner that I would have argued against Kevin getting the hoverboard, I would have done similarly if we were together due to the cost of the tour. Rufus on the other hand, had an alternative reality. He was given a heads up months ago from one of his clients that being on the glacier was a bucket list thing. Those days of what might have been were gone. Many things we forego because of its cost. He now asks, at what cost? If he worried about the cost of dating me for a year that included the weekend flights and hotels, again the book would not have been written. And the cost is only relative based on your circumstances and if it brought him joy was reasons enough because he was truly enjoying this moment in his life. Every now and again he contacted Kevin and learn he was also having the time of his life while becoming friends with student from countries he was not familiar with.

Stephanie was already skittish when she flew in small aircrafts at times when she went to St. Croix. She was soon realizing that another of her fears had to be rationalized in order that she would be able to fully enjoy the excursion. It involved a tour of snowcapped mountains, valleys and fjords via helicopter. She expressed her concerns when asking Rufus' advice of how to deal with that fear. He began by telling her that it was also going to be his first time in a helicopter. He was also smart to not tell her about his client's experience taking lessons when he described how shaky and unstable his lesson was. In the end he reassured her saying that when we fly, everyone has the faith that the pilots are well trained and will safely get us to our destinations. She later told him that was exactly what she needed to hear.

This was his first time on a Royal Caribbean cruise and he instantly love the design as he explained to Stephanie the difference. The Promenade Deck is the standard name for the deck level where you can walk the entire length of the ship where the immediate deck above is the ceiling camouflaged with mirrors and kaleidoscopic lights. In many ships designs, gift shops, night clubs and the casino can be found in this deck and it generally won't have any cabins or suites. On this ship there was no ceiling above the Promenade. It opened up several stories above to reveal the interior cabins which all had balconies and a view of the Promenade below.

And since it was an Alaskan Cruise, everyone was dressed warmly in sweater type garb which made it feel like a huge log cabin experience with stores and cafes.

Stephanie just loved wrapping her hand around his upper forearm while they walked like the first time when they had dinner at Trulucks and it's only until now I realized why. She was emulating how the actors interacted in the classic movies she loved watching. I remember when she visited him for the new year, at her behest, Rufus bought the 1958 musical Gigi and the 2010 movie The Tourist on Blu-ray and they watched them in succession in the theater. She told him that she never saw movies so brilliantly with color admiring the classic outfits. She was pleasantly surprised when Rufus sung the words to the musical while they watched.

Another highlight was when he became a karaoke sensation, again. Truth be told alert. Rufus first try at karaoke was in 2012. The three of us were cruising and had just finished dinner at the specialty restaurant celebrating Rufus' birthday. Kevin abandoned us afterwards as we walked through the Promenade Deck where the cruise director was playing a musical trivia game. The cruise director made the comment that in Prince's song Kiss, he was unable to understand a particular section of the lyrics for all the times he has heard the song. He then asked if anyone could clarify what was being sung as the DJ previewed a clip of the obscure lyric. We just happened to be walking by and was in front of the stage when Rufus detoured, walked up and took the microphone from the cruise director. There was already a crowd when they cheered and jeered him to sing, "You don't have to be beautiful, to turn me on...." And continued when he clarified the obscure lyrics, *"Ain't no particular sign I'm more compatible with...I just want your extra time and your .... Kiss."*

Then in 2014, Rufus made the colossal mistake and sung karaoke on the Tom Joyner Cruise. Black folks are absolutely unforgiving. They booed him off the stage so fast, the Sandman from the Apollo Theater would have lost his job. As he licked his wounds, I consoled him with my usual default response to everything that embarrassed him. Like the time he was beginning to go bald and I told him while we watched a commercial on television that he should use the spray hair to fill in the few bald spots...

"I won't tell anyone."

Or the time in Tortola when he was recognized as a Turnbull, we had lunch where he exclaimed the "ribs" were the best he has ever eaten, but later realizing it was pork,

"I won't tell anyone."

He was so embarrassed after they booed him off the stage, we left and I told him again,

"I won't tell anyone."

But in 2015 he made a reprieve that you won't believe unless you were on the Western Caribbean cruise with my family where he was a sensation because the passengers were not predominantly black. Like he told Stephanie in his early correspondence that he played the bass guitar, but if he had to make a living singing he would starve. He just enjoyed clowning. On this cruise with the same demographics, Rufus killed. They wanted encores and he obliged. And to bolster his ego and confidence, Stephanie was at the bar hamming it up from time to time shouting repeatedly, "That's My Man!!!" from the cheap seats. Honestly, that's something I definitely wouldn't have done.

He drew bigger audiences than usual and was recognized all over the ship the following days and she saw firsthand all the attention he was getting like he explained in the text transcript. It actuality, she never thought that she would have witnessed what he previously described.

The following evening, he left her in the cabin because she wanted to sleep in early and told him to hang out with his classmates. He eventually ran into his classmate Andrew having a drink at the karaoke bar when the bartender and other passengers recognized him. Andrew asked him what had he miss. Rufus said,

"Let me show you."

He went up on stage after the last performer finished. Turned on the flashlight on his phone and instructed everyone in the sound of his amplified voice to do similarly. Then proceeded to kill Teddy Pendergrass' Turn Off the Lights. Andrew simply laughed.

♦ ♦ ♦

Having spent more consecutive days together in their relationship, she remained true to the core. In the cabin, she made him clean up after himself – razzing him about her visit to St. Thomas and commandeered the TV remote to make sure it remained off while they slept in the dark. She sincerely believed her mother's attest that "sleep was the fountain of youth." And whenever the television was on, it either showed the ship's itinerary or the Classic Movie channels where she'd point out how elegantly the casts were dressed back then.

At the end of the cruise I was reassured. Rufus' spirit was soaring and the light that he navigated his personal warehouse was brilliantly focused on the future. And like everything of late, he wrote another journal to encapsulate the entire week's event in a short story.

Giovanni's Fable

Like Joseph and Mary away in the manger, but instead with no place to break bread, CeCe (Chocolate Charmer) and Coco were emotionally spent from the week's sojourn of wondrous senses their Alaskan Cruise vacation presented: frozen sights, delicious bites, ear piercing exuberant singing plights, innocuous sweat-filled morning workouts precluded from caresses and kisses from copulated thrilled mornings and nights.

T'was the last evening in another chapter of their seemingly fictitious romance, and a proper finale was sought to culminate what only felt like another extended fairytale week of bliss. But to their chagrin, they forgot to make the necessary reservations to dine at Giovanni's - the ship's Italian specialty culinary establishments. After last minute attempts to remedy what was immediately becoming obvious, and after being denied over the phone of the full occupancy of the other specialty dining restaurants, a select few would enjoy dining intimacy while they would wind up as social outcasts for the evening.

Being turned away and unable to break bread, instead they were left to their own devices. CeCe and Coco proceeded to embark on what had become their signature leisurely stroll down the ship's Promenade: her head on his shoulder, her hand wrapped around his arm. They felt like the characters in literary prose- walking as if they were alone. Passersby seemed to all disappear as they grew near- or others simply pause momentarily- if only to stare, allowing their access through the trove of the last minute patrons on their final spending spree from the indoor and outdoor onboard shopping venues.

They contemplated In-Room takeout from the guest services menu in the seclusion of their stateroom as they walked. Coco had a reputation of creating memorable picnic experiences in hotels suites on the fly: towels on the floor in lieu of a blanket, entre' eaten by fingertips, chased by exquisite foreign sparkly's from France or Belgian Ale...from previous chapters in their lives.

Organically, as fate seems to always been the silent companion from the inception of their relationship, instead of ascending to their stateroom floor, they descended to the level below the Promenade to Giovanni's - their original dining venue of choice where others would be in a few hours. Fate suggested the detour, and organically it felt ominous to now order room services from the limited menu they had become intimately familiar with during the week. Italian takeout would be a preferable finale. They approached Giovanni's entry to find its door locked.... fate had brought them thus far so without a second thought, they simply proceeded to knock.

Quickly ushered in by a lone waiter interrupted while exquisitely preparing the evening's table settings, Victor confirmed what was already known as far as reservations were concerned, but granted their request to have the meal taken out. So with menus in hand, and choices being made, Victor diligently recorded while suggesting complementary alternatives. At one moment he expressed concern about how the takeout presentation would appear and the amount of stone and flatware Cece would have to bare.

Upon leaving the order was repeated for confirmation and clarification as they both thanked Victor for his patience and for the exception. CeCe and Coco proceeded their invisible stroll back to their stateroom. In the midst of relishing the last hours of their vacation, they knew that dinner would be an amazing experience, having had similar indoor picnics with less preparation.

The phone in the stateroom rang and CeCe answered, and moments later hung up chomping at the bit to explain. "That was Victor asking whether we would prefer to dine in or still want the food to go." The effervescence Coco facial expression displayed at that moment was indicative of joyful exuberance she'd portrayed for the entire vacation.

Fashionably early and led to the restaurant's most intimate seating - or to both it seemed: corner table in partial seclusion, once again it felt as if Cece and Coco were alone as they sat with each other's undivided attention. Both admittedly forgot what they had earlier chosen from the menu, but Victor reassured them that he had the situation at hand. The relieved couple acquiesced to what the last evening of the cruise was about to unfold.

Performing series of gestures resembling a music-less pantomime, Victor proffering commenced with pre-appetite bread made to be fabulously broken in saucers of oil puddles and vinaigrette. Flatware changes after each course as appetizer, dual entrées and dessert were exquisitely prepared and presented with the finest culinary artistry and care.

At dinners end, the couple thanked Victor for a wonderful conclusion to their vacation.... most importantly...monetarily. The evening ended like their vacation began.... with the hopes and dreams that their next extended week together would be a continuance of their hopes and dreams for the future.

CHAPTER TWENTY-THREE

"I swear, if Rufus had taken the time to be very quiet, he would have actually heard me laughing again."

AFTER A YEAR OF WHAT can only be aptly considered as a covertly auspicious relationship, they decided that August 7th would be their official anniversary - the day they made contact on the dating site - not the actual day they met in September. And because of the priority pact they made where their sons were concerned, there wasn't a celebration even though Rufus was in Florida on the 7th. He was with Stephanie the day prior but had arranged to meet Kevin at the Fort Lauderdale airport after the basketball camp where they overnighted in downtown Miami at Hotel Beaux Arts which was now his favorite hotel. The following day they both returned home after having very eventful summers.

Later in the month he celebrated his birthday weekend with her where she prepared for him his favorite breakfast of salmon, spinach, eggs, and Veuve. She also bought a single cupcake as a gesture and upon it one candle was placed to make a wish. And she hand-wrote seven greeting card sized parchment pages of the most endearing sentiments of what he has meant to her for the past year:

To my Dearest Love Rufus

I love you so very much, words could never let you know the immense feelings that I have for you in my heart. Spending time with you are like moments in paradise. You have brought happiness, joy, peace and love into my life. I feel so blessed and happy to have you in my life. Each and every moment with you I treasure.

Rufus, you are my dream come to life. Your strong embrace makes me feel safe. Your gentle touch makes me feel deeply cared for. The care that you show me makes me feel completely loved. I feel so lucky and proud when I hold your hand, because being in your presence makes me feel so safe and protected.

Words make never be enough to tell you the oceans of love that I feel for you. But I know that I love you with my heart. I love and miss you every second we are apart. My heart beats an extra beat just for you. I will always love you.

I love you when you are happy

I love you when you are sad

I will love you when you are healthy

I will love you when you are sick

I will love you when you smile

I will love you when you cry

I will love you when we are joyful

I will love you when we argue

But most importantly

I will love you always

I will love you forever

I love you Rufus Turnbull

HAPPY BIRTHDAY MY LOVE ALWAYS

STEPH

◆ ◆ ◆

A month later in September for Kevin's birthday, Rufus again fulfilled another promise I made. In 2008 we planned another birthday party for Kevin in Puerto Rico at a new Bowling Alley in Plaza Las Americas and we were supposed to fly over in the Cessna with one of Kevin's friends. On that particular trip, Rufus had a new instructor who was a stickler for the rules as far as passengers were concerned. We had in the past traveled with two kids when my niece wanted to visit because we met the weight and balance requirement of the plane. But this new instructor not only did not allow Rufus to fly because he was not familiar with his proficiency, he also did not allow the extra passenger. He treated the trip as a charter instead of a lesson. As a result, Kevin's friend was left behind sobbing. At that time, I promised him that I would make it up to him. And as a result, we informed Cleo that if we had that instructor again, we would fly commercial. The next time we flew, the instructor was no longer there.

So in 2016 for Kevin's 16th birthday, Rufus flew two of Kevin's friends – who happened to be the similar aged sons of my girlfriends Kevin stayed with on the weekends when Rufus visited Stephanie – to Miami where they stayed at his new favorite Hotel Beaux Arts. He even rented an Infiniti SUV similar to mine to which Kevin commented that the car was a great choice. Kevin got a preview the month prior on the 7th after he returned from the basketball camp. The private concierge, private dining and modern design of the rooms were reasons why Rufus and Stephanie liked it; the game rooms and the basketball court on its 19th floor was the reason Kevin and his friends would love it – in addition to his cousins from Miami and West Palm Beach. The boys had an amazing weekend.

The following Thanksgiving again was spent in Puerto Rico even though nothing had been resolved as far as repairing the relationship. My mother was so pleased that she unknowingly repeated to her friends in Puerto Rico that the three of us – Rufus, Kevin and me – were coming over. I knew she tried to hide her depression, but that lapse of judgment was an insight into her emotional state almost two years after my passing.

It had been a while since she saw her grandson after Kevin made up his mind that he was not going to Puerto Rico unless Rufus came along. Rufus on the other hand decided to spend one day primarily so my mother would be able to spend time with Kevin, but especially because my shorter sister had reconciled with him. It was actually sixteen months since they had last seen each other.

This gathering was the same as the year before where my taller sister was cordial to Rufus, but after my shorter sister late arrival, it was as if the past hadn't happened between them. She immediately complimented him on his healthier fit appearance. He was just happy to have a real conversation other than how his business was doing. She also found it was incredulous that her favorite brother-in-law watched all 72 Spanish speaking episodes reading the subtitles of *Celia* – a Netflix documentary about the legendary Cuban singer Celia Cruz, while she only watched 50. Kevin vouched for his father saying he was kinda worried because he wouldn't watch anything else for two weeks. Kevin actually thought that Rufus had slipped back into a state of depression because the few cinematic views of the television reminded him of Puerto Rico because lots of the scenes were recorded there. And the both of them kept to themselves the fact that the series was actually recommended by Stephanie. Shortly after the meal Rufus caught a flight to Fort Lauderdale and returned on Sunday to take Kevin back home.

Christmas was monumental where Stephanie began to do things for Rufus I was unable to. Unbeknownst to him, she had one criterion that she held close to her chest that she hoped that he would soon come around. His mind was closed to new eventualities and the fact that he failed to try new foods suggested a correlation that he was content with the status quo and was potentially stifling any of his potential for growth. She had been working on him for a long time paying close attention to his needs and his diet and at the right time she got him to try new foods.

During the Alaskan Cruise, they had lunch in Ketchikan in a quaint town that was infamous for its Alaskan king crab. She exclaimed that it was the best she'd ever eaten. Additionally, she allowed Rufus a very small taste. Another time they were having dinner at the W in Fort Lauderdale where her appetizer was oysters. She commented that she grew up with that taste on her pallet on the Florida north coast. She determined that based on how finicky Rufus was towards new foods, the "rhimy taste of the slimy mucus-like" (her words) delicacy was not going to be experienced by him in his near future. On the other hand, he stayed true to himself when she wanted him to try quinoa and he stated,

"I didn't like it when Christine made it and I still don't."

But it behooves me if I did not add what happened days before her arrival. Just for the mere fact that it was funny. I watched as Rufus lay on his back staring at the ceilings: in the great room and in the bedrooms and office. He continued to stare up at the ceiling in all of the other rooms as he walked around. I was taken aback for a moment. Then he placed a ladder on the kitchen island a began cleaning the pendant lights, the wood trusses on the ceiling from cob webs, the fans – everything. I remember he told me that the interior apex was 18ft. I assumed that he thought everything below was cleaned adequately. I smiled as I immediately realized that he wasn't going to have another Home Depot episode.

During her second trip to visit him for New Year 2017 in St. Thomas, they over spent and were over dressed for what they thought was going to be a formal gala at the Ritz Carlton 2016 New Year's Eve party. Rufus thought it was going to be like the swanky parties he was accustomed to when he played the music circuit. And based on what they paid, they could have traveled to Puerto Rico and crashed one of the extraordinary ballroom celebrations with the legendary Salsa bands. But they were both spectacles as everyone looked at how they were dressed where Rufus was actually getting some compliments too.

But instead of being in one of the intimate dining rooms or a festively decorated ballroom, they were seaside at a makeshift Grill dining under portable canopies where the flooring was the sea sand. At least the weather really cooperated where the evenings skies sparkled with stars that reflected off the seemingly still ocean as the waves failed to encroach the sand. They decided to sit at the nearby Sail Restaurant instead and watch the tourists with sundresses and Bermuda shorts.

To get their money's worth, in the buffet line Stephanie placed a huge unshelled lobster on Rufus plate. And before he could protest, she said, "Eat it!" Rufus told me that he had never eaten lobster after one climbed out of a steaming pot and chased him out of the house as a kid. Stephanie also heard the story and was now adamant that he was too uptight about foods for way too long. He acquiesced. He loved it. She told him the way it was prepared was healthy being lightly seasoned and grilled. Rufus had seconds, thirds, and fourths as if he was making up for lost time.

The party lost its luster after they ate and by 10pm, they were ready to leave way before midnight. Fortunately, he remembered that two of his clients rented a club in the downtown Havensight area for the same night and were hosting an invitation only event where they hired an act from the mainland called The Dueling Pianos as the entertainment. It was interactive where the two pianists played anything that the audience requested. After calling and reporting that the Ritz party was a bust because it catered to the tourists, his client told him that the evening was young and he couldn't wait to finally meet Stephanie. Upon their arrival, I thought it was cute how one of Rufus' friends referred to Stephanie as *Fort Lauderdale* before she was introduced.

◆ ◆ ◆

2017 began tumultuous for Stephanie in many ways. After a year and a half of being in business, her business partner's husband wanted out because they weren't showing any growth and weren't profitable. They were not profitable because her partners did not do their part. Frankly, they failed to advertise; they thought that the clients that followed her from her last employer and word of mouth was going to be sufficient.

Rufus was the rock she needed in those uncertain times. One time she asked that he make a special trip so they could discuss her options. They had a last gasp attempt to spur up business with a social media campaign of video clips and social networking. He videotaped a Saturday class with his camera equipment. He was even her Plus One at the trendy parties like the Venice Magazine 10th year anniversary where the bartender destroyed a guest's fabulous dress. I remember in preparation for that party, he went to a Men's Warehouse looking for pastel colored linen slacks and the older salesman actually told him,

"If I had an ass like yours, I would fill out my pants better."

Rufus again looked at the man sideways feeling a little put off wishing the comment was from a female. He bought two and had the perfect sandals from Born where he had several of the same pair.

But in the end it was too late.

Another weekend they spent a Saturday looking at potential places to lease. The fact that she insisted that she didn't want him to fund her future endeavor was telling. As a result, a closing date was established in the fall which gave her the opportunity to consider what she really wanted to do in the future.

What happened next began a chain reaction of events that I am very proud to have been a part of. Remember when I saw her potential in my recognizance I said Rufus would really compliment her? After one of her clients realized what was happening to the studio, she reminded Stephanie about building her online business with workout videos. Now the client explained further than she was 70 years and would be going away to Europe for a few months and needed workout content from someone she knew and trusted. And to that end, she left a blank check for the cost of producing the videos and would subscribe afterwards.

Stephanie called Rufus and sought his advice because she quickly became overwhelmed. That was his strength. He quickly learned that she had begun procuring equipment like a DSLR camera and lighting. Her son commandeered the camera for his own use and the 3 lighting kits she bought remained in their unopened boxes. Rufus noticed everything back on the first day they met and had suspicious thoughts back then. Now for the very first time those boxes were opened by him. He also had the perfect cameras and expertise. So on the following day after their heated discussion about the classification of the piano and the follow up jab about a luthier, they recorded their first of forty intense 20 Minute workout videos. He sought and bought the necessary monitor, microphones, and rigging to make it very simple for her to produce the raw content at home. She then emailed him the video file and on St. Thomas in his office, he edited and added music then uploaded the finished content to their video hosting site which was later linked to their website.

While Rufus was in the process of setting the audio levels before the first shooting, he recorded her talking freely expressing her hopes and dreams for their future without her knowing saying the following:

"This right here, there's a lot riding on it. You know, I feel like this is not only my future but it's our future; it's the future of our children. Because what I want to be able to do with this, is to buy our children homes. This is what I'm talking about - I mean with what we do, together. This is what I want to do: college paid for, buy them homes. I mean, what a great start in life, right? A great, great, great beginning. And then it's like.... go on (deep voice) young men... and prosper...thrive, and prosper. That's what I want - this is what I want to do- it is just my dream - Kevin and P - we buy them homes .... Done. Paid for.... done. It's not much money. And we just do our thing. You know we're in some lil beach house somewhere - you know doing our thing: going for walks in the morning...on the ocean - just doing us. Nothing like - you know that I don't like big houses in the first place. I need to be able to say, "Honey" and you are right there."

During the year they were both hitting their strides. Their weekends were mainly learning more about each other while lying under a cabana on Hollywood Beach, experiencing all of the different therapeutic water modalities at the Russian and Turkish Bath House in Miami Beach, going to the theater where he struggled like a baby to stay awake, attended different soirees or simply hanging out on the first story screen porch watching iguanas and ducks in the nearby trees and man-made pond with a spectacular fountain.

They began to establish what they truly enjoyed together - what she would do that was important to him even though it may not hold the same significance for her. Like they both looked forward to their honeymoon around spring break when her son now spent that time with his dad. It was aptly named when an Uber driver referred to her as his wife and she simply smiled seeing no need for corrections.

He loved Blue Martini and quite frankly would go every weekend, but she said once every other month was her max.

Additionally, she became a cruise convert after the same client that kept referring to her as Fort Lauderdale at the New Year's Eve party told him about The Haven on NCL. The epiphany about her social anxiety made The Haven option perfect. And again, even though the added conveniences inexorably cost twice as much for a standard room, Rufus justified the cost comparing it to the Tom Joyner Fantastic Voyage which is priced similarly.

The Norwegian Cruise Line 'Haven' package could might as well be named Heaven. But as scripture would have it, one has to die and be a believer first along with other prerequisites. As far as heaven was concerned, Rufus often expressed quite poignantly that the happiness he felt when we were married and the life we lived was Heaven to him. Kevin expressed similarly but in his own way when he stated that our life was perfect before 2012.

But The Haven is the best unkempt secret because a majority of the regular passengers - like Milton - doesn't even know it exists on the NCL ships. The experience is like having a smaller ship within a ship. Expedited embarking and disembarking, private butler, concierge and open bar is where it begins. Private pool in a covered atrium where instead of hearing the crowd waller of hundreds of people frolicking to loud music by the rotating DJ's, instead all you hear is peaceful serenity music as you lounge in or around the air conditioned huge private pool deck. Unfettered access to the water spa that exceeded the experience at the Russian and Turkish baths, and specialty dining your way.

Rufus told Milton about The Haven experience and they were at it again. Milton expressed,

"I've been on Norwegian way before you Dred. And I've even been on the same ship the Escape," he began to solidify is point. Then continued, "You know I'm always in the gym when I cruise. Now you've been on that ship one time and you're claiming that there were cabins right outside the entry to the gym on deck sixteen?"

"I don't know that you are always in the gym. On the Tom Joyner Cruise, I had to wake you up to go walking, remember?" Rufus reminded.

"Walking and the gym ain't the same – and you know it was raining on the track." Milton added trying to keep a straight face.

Rufus calmly explained to his skeptical best friend the following,

"When you left the gym corridor, on the left led you outside through automatic sliding glass doors to the starboard balcony."

"What's starboard?"

"The right side of the ship."

Milton concurred. Rufus continued,

"To the right led you to the elevators on the left and the stairwell on the right."

Milton again agreed. Rufus further explained,

"And if you continued to walk straight ahead, there was the opposing automatic glass doors that led you to the port side balcony."

"That's the left side of the ship" Milton deduced then agreed.

Rufus then concluded,

"Between the port side glass doors and the stairwell was a dark paneled wall with a discretely place black card reader that opened an equally discrete dark paneled door into the concierge, private bar, cabins, and covered pool."

"There wasn't any magic door there Dred." Milton excoriated.

♦ ♦ ♦

The two Category 5 hurricanes during the fall of 2017 were really trying for Kevin and Stephanie. Rufus was scheduled to attend the

Electronic Trade Show in San Diego California and his sister Lena was supposed to spend a week on St. Thomas taking care of her nephew. And as a result of the frequent flyer miles and points accumulated, Rufus had already booked flights for biweekly returns to Fort Lauderdale from October to February 2018. The hurricanes permanently changed all those plans. Rufus basically went into hurricane preservation mode.

In previous conversations leading up to the first storm Rufus told Stephanie about all of the precautions we had to do. And being the great listener she is, Stephanie later reminded him of things she thought he had to do. She told him to cook all of the perishable foods in the refrigerator and to double check his checklist.

It was trying unable to communicate in the immediate wake of the first storm after Sprint service was out. Fortunately, Kevin's phone by virtue of maintaining the service on AT&T was their life line having never losing its service. The cells were overloaded at times but in spite of what had happened they were able to communicate. My family all called instead of texting to see how they feared.

The storm that had just decimated St. Thomas and the Florida Keys was now forecast for the I-75 corridor. Stephanie was supposed to drive north to visit her family for her father's 70th birthday but all of the gas station in her area were out of gas and there were reports of lots of cars being stranded on the evacuation routes. Since she didn't want to be in the same boat as the many stranded along the turnpike, she decided to stayed put.

In the storm's wake, she actually had a sense of adventure similar to the surfers you see on television waiting to catch the big waves. She did the land based equivalent in the desolation that was seriously crazy and cool. She and her son drove to the nearest interstate exit ramp, got out the car, and proceeded to run back and forth across the lanes of I-95 because there were absolutely no other cars in sight.

During the storm she hunkered down in her apartment until it passed. But Rufus chided her for going outside to charge her cellphone in the car after they lost power. He told her that her laptop could have charged her phone several times and she agreed that it was dangerous.

Before the second storm hit St. Thomas, all of the mitigation measures remained and this time Rufus invited Milton and his family to stay with him downstairs because they sustained damages to their home from the first storm. The client that referred to Stephanie as Fort Lauderdale allowed Kevin and Rufus refreshing nightly hot showers and a place to hold their cold storage. To recompense Rufus installed a DISH Network antenna so that he could see television. And his neighbor two houses away allow everyone who had extension cords long enough to plug into her standby generator that powered her entire house. They connected their wet bar appliances of the mini beverage cooler and microwave, a power strip to charge cell phones and they watched television via the DISH Network Hopper, a router, small LED TV, and iPad so he could watch something different. And a month later, Rufus bit the bullet and finally bought a diesel generator.

In addition to seeing the second storm coming on television, he also realized that it was going to hit Puerto Rico directly and became very worried. He showed his concern instructing them what to do in case of the worst: fill bathtub with water, sparingly bathe in the other bathroom shower, and charge all computers to recharge cell phones. But what he impressed the most was that the storm was huge and it was going to last for a very long time. And to provide a visual reference for them to monitor knowing they would undoubtedly lose power, he emailed a charted map with the forecast path with the estimated time stamped at every two hours.

In the end, my niece and sister confirmed his worst fears and thank him for his foresight about using their computers to charge their phones.

It took six weeks to finally get off the island and to make a case of honesty, Rufus told Stephanie he just wanted to relax – none of the usual outings that they were accustomed to. She recommended that he travel with his laundry after he complained that the line to the laundromat was a half day experience. She also suggested that he shopped for cold storage and buy a cold storage bag to return with. He even changed his cell phone carriers to AT&T and took the opportunity to install the music system in her newly relocated Pilates Studio with her new business partner.

The subsequent Thanksgiving was spent in New Jersey at my aunts and it was the most festive they had experience in the past three years. Again, unbeknownst to my family Rufus made those arrangements months before the hurricane. And again he purposely chose to layover in Puerto Rico for the purpose of them being able to see Kevin. That evening my shorter sister suggested that they go dancing in the hurricane damage island where live music was being performed. He reluctantly agreed but from his Facebook live posts, it was again like it always used to be when they first watched boxing together. It was apparent that he missed those times.

The next day before they went to the airport where no attempts to in-authenticate the holiday by sitting down around a table and pretend like nothing happened two years before, everyone present were having dinner at friends which also bode true for Kevin and Rufus arriving later at Debbie's in the evening in New Jersey. This time, it felt like home. It felt like home because the mood was festive.

On the Saturday morning Stephanie recommended that he should go to a basketball game with Kevin. Again that was my passive influencing at work. Rufus chose the Philadelphia 76ers game instead of the New Jersey Nets. And they had an amazing time sitting floor level and were allowed early entry where Kevin was able to see the players parking lot and watched them in the pre-game shoot around.

Upon their return to St. Thomas, the north Florida country girl persona that Stephanie keeps hidden expressed poignantly that she was a little jealous when he described the quiet of the nights. And during the evening of the full moons in the storms aftermath, the stillness and silence inspired him to start drawing again.

I always knew that he drew and painted because of the few times he did during our marriage. But the void of noise precipitated a resurgence in his artistic prowess where scores of nude portraits and drawings began to populate the lower guest bedroom. He bought all of the discounted 25 sheet 18x24 canvas pads from a local store that was going out of business. The subsequent time he was in Fort Lauderdale, Stephanie took him to Blicks to stock up on art supplies. And for Christmas he bought a box of 250 sheets of 24x36 paper from Amazon. All of the inspiration for creating seemingly derived from 1000 miles away.

Because of the devastation that remained in the islands, Christmas 2017 was spent downtown in Miami and for the new year Stephanie thought he would enjoy a slow train ride to Tampa instead of flying commercial. They chose to have a cabin and thoroughly enjoyed the experience. The highlight of that trip was the inconsequential dinner they had at the Bazille restaurant at the mall that wound up being so significant. Later Stephanie admitted to purposely choosing other restaurants since they have known each other because it was his favorite in Puerto Rico and she wanted it to remain that way. She told him that she didn't want to conflate those memories. But again by happenstance, on the last evening of their Tampa getaway and all of the other options for dining had long waiting lines, the following actually happened.

Unbeknownst to Rufus, Stephanie was purposely avoiding the Bazille Restaurant and was about to go to a café they had earlier eaten when someone tapped Rufus from behind. It was the waiter from the Bazille Restaurant in Puerto Rico. The same restaurant at The Mall of San Juan where the last time he was there, he was so angry that he left his entrée uneaten. Rufus and the waiter hugged and he asked him what he was doing in Tampa when he explained that he had to relocate after the storm and was fortunate to find a place in Tampa and kept his job. Although they both did not know each other's name, he remembered what Kevin and Rufus always ordered. He even asked how Kevin and my mother was doing. For the moment there was now no doubt where they were going to dine. The waiter escorted them in the restaurant and only gave Stephanie a menu and proceeded to not make Rufus a liar when he memorized his order from Puerto Rico. After dinner, Rufus left a larger than usual tip.

♦ ♦ ♦

The final months of the 2018 school term was nearing and Kevin began to show interest in Accounting. As part of the business curriculum, they partnered with businesses to help the students get On the Job experience and one of Rufus' clients offered Kevin a paid internship in high school and the ability to work at his leisure while attending the local university after graduation. Additionally, as a class project, each student had to prepare a dessert to be critiqued. Rufus knew Kevin wasn't going to do it and scoffed by asking Kevin whether the teacher knew about their circumstances after the recent hurricanes as a cop out.

You see, Kevin assignment was to have a pie Key Lime Pie presentation. Rufus even reminded Kevin how long ago he was out of school. I knew he was going to tell Stephanie and when he did, the discussion would be over.

He found a recipe online and saw that he had to go shopping. He couldn't find anything on his own and was quickly becoming frustrated. He even thought about buying a Key Lime Pie. Then I sent a familiar face to his rescue. Another one of his Caucasian clients said hi in the supermarket and he asked her where to find heavy cream because there weren't any in the dairy section. She helped him get all of the ingredients including twin pie crusts.

To extract the yolk from the egg I compelled him to remember that when I baked, in addition to having several baking pans and cake molds, he would find it bubble extractor.

He soon realized that it was very simple whisking the wet ingredients and after it was all said and done, it was perfect. He took a very small slice and was totally enamored with himself. He even called Milton who said,

"You know you didn't make no Key Lime Pie Dred."

He then knew where to go to get the kind of praise he was looking for so he called Stephanie after sending her a picture.

"I'm so proud of you honey." she began, "... so you have another to send Kevin to school with, right?"

"No, I didn't eat much. I'm going to send him to school with the remaining."

What she said next was priceless.

"Are you nuts?"

"What?" Rufus replied.

"I said, are you nuts?" she repeated emphatically.

"I only ate a very small amount." he tried to rationalize.

She already knew that the pie was cut because it was evident in the picture he sent. That is why she asked whether he had another. After his continued bellyaching, she interrupted to insist,

"You are not going to send him to school with a half-eaten pie." And to make it perfectly clear she continued, "You are not going to send him to school with a partially eaten pie either."

I swear, if Rufus had taken the time to be very quiet, he would have actually heard me laughing. Then he sheepishly asked.

"So that means that I have to do it again?" She replied incredulously,

"Ya?"

◆ ◆ ◆

In June 2018, Kevin graduation from high school was momentous in more ways than I am able to mention. He too has been through his own Hero's Journey where the lowest point in his short life was when I passed away. Despite it all, through the love and support of our families and friends, he came out on the other side. That weekend began precariously when my family came over and decided to stay at a hotel instead of visiting and staying at the house. It was that kind of energy that made Stephanie change her mind about attending. She appropriately deduced that if she did, she would have otherwise been the unintentional center of attention. Nonetheless, on the day before the ceremony, Rufus took them out for a pre-graduation dinner at the Greenhouse on the waterfront.

In hindsight I truly wish that the circumstances were different so I could be there physically and the dynamic between my family was more amenable. The way it worked before, I made the tough choices that we all collectively supported where my family was concerned. Now it is quite obvious that my taller sister now occupies that role. But after it was all said and done, I was there otherwise and I was able to contribute in my own inimitable way.

You see, only four tickets were afforded to the graduates and my mother wasn't certain whether Rufus was going to secure a ticket for her. So instead of asking him directly, my shorter sister was chosen to. Rufus already told his sisters who were coming that he really did not know how many tickets were to be distributed, but the first two were going to him and my mother. That was also the message he relayed to my sister. Again he was disappointed that my mother did not call and ask herself. But in the end, Kevin was able to secure enough extra tickets from his classmates in order for everyone in our combine families to attend his graduation.

This moment of accomplishment makes me reflect on how it all began; the chanced meeting over Happy Hour, a year later married, and Kevin a decade removed. I even remember all of the small celebrations in between; his first steps, Rufus on the toilet with a strained face while Kevin was on the potty to teach him how he should look when he pooped.

When he learned to swim was huge because Kevin knew we couldn't. And after I passed, I saw how proud Rufus was after he viewed the video while on the barge returning from working on St. John when he programmed that car in his technology camp.

I remember when Kevin saw me physically for the last time in the Intensive Care Unit at the Auxilio Mutuo Hospital in Puerto Rico. Rufus had just gotten the news from my taller sister when his disposition immediately changed. After being led into the ICU, he saw me in my stillness, went to my bedside, and he dropped to his knees sobbing. From Kevin's vantage, he saw his father from a perspective he had never before witnessed. He was visibly confused and in a state of shock asking several times,

"what happened.........what happened....... what happened?"

Rufus realized then that Kevin was behind him when he gathered himself and told him,

"Mom's gone."

Kevin immediately went limp and Rufus caught him from falling. He remained limp physically unable to walk at times on his own after being grief stricken even when they later left the hospital. For that entire evening he never cried outwardly. And as this book come to its conclusion, for the last time I am going to preface that the following actually happened.

When Kevin was preschool age until six, he always cried when he was on stage for the school ceremonies and church holiday programs – without fail. Rufus became annoyed after a few times. Even at his graduation ceremony from kindergarten, he was the only child on stage crying. At the subsequent first grade play, he cried. I was also at my wits end wondering what was wrong and I even thought that the people in the audience thought that we were abusive.

Then we sent him to summer camp at the Moravian Church and the counselors told us one afternoon when we picked him up that Kevin won the hula hoop contest stating "he never stopped ... he just kept going and going." So we bought him a hula hoop over the weekend and as she reported, he just kept going effortlessly. At the end of the camp they had another ceremony and as it began, you guessed it, Kevin began to cry again.

Then again Rufus had another one of his brilliant ideas that I totally did not agree with. He said,

"Let's leave."

"Absolutely not!" I whispered back vehemently.

Rufus continue to suggest that the other kids are singing and Kevin is disrupting the show. I was firm until he said,

"I don't mean that we are going to leave. We are just going to go where he cannot see us."

I reluctantly acquiesced and as we got up and proceeded to walk out of the church. Everybody looked at us and I felt like I was walking the plank. We exited the church and snuck around to a window to see that Kevin had stopped crying and began to re-engage with his friends. During a break in the show we asked him what was the matter to which he responded,

"I don't know."

Rufus told him that his crying was disrupting the ceremony and people are recording him 'bawling.' I told him that I wanted to enjoy the program inside and it wasn't fair that I have to watch it from the outside. And we both want to see you win the Hula Hoop contest. He gave me a huge hug and promised not to cry anymore.

That was eleven summers ago. But after the high school graduation ceremony - after driving himself to the auditorium in his own car, after stoically walking with his classmates in the procession, after hamming it up on the stage when he received his diploma while Rufus recorded and posted it on Facebook for perpetuity, and after it was all over, outside of the auditorium he was the only person uncontrollably crying. He was crying because he knew I was there. I take eternal solace knowing that with each tear he realized that I saw him through it all. It was as if in his very short life everything came full circle from the first time he attended preschool. But that's his story to tell if he allows me to.

♦ ♦ ♦

Two months later Rufus and Stephanie were celebrating their 3-year anniversary on the cruise ship MSC Seaside and the following occurred that otherwise shouldn't have. While on a day long excursion to the Bob Marley Museum in Jamaica, his cellphone unexpectedly rang. The fact that his phone rang was as curious as that notification Stephanie received from the dating site 3-years earlier. He knew that while on the cruise he would be unable to receive calls due to his default settings to not recognize international carriers. That was reason enough for his phone to remain silent; the limited cellphone coverage and service in the remote area where the museum was located was another. He merely took his phone on the tour to use it as a camera. When he opened the phone he immediately recognized the number and promptly answered. The call was brief and when he hung up, he sighed and began smiling.

Stephanie knew it was good news and before she could ask Rufus reported,

"That was UVI (The University of the Virgin Islands) on the phone. They told me that a dorm became available for Kevin."

He continued to explain that Kevin has to move in immediately. Rufus tried to call back but could not get through. He knew normally he should not have received that call. But at the same time, he knew that he would be able to immediately when they returned to the ship when his phone connects to the WiFi and he can contact Kevin via WhatsApp or Messenger.

Rufus felt a little conflicted wishing he could be there for Kevin's transition from home to college. He was on the waiting list as the dormitories were being repaired from the storms and it was expected that he would be commuting to his classes. If he was in Fort Lauderdale, he most definitely would have returned home to be with him, but he was also secure knowing that Kevin has a credit card on his account and could get everything he needs at Kmart. But at the same time he knew everything was going to be alright.

The following week upon his return, Rufus delivered a dorm-refrigerator when he visited Kevin's room. He immediately noticed that Kevin commandeered the framed pencil portrait of me from home that Rufus drew in the nineties and hung it over his bed. With that gesture, he realized that I helped him with his transition into the dormitory and will always   continue   to.

EPILOGUE

There was an incident that occurred in 2017 that I purposely did not include in the storyline. After the weekend breakdown in 2016, Rufus was in very good spirits for the entire year that followed and I wanted to chronicle the story in that manner to maintain that tenor for the following two years.

Everything was promising where they even considered eloping. It was Stephanie's idea and he concurred. She wanted it to be totally secret, but Rufus insisted that he had to tell two people: Kevin and Milton - and particularly in that order. She agreed at first and later had second thoughts. Her apprehension wasn't against marrying him, but it was about the potential repercussions if her ex found out and how much of an asshole he can be. After her son leaves for college, the subject at that time will be revisited. So Rufus went along with her wishes, but also told her,

"I am not going to ask you to marry me again." She corrected him by saying,

"You never did."

"I am not going to ask you again anyway" He repeated again. And in the back of his mind he was smiling to himself thinking,

"*...this five or six year waiting seems to be working out.*"

But in all honesty, she knows when that timing is right, he is only a "Yes" away.

So with all that positive energy and joy abloom, I didn't want to include that last salvo that began another vortex that was about to create another rabbit hole. By this time, his emotional reservoir was overflowing where anything that caused despair would have been filled.

My shorter sister texted him about Kevin not returning their calls nor texts. In actuality, she was communicating the concerns on behalf of the others because she and Rufus communicated monthly and if she wanted Kevin involved, she added him into the chat. Additionally, Rufus made a point to always tell him when his "Titi" called or texted and to relay what they discussed even when she only texted,

"Rufie, how are you doing?"

Rufus was in Fort Lauderdale when he received the message and he had no intention to address it while he was there. He responded upon his return. She was trying to make the point that he should teach Kevin how to behave as it relates to his aunts and grandmother. He was incredulous that they were having this conversation again and he was visibly getting upset. He was becoming upset at the fact that they were still able to make him upset. He took a step back and this time did not parse his response telling her back when he informed everyone about what was going on in his life, they took it to another level. And after all the time that has passed, quite frankly he no longer cares. And quite frankly, he was teaching Kevin how to respond if the unfortunate situation happened to him. A riff ensued where in the end he promised to have Kevin call her so he could express how he really feels.

He later expressed what happened to my aunt Debbie. Debbie was another sounding board of support he had and an advocate behind the scenes trying to mediate when at times my taller sister actually told her it wasn't any of her business. But before I continue, since Debbie was so instrumental in Rufus' healing – giving her updates bimonthly - I think it's best that he introduces her in only the way he can.

First of all, Debbie is not really Christine's aunt; she is simply Christine's mother's childhood best friend. Just in the same manner Anna is not Christine's cousin; Anna's father was raised by her grandmother when his mother died in her teens. I used to tell Christine if somebody came by their childhood home too often they became relatives.

Anyway, I liked Debbie immediately when I met her for the first time in Puerto Rico at our ruse of a wedding. And since I am being forthcoming and truthful, I liked her immediately because she was the only person in the whole congregation that gave me a wedding gift. It was a bath towel with a Velcro tab that made it easy to wrap around the waist. When we were introduced for the very first time after the ceremony in the church, she held my face in her hands like The Lord of the Rings' Gollum handling the 'Precious' and hugged me like my mother does. Which again suggests that Christine spoke highly of me.

Over the years she has become hearing impaired where she now wears cochlear implants which effectively allows her to hear most sounds, but not my voice. She explained that the frequency of my voice is too low to understand clearly and it's worse over the phone. So while she has conversations with most people over the phone – and we have tried once – she can't with me. So in person she reads my lips and otherwise, I have been texting and emailing bimonthly since Christine's passed. And to prove that she is not faking about her hearing issues, I remember a more recent time when the three of us were visiting at her home in New Jersey. She left to go to work and forgot to turn off her alarm. After reading this passage you will agree that a petition is necessary to come up with another name for what woke us up. Let me begin by saying it was the worst manner I have ever been awoken in my life. We were all hightailing down the stairs when we heard what sounded like loud jack hammering that made the entire house vibrate. I know I am being overly dramatic but we really thought we were being under attack. Anyway, since the sound was prolonged and we didn't appear to be in harm's way, Christine sent me back upstairs without a weapon when I realized that the sound was coming from within the walls. It timed out in a minute and I returned laughing and explained to Christine and Kevin.

Now with this potentially manufactured derailing situation of Kevin not answering their calls again, Debbie to an extent agreed with my sisters and mother. She was channeling Rodney King's in hopes that '*they all just get along.*' Rufus referred to the entire situation as the Elephant in the Room where they just wanted to conveniently forget that my taller sister accusation was a figment of nobody's imagination but her own. And they really didn't what to hear anything about his affairs in Fort Lauderdale. Rufus reiterated the fact that he was teaching Kevin to make prudent decisions and not to be manipulated or disregarded in the manner he was being treated. After all, my family have existed as a tribe of women for most of our lives and their behavior towards Rufus directly affects how Kevin sees them and he is reacting accordingly. So in the end he told my sister he would have Kevin call her.

Again, the following actually happened and the actual text transcripts with time stamp are included. (the parenthesis are where my family member's names were)

April 19, 2017 6:53pm
Kevin and (my sister) just ended their conversation...again I wish I had a voice recorder. He told me nothing was resolved but at least they spoke to each other.

The most profound thing I thought that he said to her was, 'it took the fact of him being 'distant' for them to recognize the situation that was created by them has not been resolved after all this time.' (My sister) also remarked that they know that my life is none of their business.
Frankly, that IS the point - the Elephant. It wasn't their business to disparage me and later act like everything was okay without remorse... (not including my mother-in-law and niece)

Remember I told you about the few times when Kevin went to Puerto Rico, they would tell you how they felt he enjoyed himself and he told me how it really went. Back then the only time he really felt distracted and had a good time was when (his cousin/my niece) was home from college. I recalled one time he told me that he didn't want to go back unless I went.

[I fell asleep...]

The next morning, he awoke and the following is the transcript from the end of the text messages that he sent to Debbie

April 20, 2017 6:53am
I thought long and hard early this morning and I have been struggling with my feelings. It's like everything has been re-hashed again. I was in a very good place mentally last week, but I have dedicated too much energy and emotion to a situation that won't be resolved anytime soon.

At this point I don't care if they accept my relationship. I do care that Kevin maintains a relationship with everyone in Puerto Rico - that's the best I can guarantee. This situation is affecting my work again where I can be doing something else. I need to refocus on what I was doing before this came up.

April 20, 2017 6:56am
Something weird happened when I sent my last messages I'm not kidding ... I sorta got the chills.

April 20, 2017 6:58am
This picture just appeared after I pressed send [A picture of Christine and Me inserted itself into the chat]

April 20, 2017 7:01am
I found [the picture] it in a message I sent your way earlier. I try to find meaning in everything and I think my mind is telling me that Christine is fine with my decision.

Debbie
April 20, 2017 7:02am
U wanna hear weird. I just woke up from a dream Christine called me on the phone n said she had something to tell me. I started crying telling her how much I miss her n so happy to hear her voice n then she wasn't on the phone n I cried like a baby. Woke up n found your text.

April 20, 2017 7:03am
It tells me that she knows that we tried (I'm crying)

Debbie
April 20, 2017 7:04am
I'm crying also

NOTE FROM THE AUTHOR

This story isn't unlike many others who have unwillingly became members of this fraternity that has no age, religion, race, nor gender requirements, while its membership unwittingly increases every day. The only prerequisite is that you were married. And after a year or two, decades, generations or fewer, when one finally succumb to the natural order of life, the other is left remaining to pick up the pieces and hope to have the capacity to move on.

This memoir isn't about the stages of depression that is a result of its membership, but it is a story of hopes and dreams that abound where at the same time forces – seen and unseen – try to guide you along different paths when you are most vulnerable. And based on the choices, you either wind up slightly unscathed on the other side or the elements that led you down the rabbit hole eventually swallows you up.

I also recognize that this story isn't for everyone because it may conflict with deep seethed religious beliefs and practices. But in the end, this is my story and it's told from my late wife's point of view.

Writing really helped me through those moments of deep despair when at times I did not know what to do. When I was paralyzed with grief, it fit everyone's narrative of how I was supposed to act in the aftermath of my late wife's passing. And when those unseen forces began to pull me out of my sorrow, another narrative ensued. But in the end, you are still left asking yourself, why?

Were all those years a rollercoaster ride or blissfully optimistic? Was it a life cut short or an illness prolonged? Or was it what we all hope for, longevity way beyond retirement age and in good health against all the odds? That encapsulates what it really means to be widowed.

In a small community like mine in the United States Virgin Islands, the daily obituary has been a mainstay twice on weekdays for longer than I have been alive on the People's Radio Station WSTA. So in essence, everyone hears about the dearly departed and many are familiar with the bereaved to which their condolences and sympathies go a long way. But after enough time has passed, then what?

Obscurity becomes one's comfort until you are no longer comfortable. Overt exuberance is shunned upon when expressed too soon. But again - too soon for whom. And whenever the time is right, you hope that you carved out enough space when you ultimately decide to invite someone in your room.

In my deepest moments of despair, I became so insulated from the outside world that I didn't realize that I had created a quagmired state of existence to the point of using humor as a cloak. Only my son saw what I was really going through. And after he gave his blessing when I decided to move on, then and only then I really knew what to do.

I actually told a friend thanks for being honest when he told me he didn't know what to say immediately after learning my wife of twenty-five years had passed away. So his consolation instead was to talk to me about sports because he knew that brought me comfort. And I told another friend that I won't wish that kind of emotional despair of losing a loved one on my worst enemy. But while you grieve like you think you are the only one who has gone through the fire, the world continues to spin and with each new day, life goes on. And if you fail to live your life, it simply passes you by. But when you finally come to its terms, take solace knowing that from within oneself, only you know when it's time to take another turn.

Upon completing this book, I now chuckle at the thought of being a ghost writer because at least for this memoir, it's appropriate. But initially it didn't start out that way. I actually began writing this in the First Person that evening after Christine passed away when I couldn't sleep. I did it to simply remember all the things we did, document all the good times we had in our lives and possibly later to share with our son Kevin.

But a few things happened before it developed into being a book. It didn't read well from my perspective even though the excerpts went over well at her memorial service. Otherwise, it sounded like I was tooting my own horn and I was purporting too many of my personal beliefs. And after 100 pages or thereabouts, I took a huge step back allowing months to pass which allowed the various narratives of contention to develop. In a nutshell, I took the subliminal advice of Priscilla and my high school band mates. I am not a lead singer. It is my nature to be more comfortable laying down the backing tracks of support while the true artists sing the blues up front - that's what bass players do.

But in all actuality, I honestly thought that no one would want to hear what I had to say. Not to mention, all the weird things that occurred that led me to approach writing the book another way. I know people may think that my persona appears more enlightened, I also know that others may think that I'm a little crazy.

Like on the morning after Christine passed and I couldn't find her cellphone that I knew I had with me in bed during the night. After removing all the bedding revealing the mattress and asked everyone whether they had it, moments later after I dialed her number it rang under the same disheveled bedding I had just removed and replaced.

I even looked for the signs of the mccobb that were fabled but still repeated over the centuries stating that on the days of funerals, it rains because the dearly departed is crying. That actually happened in Puerto Rico for a brief moment on the way to the crematory chapel on an otherwise sunny early afternoon. But on St. Thomas it didn't rain at the church. I attributed it to the change in tenor after I read excerpts of my life with her that had the congregation mostly light spirited and laughing.

Now as I reflect on those twenty-five years of personal discussions and more recently being able to review old pictures, videos and retrieve some transcriptions, I think Christine would be equally pleased and smile knowing that she is also a published author in absentia. Early in our marriage she even played a joke on me when she bought a paperback book where the author's name was Christine Bell and she briefly suggested that she had already published a book before we were married.

In closing, I highly recommend documenting as much of one's life's experiences for perpetuity to be later shared with the small world that revolves around you.

APPENDIX

As the storyline developed, everything seemed to write itself where the story wove back and forth between the present and past. It was like seeing my life being replayed several times in my mind causing me to remember so many things I had forgotten. And as expressed in the foreword, everything in the book is accurate.

My Playlist on the plane was an insight to my emotional state evident by the Corrine Bailey track on September 4, 2015 and prior to how it changed to the Ledisi I cued up on Rhapsody on my return flight. And for more clarity, the various YouTube links allows you to see what we saw as a digital third eye.

I even sought clarification from some of the persons I mentioned by name to make sure the details were correct as I recollected. Like my classmate Amazia with that episode in the gym on the ship. She is notable and dear to me - notwithstanding she suggested that Christine be an honorary class member because she attended more fundraising activities than members of our graduation class locally, but she too has endured the debilitating cancer treatments and initially informed only Milton, Andrew, and myself outside her immediate family.

Additionally, I apprised Milton about the garlic episode where he laughed after reading it and immediately respond saying, "You got it right Dred." [Note: Dred is an endearing local island term from the 70's that never caught on. It's equivalent to when you hear us say "mehson" that means 'man' or the urban substitute 'my man.' I am of the opinion that Milton still hangs on to the term because in high school he was the trombone player in the local calypso brass band The Dred Ones.

Priscilla reminded me about how distraught I was when she learned about the breakup with Ms. Credit Card telling me how we talked often over the phone remarking that 'I was in a bad way' unlike the enigmatic person that she had known me to be as band mates. I don't remember the calls, but if there was anyone I would have apprised at that time of my life, Priscilla was top three on the list.

My sister Linda also corrected me when she EMPHASIZED whether I was "crazy in the ass" in 1989 with the Ms. Credit Card episode. And when she stayed with me in April 2016 when she attended her ex-husband's funeral, she told me about Stephanie's concerns and apprehensions. She explained that she told Stephanie to talk to me directly to get it off her chest - not expecting that she would write an email instead to dissolve the relationship. As one of my favorite comedian's catch phrase states, "these ain't jokes," ... it's the truth.

I purposely left out names like Stephanie's son, her ex-husband's – where he consequently is the only person I have not to this date personally met. When I learned that one of his email accounts began with my name, I was taken aback similarly like he was when Stephanie relay the episode about finally telling him about me.

And please forgive me for the obscure manner that I described some of my in-laws and sisters having intentionally left out all the names of my family members that are estranged. They quite possibly would not be pleased nor would agree with some of the things described. I know that they may have their own facts to what transpired but as I later learned in the book The Five Agreements, that is their own individual points of view.

I even considered the probability of writing an amicable reconciliation between me and all of my other in-laws in the end, but I was reminded that then the story would no longer be nonfiction.

The only exception where I used creative license was the St. Croix restaurant storyline. Stephanie simply told me that for over a year she traveled to St. Croix on weekends when she dated the doctor. I extrapolated the fact that Christine also worked on St. Croix almost every week around the same time. And the way I have observed how Stephanie becomes the center of attention whenever we go out where older women always compliment her attire and younger women tend to glare, while on the other hand men older and young at times would swivel their heads and stare were the factors incorporated in developing that train of thought. At the same time, I conveniently discovered an SD card in a camera with picture files of Christine and her coworkers on St. Croix at a restaurant which solidified that storyline. And as I reflect, it is quite plausible that Christine could have actually seen Stephanie before I did and she remained in the back of her warehouse similarly to seeing me playing the bass in the Hotel Bar & Lounge.

Subsequently, I only had to rewrite one storyline for accuracy after I learned that the circumstances which led Stephanie to respond to my comment about her motorcycle certification on the dating site conflicted with how she remembered it. I initially wrote it having assumed that she saw my profile pics on the dating site. She expressed with 100% certainty that I had not posted any profile pictures of myself because she didn't see any. She continued to presume that "I must not have been serious."

I am 1000% certain there were profile pictures because I posted three. To bolster my position was the fact that the administrators certified my profile with the VERIFIED label. But she was adamant as we went back and forth similarly like when we had the piano classification dispute. I immediately saw another opportunity to develop that storyline. So I rewrote that section to satisfy both of our points of view. Additionally, I was able to add the necessary angst when she informed me that I am the first African American guy she's ever dated as it was appropriately suggested that the oversight was as "plain as night and day."

It wasn't until I had to address the proverbial Ghost in the Room when the momentum and excitement really took off. Many times Stephanie and I would be otherwise oblivious of our surroundings and find ourselves simply staring at each other like we initially did at the Pelican when we hardly ate our breakfast. I even told her about my otherworldly experience an hour earlier on the plane before I landed. And for some reason that moment wasn't awkward for me because I was just being totally honest with her.

But those moments continued to linger when we sat outside on her fifth story apartment balcony, or spending quiet time in the lower level apartment screened porch in Oakland Park. We'd simply stare at each other deep in thought at times knowing what was on the other's mind but both not wanting to be the first to say.

Then that incident at Blue Martini when she said that her happiness was attributed to Christine actually occurred twice on different occasions. She simply cut through the chase and revealed what at the moment was seemingly true to her. Both of us agreed unequivocally that under normal circumstances, we should have never met. The distance between us withstanding was reason enough. And the way she isolates herself from distractions like television and all social media was evident and still remains today.

We even had existential conversations like if it was possible to talk to anyone from our past, who would it be? She asked that question and answered first then allowing me a moment to really consider when I came up with my oldest sister whom I never really got to know. I told Stephanie that sibling passed away when I was three. There were two things I remember about her: when she held me I felt a calming peace while my other sisters exuded mayhem - I am just being honest now. And at her funeral I remember walking from the Methodist Church to the Western Cemetery in the funeral procession. Our family doesn't have any pictures of her so I have no visual reference of what she looks like. But if someone were to present me with a photograph and my mother or other siblings confirm that is her in the picture, it will undoubtedly be the best present I can receive. Her name was Geraldine. Oh yeah, Stephanie said that she would like to speak with Christine.

But realistically, Stephanie and I simply did not tread in the same paths and circles. I knew nothing about Pilates and only read female fitness magazines in the eighties and nineties for their artistic stature of their bodies. Truth be told, I also read Playboy for the articles. And even though her choice of music ran the gamut, where we differ again is the fact that she is actually a 'head-banger.' She does that 'whiplash thing' swaying her head back and forth with one hand in the air as if her fingers are cramped or deformed when she hears classic rock and roll telling me that Bon Jovi's *Livin' on a Prayer* was her graduation class song while mine was Larry Graham's *One in A Million*. And I kid you not, until September 4 2015, she probably heard scores of their songs, but she never heard about the hands down, bar none, Greatest Band of All Time, "The Elements of the Universe." Forty-five years of her life had passed and on that first date when she introduced me to pretty bottled Belgian beer, I introduced her to Earth Wind & Fire. She later asked her older clients the following week after where they confirmed that I knew what the hell I was talking about musically.

In addition to both expressing how happy we are to have met, she gets her jabs in from time to time saying if I had not met her, I would be fat from eating eleven Guys Burgers on the Tom Joyner Cruises actually saying, "Nobody should be eating regularly at midnight." She also loves to remind me that when she fell in love with me, I had a gut.

So as the story developed from Christine's point of view, I researched the internet and found out how to retrieve original text transcripts from my cell phone. As I reread the texts and recalled those concurrent days of communication, I realized how our worlds evolved from innocence to more. All of the emotions were there: love and lost, heartache and pain, innocence and optimism, anger and disdain. As a result, I decided to let those words speak for themselves by including the transcripts and it actually felt like all of the ingredients to the story was being realized. In addition, the audio links of the video logs were included audibly to express our personalities.

Being an avid reader, Stephanie would recommend books from time to time like Ralph Ellison's *The Invisible Man*. That book didn't move me in the manner she thought. Frankly, the way the protagonist allowed himself to be subjugated was a dynamic that totally runs counter to how Caribbean men behave. And as Natalee suggested, Caribbean men don't have to look far for role models and don't consider themselves invisible. She later commented that after hearing my personal stories she was not surprised that I was self-employed.

On the other hand, she also suggested that I read Ray Charles autobiography although I admitted to have watched the movie *Ray* at least five times. It was viscerally stimulating – so to speak. The unabridged book was very descriptive in the manner it told his story from a blind man's point of view. That was consequential in writing from Christine's point of view. The book organically challenged me to broaden my horizon way beyond what I can see.

But the most impactful book she suggested was most definitely *Dying to be Me* by Anita Moorjani. I was able to visualize another point of view of life and death from someone who had actually died in all medical sense of the word by her doctors, lived to talk about what she experienced, and is still alive. (Read the book with an open mind; it will change your life.) And what I love about that author is, she is not telling anyone what to believe when others have tried to dispel her testimonials.

Her insights led me to the concept of the *Warehouse* where I further incorporated the Ideology of Light from the basic rudimentary Principles of Physics that I have come to my own personal conclusion is now my late wife's vehicle of eternal existence. That's a mouthful, and it's what's simply makes sense to me.

And as if everything up until that point was researched for a postgraduate dissertation, I have been learning more about myself every day as I allow myself to be open for new opportunities: like trying new foods having finally dispelled that very old notion that later became a refrain in a calypso, "...stay off the swine." Pork is fine as long as you eat something green every day. And I still don't like quinoa.

The book The Four Agreements by Don Miguel Ruiz became my daily bread so to speak as I listened to it while I walked in the mornings. Then the sequel book, The Fifth Agreement got into my rotation. All those books basically changed my thought process where although I always questioned social norms, my convictions became resolute.

After all is said and done, timing was the catalyst that brought it all together. Throughout the entire ordeal there were advocates on both sides that truly wanted the best for us. Specifically, her 70-year-old Jewish client Ina whom she shared all of her deepest secrets over scheduled lunches and private workout sessions and of course Milton from my perspective. He was totally green when I explained the proverbial quagmire of online dating. I told him that "It is literally a virtual crap shoot" not knowing whether you are dealing with someone real or their alter egos. And there something inherently daunting about how much personal information you can tell a stranger and whether the reciprocation of information was true and forthcoming.

I actually met Ina once on my third visit at the River Market parking lot in Fort Lauderdale outside Whole Foods. Stephanie saw her in the distance and called her name to get her attention. I swear this diminutive lady looked at me as if she knew me forever as I bent over to give her a hug. It felt like an embrace from my mother. I immediately knew then that Stephanie was speaking highly about me. But what I learned was the wisdom that Ina later conveyed. She told her simply that the timing was not right for the other relationships to materialize. The universe's clock runs constant in relative time based on our state of mind and where you are in your life. Timing seemingly put our future on delay where both of us are content knowing that added pressure can derail what we have sustained. Waiting four years for both of our sons to graduate from high school is another example of timing again at play, opposed to us having offsprings whose ages are significantly different in the stages of our lives. And even though she now expresses signs of another form of anxiety explaining that her son's leaving for college next year rehashes the separation memories of the loss of her daughter, I totally understand. With that said, I honestly would wait another year if she requires a little more alone time to reflect. But to be fair to myself, I am not certain is in any of our best interest to wait another two - inasmuch as I love to travel. In the end timing will tell us what to do.

During the several months of writing, at times I became very introspective as my entire life was revealed with each touch of my thumb on my handheld touch screens as sentences seemed to materialize on their own. It was very therapeutic as the realization of why I currently do a lot of the things I do was revealed. I guess that laying on my bed writing was as effective as me laying on a therapist's chaise. Not only were these truths self-evident, but they were realized. Like why I have an affinity for frequent travel.

Before the incident with my demure sister, all of my travels were generally for business while I worked at the bank and at my cousin's electrical contracting firm having to travel several times to Puerto Rico. After the incident it was like a flipped switch where I felt the need to protect my wife from my sister's wrath when she repeatedly told me that she had never been treated like that before. So getaways to hotels around the Caribbean were the norm we both looked forward to weekly.

I also remember not being much of a book reader before I met Christine, but I immediately emulated her. She later was adamant about having an area in the lower renovation to get away from her Guys to read. When Stephanie asked me about the books I'd personally read, I had to return downstairs to our library to recount my considerable few. I have all of the early John Grisham hard covers, Booker T Washington's, Up from Slavery, Miles Davis, the Autobiography, I'm Just a DJ by Tom Joyner and another twenty.

Then I saw the spine of the book that was most impactful in shaping my innate personality, *Why Should White Guys Have All the Fun.* It took me back to when I saw it in the book store 'literally' calling me to explore its contents. It is the biography of Reginald Lewis who was the first modern day African American to build a billion-dollar company. His net worth was not the part of his story that compelled me. Quite honestly, when I saw the spine of the book it suggested otherwise. It was the point that in his life, no one saw him coming because he operated below the radar. He lived life on his own terms foregoing his personal health and dying very young at the age of 50. In the book I also learned that a local Virgin Islands architect by the name of Robert DeJongh was on the board of directors of Mr. Lewis' corporation. And as irony has it, I was in the early phases of a renovation project with the DeJongh Group when I had to withdraw after Christine passed. And as Natalee purported, role models everywhere locally.

That chapter of my dating tendencies I now realized were all predicated by the validation I received in the eleventh grade clandestine class taught by Dr. Emanuel and reinforced by my Presidential Classroom alumnus Rochelle when she complimented me on the darkness of my skin. That was huge. In hindsight, I know that's why I immediately got along with my shorter sister-in-law. I am now kidding when I say it was like out of the scene of the movie *Lethal Weapon* 2 when Joe Pesci and Danny Glover were in the South African embassy when Murtaugh was requesting asylum when the embassy envoy said, "...but you're *bleck*." Instead my sister-in-law lovingly calls me '*Prieto*' – a Black guy. Hence anyone who had an issue with my appearance personally was not a relationship that was sustainable.

At the end of it all, it would behoove me if I did not acknowledge that I also got a lot of unexpected inducement from Stephanie. In addition to the text transcripts during the first month, we talked for hours on weekend hiding from our sons. I shared more initially and at one point she later told me that she knew I was someone of substance after the story of me remembering Christine's makeup on that surprise trip. Even though her contributions were only limited to subjective references here and there suggesting a book to read every now and again, she absolutely did not provide any plot details. She did explain to me Joseph Campbell's concept of the Hero's Journey after suggesting that everything I was telling her about myself sounded like the makings of an extraordinary life story: Call to Action, Supernatural Aid, The Threshold when Temptations and Challenges abound, then you hit bottom in the Abyss. From the abyss you are Transformed and Atonement is made. Until the point you Return to another Call to Action.

And even though I have shared the Preface and Foreword to a few friends when asked what am I up to, Stephanie only wants to read the book after it's published. I asked her whether she wanted the opportunity to redact any part of what I have written and she simply stated, "I trust you with my stories."

Inasmuch as she has been very instrumental in my personal recovery and a great source of inspiration, Stephanie too is in the process of writing and publishing a book. When I told her that I had an idea for her cover, she chastised me for thinking that it was about me. Based on the title and her outline, I forwarded my idea anyway and waited for her apology. So look for my name in her book for the illustration credit.

Writing this book has been truly an incredible ride. Rollercoaster highs when I travelled back and forth and similar lows in Christine's passing, the brief breakdown and the various twists and turns. In the end, the following summarizes everything I've learned to date as it augments the poem in the beginning pages of the book.

The Choice is Yours

After it is all said and done, the most important thing is what you choose to believe.
Whether those things described were coincidences or phenomena to be accepted or deceive.
Maybe during Operation None of Your Business, he woke up on his own and drove to his mother's so he won't be alone,
Or on the plane he really heard the original chorus to Corrine Bailey Rae's song,
And choose to cry anyway because he hadn't cry for so long.
Or on that day my mother called him Honey he didn't really hear my voice,
Instead he heard what was comforting to his ears and simply made that other choice.

So ask yourself haven't you experienced anything that to this day you chose not to believe,
Accepting everything else you experience blindly without vetting the information you receive.
I know my mother on that fateful day called him Honey and maybe he heard my voice,

I also know that Corrine Bailey song on the plane made him cry over something he
may or may not have heard - but again – that was entirely his choice,
After it was all said, it simply made his heart rejoice.
And after it is all done, it's still what you choose to believe.

LAST WORDS

She now sees him the way I did - and for the time being – I see the manner
how she cares for him similarly too.
Finding love again with someone from a faraway place, totally different in
every sense of the word and plays her favorite instrument too?
She no longer looks at him like her poem suggests – a continuous dream
she made up while lying in bed.
I simply think they're going to make beautiful music together.
And as for him, all he yearned for was the capacity to move on.
Possibly finding another soul whose path to walk along.
From my perspective their future is clear.
And for all intents and purposes, my work is done here.

As I pat myself on the back, there's no illusion that my quest is yet
to be over; my quest persists for eternity for as long as those whose
memories of me are in my company. And for the moment being, I have
passed my Law of Attraction test – manipulating the cosmos and
scavenging for proverbial treasures in warehouses has brought me so much
pleasure in bringing two lost souls together. It simply proves over and over
and over again, 'when you wish upon the light of a star, dreams do come
true.'

SNAPSHOTS FROM MY LIFE

Pre-School   High School   1st Time to St. John 11/5/89

Our 1st Trip Together During the Summer of 1990 When I Over-packed

One of the Happiest Days of My Life.   Dancing in the Sunset   2nd Day Married on
Honeymoon.

Rufus Birthday party & 1st Flying Lesson with Cleo 1992   Mrs. Hawaii's Family 1999

After Babysitting her, we *got*
serious about getting pregnant

Rufus built the Changing Station

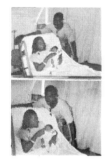
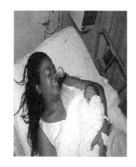

September 29, 2000, We became a family of three.

329

Our 1ˢᵗ Trip as a Family to the Mainland to visit Maxentius in Houston December 2000

Striking a Pose   *On St. Maarten where My Dad Met Kevin*   *The King and His 1ˢᵗ Car*

1ˢᵗ Day at Pre-School   *Pictures Taken After Returning From His First Day of Pre-School*

T-Ball Game

My Favorite Picture of My Guys

Rufus Featured in the Last Issue of Tradewinds Magazine 2007   Family Portrait

Sporting Short Hair for the 1st
After my Dad passed in 2008

Celebrating Rufus' 30 Year
High School On Virgin Gorda 2011

2012 Celebrating
Lena's Recovery

December 2012 our Christmas Picture with Personalized Yankee Jerseys With Our Ages on Our Backs. True Fact: That's What Rufus Wore at the Pelican That Fateful September Morning 2015

Embracing My Hair As It Grew Back

2013 1st Baseball Game Thanks to the Philly Mogul. Parent/Student Gala   8th Grade Graduation

Tom Joyner's Fantastic Voyage 2014 Celebrating being Cancer Free. Sailaway Party Jerseys, Rufus' 70's Outfit was way Too Small with me in my Go Go Outfit, He Bought Me The Dress and Shoes for White Night

Celebrating the Homegoing

In *Loving Memory* of

Christine Turnbull

Sunrise: December 30, 1966 – Sunset: January 20, 2015

Saturday, January 31, 2015

3:00 p.m.

St. Thomas Assembly of God

#133 Estate Contant

St. Thomas, VI 00802

Pastor George E. Phillips, Officiating

New Business Cards

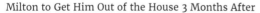

Milton to Get Him Out of the House 3 Months After

My Profile Pic on His Phone

Fall of 2015 Amazed at How Much He's Grown Fall 2017 Outside The 76er's Arena & Introductory Night

2018 Prom Wakanda Outfit   *I Think We Did A Very Good Job To This Point*

Kevin Has This Original Framed Portrait
Drew of Me Hung in His Dormitory

I LOVE YOU GUYS!!!

Christine Turnbull

Made in the USA
Middletown, DE
06 June 2021